LANGUAGE, LITERACY, AND CULTURE: ISSUES OF SOCIETY AND SCHOOLING

edited by
Judith A. Langer
Stanford University

ABLEX PUBLISHING CORPORATION
NORWOOD, NEW JERSEY

Library of Congress Cataloging-in-Publication Data

Language, literacy, and culture.

   "This volume grows out of a two-day conference...organized at Stanford University in the fall of 1985"—Introd.
   Includes bibliographies and index.
   Contents: A sociocognitive perspective on literacy / Judith A. Langer—Second game : a school's-eye view of intelligence / Robert Sternberg—Metacognition in second language behavior / Richard Duran—[etc.]
   1. Literacy—Congresses.   2. Educational sociology—Congresses.   3. Socio-linguistics—Congresses.   I. Langer, Judith A.
   LC149.L25   1987   370.19   87-11450
   ISBN 0-89391-437-1

Ablex Publishing Corporation
355 Chestnut Street
Norwood, New Jersey 07648

Contents

Introduction   **v**

1.   A Sociocognitive Perspective on Literacy   **1**
Judith A. Langer

PART I. PSYCHOLOGICAL ISSUES IN LITERACY   **21**

2.   Second Game: A School's-Eye View of Intelligence   **23**
Robert J. Sternberg

3.   Metacognition in Second Language Behavior   **49**
Richard P. Duran

PART II. LITERACY AND THE LITERARY EXPERIENCE   **65**

4.   The Orality of Literature and the Literacy of Conversation   **67**
Deborah Tannen

5.   The Literate Essay: Using Ethnography to Explode Myths   **89**
Shirley Brice Heath

PART III. THE INFLUENCES OF SOCIETY ON LANGUAGE SHIFTS   **109**

6.   Literacy and Language Change; The Special Case of Speech Act Verbs   **111**
Elizabeth Closs Traugott

7.   The Community as Educator   **128**
William Labov

PART IV. CULTURAL AND HISTORICAL EFFECTS ON LITERACY   **147**

8.   Opportunity Structure, Cultural Boundaries, and Literacy   **149**
John U. Ogbu

9.   A Socio-Historical Approach to Literacy Development: A Comparative Case Study from the Pacific   **178**
Thom Huebner

PART V. TECHNOLOGY IN EDUCATION   197

10. New Technologies, Basic Skills, and the Underside of
     Education: What's to be Done?   199
     Peg Griffin and Michael Cole

     Author Index   233

     Subject Index   237

Introduction

This book offers a multidisciplinary view of recent issues in the field of literacy theory and education. It is different from other books on similar topics in two ways: First, because it brings together scholars from anthropology, education, literary theory, linguistics, and psychology—a variety of the disciplines concerned with literacy—and second because together, the authors make a very strong statement about new and broader ways of looking at literacy. Despite the importance of literacy issues and despite the current attention literacy is receiving, inquiry into literacy research and practice has tended to be the specialized domain of scholars in the particular fields—who generally talk among themselves. This volume gains its power from its multidisciplinary perspective. While each author is known to broader audiences, this will be the first time many have published together.

This volume grows out of a 2-day conference I organized at Stanford University in the Fall of 1985; Language, Literacy, and Culture: Issues of Society and Schooling. Generous grants from the S.W. and F.E. Terman Memorial Fund and the Stanford Humanities Center permitted speakers and participants from a variety of disciplines to listen, and talk, and argue. The goal of the conference was to bring together scholars from the various fields to present their most recent thinking on issues of language, literacy and schooling. Although they come from different disciplinary backgrounds with different ways of conceptualizing issues, conducting research, and presenting arguments, each sees issues of language and literacy learning and change as inseparable from issues of society, its interactions, and its institutions. Each believes that literacy development is affected by who people are —their cultural histories and ways of doing—as well as by the societies and institutions they encounter.

Why expound upon what seems to be so sensible a notion? You will see from the first chapter, which serves as a conceptual introduction to the sociocognitive thrust of the book, that I believe issues of literacy are being too narrowly defined by people in many fields (researchers, policy planners, educators), and are therefore being underconceptualized. By its very nature, an understanding of literacy calls for an understanding of the complex cultural and human roots that underlie thinking and learning. The topic of the conference (and this book) suggests this interplay. Across the variety of chapters intelligence, learning, cognition, interpretation, and schooling are socioculturally defined and related to context and use.

This volume serves as a step toward making these connections. Chapters reflect five differing approaches to the study of literacy: Psychological

Issues in Literacy; Literacy and the Literary Experience; The Influences of Society on Language Shifts; Cultural and Historical Effects on Literacy; and Technology in Education.

The chapters in Part I focus on psychological issues in literacy and learning. Sternberg argues for the notion of several kinds of intelligence, influenced by society as well as nature. He sees perceptions of intelligence as growing out of socially learned and domain-specific ways of behaving, and illustrates how erroneous decisions about brightness and ability occur when an individual's conception of how to use and display knowledge—how to play the game of schooling—differs from that of the teacher or the institution. Duran focuses on another psychological issue, metacognition, as it relates to bilingual learners in particular. He reviews literature in second language education, psychology, and sociolinguistics, and discusses issues that are relevant to metacognitive development, literacy education, and assessment.

The chapters in the second part discuss issues of literacy and the literary experience. Tannen argues that oral and written languages are intertwined rather than dichotomous, and that descriptions of similar as well as different linguistic patterns within particular oral and written discourse types are needed to help explain the ways in which the overlaps occur. With examples from literature, student writing, and ordinary conversation, she goes on to demonstrate ways in which literature and oral language each contains features of the other. Also focusing on the literary experience, Heath exposes and dispels several myths about a common literate genre, the essay; she discusses what people do when they write essays, and how composition can and cannot be taught. She does this by leading the reader through the writer's world and illustrates by experience how the essay is created, why it is constructed in a particular way, and what makes it both literary and literate.

Part III focuses on the ways in which society influences shifts in uses and structures of language. Traugott challenges the view that oral and written traditions create separate ways of constructing consciousness and of using language. In particular, she argues against the view that modern thought distinguishes "meaning" from "saying," and that literacy is related to the appearance of related speech act verbs. With evidence from historical studies of word meanings, she demonstrates that such speech act verbs are a function of structure and experience in both literate and nonliterate societies. Labov, also interested in the effects of society on linguistic systems, focuses on issues of dialect, looking at the ways in which language learning takes place outside of schools, within the community. With evidence from recent studies, he demonstrates that language learning is fluid and changes throughout life; he also shows that linguistic features that minority students do not learn in school are acquired through interactions with dominant dialect speakers in the larger community.

Part IV addresses the ways in which the cultural history of a people affects literacy development and learning. Ogbu addresses the issue of restricted literacy learning among minority group students. He explores the differential success among various kinds of minority groups, whose perceptions of group status and mobility differ based on their historical experiences. He argues that attitudes toward literacy and schooling can be best understood by examining the perspectives of a particular group in terms of its long-term exposure to domination and deculturation and its opportunity to use the skills of schooling in personally rewarding ways. Also emphasizing the importance of cultural history on learning, Huebner traces the historical concomitants of literacy development that affect different countries in different ways. By examining the history of literacy development and schooling in Hawaii and American Samoa, he demonstrates that issues of current educational concern can best be understood within their broader historical contexts, and that educational planners would benefit from incorporating such an approach in addressing policy issues and their implications for schooling.

Part V turns to the issue of technology in education. Regarding computers as tools for language use and interaction, Griffin and Cole review the changing literacy conditions in the United States and then consider particular uses of computers in fostering literacy learning. They make distinctions between Level 1 learning (rote), and Level 2 learning (thoughtful reasoning), and distinguish ways in which the second kind of learning can be achieved in schooling through language-fostering uses of the new technology. They close with particular suggestions for computers in literacy education.

Chapter One
A Sociocognitive Perspective on Literacy

JUDITH A. LANGER
Stanford University

Issues of literacy are critical to society—to its innermost workings at economic, political, and social levels. Literacy involves how people think, and learn, and change—and how society changes as a function of the changes in its people. I will argue here that many scholars, as well as the general public, have regarded literacy somewhat narrowly—as the ability to read and write and get on at some minimal "functional" level in day-to-day life and work —and that because of this restricted view, our solutions to very pragmatic issues of literacy learning and instruction have suffered, as have national interpretations of literacy-in-society for policy and planning.

While the marks of a literate person have changed over the years (Resnick & Resnick, 1977), such changes have not led to broader definitions of literacy for society or schooling. In the United States, school-based notions of literacy have progressed from literacy as the ability to read a simple, familiar passage aloud, to the ability to answer literal questions about the passage, to the understanding of word and sentence meaning in an unfamiliar text— a progression from rote to functional performance (Clifford, 1984; Kaestle, 1985; Resnick & Resnick, 1977). Before the mid-19th century, writing was taught as copying (Heath, 1981), and until the beginning of the 20th century reading instruction focused on syllables, sounding, and memorization (Resnick & Resnick, 1977). During World War I, the Army Alpha and Beta tests emphasized that a broader set of literacy skills were needed even for routine army tasks, and literacy training was offered to those who failed. And by the 1970s functional literacy, the ability to participate in the reading and writing demands of everyday living in modern society, was considered essential (cf. Adult Functional Competency Report, 1975). Most recently, the National Assessment of Educational Progress undertook a literacy survey of young adults, aged 21 to 25 (1986). For this survey the criteria for literacy changed once again: The Profiles of Literacy: Assessment of Young Adults (NAEP, 1986) describes literacy as the use of written information to function in society to achieve one's goals and to develop one's knowledge and potential. Literacy is seen "not as a set of independent skills associated with reading and writing, but the application of particular skills for specific purposes in specific contexts." This view marks an end to the simple dichotomy between

1

literate and illiterate citizens in favor of a literacy profile, based on the variety of contexts and uses of literacy.

However, while definitions have changed in response to changing societal uses of literacy, the focus has remained solely on the uses of reading and writing. It would be more productive to view literacy in a broader sense, from what I call a *sociocognitive* perspective that incorporates social practices, conceptions of reading and writing, and literacy as a way of thinking into the definition of literacy. Viewing literacy in this way would lead to a radical change in the ways in which literacy learning, social and cultural issues involving literacy, intellectual effects of literacy, and issues of schooling would be addressed. If we view literacy from this broader perspective, we can show that some very basic aspects of literacy have been changing but have gone unnoticed. Further, these changing aspects of literacy make all the difference in what people learn, how people learn, and how they think—it is these aspects that make issues of language, literacy, and culture inseparable.

In this chapter, I will develop this sociocognitive view of literacy and show how from this view literacy (a) is culturally based, (b) involves the higher intellectual skills appropriate to the culture, and (c) is learned by children as they interact with their families and communities. I will also describe the relevance of the sociocognitive view of literacy learning for schooling, suggesting ways in which schools can capitalize on the social nature of literacy learning and create instructional experiences where students gain literacy skills as they engage in broader and more purposeful literacy activities.

LITERACY AS LITERATE THINKING: A SOCIOCOGNITIVE VIEW

There are two ways to regard literacy. We can think of literacy as the ability to read and write (Kaestle, 1985; Graff, 1979; Resnick & Resnick, 1977). This is the common dictionary definition, and the one that is generally reflected in statistics on literacy rates and in assessments of the success of schooling.

We can also view literacy another way—as the ability to think and reason like a literate person (Kaestle, 1985; Langer, 1986a, in preparation; Traugott, this volume). Here, the focus is not just on the reading and writing, but also on the thinking that accompanies it. In this case, literacy can be thought of as a tool. The thinking skills that a person uses when reading and writing are generalizable to, and occur in, many other situations—situations where people talk about language (written and spoken), are conscious of the distinctions between the discourse (speaker's or author's) meaning and their own interpretations—where they use their knowledge to read, write, think, and communicate in new ways. Literacy enables a thinking about language and about oral and written discourse, using language to extend meanings and knowledge about ideas and experiences. It leads to the spiralling change that comes about when people use their literacy skills to think, rethink, and reformulate their knowledge and their worlds (Bakhtin, 1985). This view of literacy is not text-based. It values both the reader and the discourse—and depends upon and fosters the kinds of metalinguistic and metacognitive abilities that are found in the most successful learners.

For example, when a group of people read one of the classics and then discuss the theme, motives, action, and characters at a Great Books meeting, I would say they were using literate thinking skills. If the same people happen to read a best-selling gothic romance and discuss the plot and the motives of the characters, I would also say they were using literate thinking skills. Further, when those people see a movie and then discuss the plot and the motives and alternative actions and resolutions, I would again say they were using literate thinking skills even though they had neither read nor written. And if the people engaged in that very same conversation about a movie, but did not know how to read or write, I would still say they had engaged in literate thinking.

The distinction I wish to make is between literacy as the act of reading and writing and literacy as a *way* of thinking and speaking. Reading and writing as low level activities can involve little literate thought, and using literate thinking skills when no reading or writing has occurred may involve a good deal of literate thinking. It is the way of thinking, not just the act of reading or writing, that is at the core of the development of literacy.

Of course, I am suggesting that certain uses of language and certain kinds of thinking may be related to certain kinds of literacy practices—not to literacy in the narrower sense of being able to encode and decode written language. And it is through engaging in particular uses of literacy that a wide range of intellectual behaviors are learned and refined.

While literacy involves special uses of language, these uses and the cognitive behaviors they invoke may take place orally as well as in print, and literate thinking about ideas can occur even when no reading or writing has taken place. Literate thinkers objectify the subject matter, making it opaque and malleable, thereby permitting self-conscious distinctions to be made between language structure, discourse meanings, and interpretations. For example, Olson (1985) describes the language lesson inherent when a parent says to a child looking at a frog in a pond, "See! Jumping." The parent's emphasis urges the child to focus on the instance of *jumping* as a present tense verb representing the observed action, and on the *ing* form used to convey it. Because this type of objectification and logical treatment of language and ideas can occur in a variety of contexts, there is an overlap in use (and in the types of thinking) between oral and written modes (see Tannen, 1982; Chafe, 1980; Stubbs, 1980), rather than a great divide between oral and written language (Goody, 1977; Ong, 1982).

Narrow definitions of literacy as the act of reading and writing are also becoming blurred by the rapid development of mass media and computer communications in our society. Traditional genres such as newspapers and magazines are breaking down, causing us to "alter our ideas about what constitutes a 'book,' what separates an 'academic work' from a popular one, indeed what body of data should properly be considered a book or an 'author'" (Smith, 1982). Television has replaced many of the news, editorial, and literary functions traditional forms had served in the past, while the print forms have enlarged such "neighborly" feature sections as health hints, personal living, and advice columns. Shared contexts of communication now reach well beyond the here and now to people in different places and different times. Television reports use such "literate" conventions as logical argument, and careful analysis of issues, but also rely on such "oral" language features as formulaic devices, repetition, emotional appeal, and reliance on the shared situation. (See Ong, 1982, for a contrast of oral and written features.)

Lakoff (1982) suggests that as a result of technological progress, modern society is changing to one where features of the oral and written traditions have become merged, with each incorporating linguistic features of the other (see also Tannen, this volume). She goes on to suggest that in our age of mass communication the oral medium is often considered a more valid conveyor of ideas than is print (cf. the "truth" of the evening news report), and that written documents are being rewritten to more closely approximate the oral mode. The point is that in modern society, a focus on simple reading and writing skills as defining "literate" thinkers, and on uses of oral and written language as involving different intellectual dimensions, are unhelpful distinctions. Uses of oral and written language mix and blur and vary as the language situation changes, and these complexities need to be considered if we are to understand the literacy demands that occur within a technological culture.

Literacy is an activity, a way of thinking, not a set of skills. And it is a purposeful activity—people read, write, talk, and think about real ideas and information in order to ponder and extend what they know, to communicate with others, to present their points of view, and to understand and be understood. In doing this, sometimes they read and write, sometimes they talk about what they read or wrote, and sometimes they talk about ideas using the ways of thinking and reasoning they might also have used when they engaged in directly text-based activities. According to this expanded notion of literacy, a society does not grow less literate as its modes of communication change to more oral media; instead the functions of literacy modify in response to these shifts, as do the particular ways of thinking.

Literacy in Society

Nations profess concern when many people cannot read and write, and they develop literacy programs as a remedy. At times programs are developed by the government (e.g., among the Mossi people in the Upper Volta) because literacy is "good" for the people; at times they are offered by the church (e.g., the Kaluli in Papua New Guinea) to enable people to read the bible (see Schieffelin & Cochran-Smith, 1986). Sometimes these efforts fail, as they did with the Kaluli, because the ways and uses of literacy introduced by the program have no basis in the people's culture. Cressey (1983) would consider such a failure the result of a "push–pull" imbalance, where the conditions in society make it unnecessary and even unproductive for the target population to become literate. Push factors are the external ideological or political forces that attempt to influence people, while the pull factors are utilitarian, internal concerns. Some balance of internal and external factors seems to be needed to make a difference in the development of literacy within a culture.

When literacy is successfully introduced into a society, it also changes the culture of which it becomes a part. With the Vai in Liberia (Scribner & Cole, 1980), for example, letter writing in the Vai language became a frequent way of communicating with distant relatives, and the decontextualized nature of this writing activity was transferred to other tasks where specific and non-situational language was needed. As with the Vai, the onset of literacy creates initial changes within a culture, and the members of the society who use literacy are then free to modify the uses to which literacy is put and to further change their culture. In this way, literacy can change across time within a particular culture, and it can change differentially at the same time across different cultures. Both of these processes need to be addressed when considering issues of literacy in society.

Social Origins of Literacy.   The practices of literacy, what they are and what they mean for a given society, depend on the context. They are embedded in a cultural way of thinking and learning and although they may appear stable in the short run, they are ever changing, reflecting the growing and changing ways of thinking and doing enacted in the population at large. Thus, how literacy skills are learned and taught and used by individuals not only depends upon, but also deeply influences, literate activities of the society at large.

The skills and concepts that accompany literacy acquisition do not stem in some automatic way from the inherent qualities of print, but are aspects of the specific uses of and approaches to literacy that are implicit within the social, political, and intellectual forces that constitute that society.

Vygotsky (1962, 1978) stresses the social origins of language and thinking and begins to conceptualize the mechanisms by which culture becomes a part of how each person thinks, learns, and relates to others and the environment. At the root of his theory is the notion that humans "master" tools and signs to serve their own ends, and in doing so, they take part in modifying their own environment. Tools and signs, he argues, are created by society and change with society. As people learn the rules for manipulating these culturally produced sign systems there is a transformation in the way they behave—they learn to interpret the signs and since the signs are part of the culture, they learn to become part of the culture as part of their learning. And, because they learn to understand and master the environment through mastering the signs, their ability to think and reason also changes and develops.

In short, the literacy skills societies (or institutions) value are those that people learn (Au, 1980; Heath, 1983; Scribner & Cole, 1980; Sternberg, this volume; Vygotsky, 1962, 1978). Literacy behaviors gain their functional value from the contextual settings that cultures and subcultures provide for their uses; in each case these may reflect different modes of thinking and reasoning (Applebee, 1984; Langer 1985b, 1986a, in preparation; Langer & Applebee, 1986; Olson, in press; Scribner & Cole, 1980). The outcomes of an individual's literacy learning are shaped by the social contexts in which they are embedded and can only be fully understood in relation to these social contexts.

Intellectual Effects of Literacy.   Some scholars (Goody, 1977; Olson, 1977; Ong, 1982) make claims for the cognitive consequences of literacy, suggesting that written text evokes a very different way of thinking from oral modes. While oral thinking has been described as emotional, contextualized, and ambiguous, literate thinking has been described as abstract, decontextualized, and logical. Tannen (1982), Chafe (1980), and Scollon and Scollon (1981) argue instead that the literate tradition does not replace the oral. Rather, when literacy is introduced, the two sets of skills interrelate with one another. People use both ways of thinking for differing purposes in specific settings. Others (Bruner, Olver, & Greenfield, 1966) suggest that intellectual differences in literacy are based on the effects of schooling. However, Scribner and Cole's (1980) work with the Vai people of Liberia suggests that the intellectual differences are not dependent on schooling, but are rather a function of the ways in which particular literacy activities are used within a culture; it is the particular uses of literacy rather than schooling per se that makes a difference in cognition.

Higher mental functions are social in two senses: (a) their development is part of the development of the social system, and their existence depends upon the communication from one generation to the next, and (b) they are seen as social relationships that have been taken over by the individual and internalized. Vygotsky (1962, 1978, 1979) suggests that higher psychological processes are direct reflections of social processes in which the child participated at an earlier stage—that processes evolved from *inter*psychological to *intra*psychological. Of critical concern are the social processes used by the adult and how these are taken over by learners—allowing them to act as independent thinkers and doers. How people think and reason depends upon the uses for literacy in the culture and the ways in which those activities are transmitted to younger generations.

As learners assume ownership for their literacy activities (i.e., as the child attempts to master the environment by using a written sign to stand for something to be understood or remembered), they are in a sense learning to master themselves—they gain control of their own abilities as literate thinkers and doers, using language to serve their own ends. The act of mediation, of using signs and symbols to stand for something else, actively and fundamentally changes cognitive behaviors. As such, literacy activities (as mediating behaviors) are acts of higher mental thought, and these higher mental acts have their roots in social (cultural) interaction.

Children learn such higher level skills as they engage in socially meaningful literacy activities. Interactive social experiences are at the heart of literacy learning; they involve children as active learners in cooperative social environments where an adult (or able other) serves as a model or offers some direct guidance that governs the children's initial engagement in the activity. After successive experiences, children develop their own self-evaluative and self-regulatory abilities. They first learn the activity in a social setting in which cultural interpretations are embedded and communicated by other members of the society, and with experience they internalize the skills needed to complete the activity and also the socially or culturally accepted way to evaluate the meaning and relative success of that activity. In this sociofunctional manner, they learn metacognitive and metalinguistic skills (Duran, this volume). Both Vygotsky (1962, 1978) and Bruner et al. (1966) argue that literacy learning grows out of such communicative relationships, and that these joint learning activities support higher levels of cognitive development. (See Langer and Applebee, 1986b, for an extended discussion of adult–child interactions and literacy learning.)

Culture and Literacy Learning. Just as culture affects the intellectual effects of literacy, so too does culture affect the process of learning to be literate. Detailed studies of literacy from historians and anthropologists have been culture-specific (Goody, 1977; Cressey, 1983; Furet & Ozouf, 1977; Clanchy, 1979), attempting to explain relationships between particular cultures and ways of learning. This has provided an understanding of literacy uses and developments within and across certain cultures at particular points in time. However, educators and development planners often fail to consider literacy in similar ways, as a culturally specific phenomenon. They look at reading and writing as an expected part of the general changes that come with modernization, industrialization, and urbanization. Issues of biculturalism and co-culturalism (see Griffin & Cole, this volume) are often overlooked in attempts to deal with literacy learning, although such issues are particularly important both in the United States, where students from many cultures come together to learn, and in many developing nations where a variety of peoples speaking different languages are trying to establish a sense of national purpose. Similarly, any nation that wishes to participate in the world economy and world culture needs to extend its views of literacy to include an understanding of its cognitive and cultural underpinnings. To do this it is necessary to look at societal as well as individual universals and differences—at the ways people acquire literacy, and at the social environments and institutions in which literacy learning takes place and in which literacy is used.

Ong (1982) has stated that cognitive growth "occurs as much from the outside as the inside. Much of it consists of the person's becoming linked with culturally transmitted amplifiers" (p. 109). Words are embedded within cultural meanings. From a Vygotskian perspective, culture plays a critical role in how a learner gains access to the signs and symbols in the environment, and learns to imbue them with meaning. Culture is the product of social life and human social activity. As people learn the signs of a culture, they learn to use these signs to mediate their thinking, and thereby gain the tools to change the culture. The signs of a culture, the symbols of that culture, and the meanings (how to read that culture) are all accomplished first in interaction with others, and later internalized for personal use.

While Vygotsky begins with the social origins (at the interpersonal level) of these processes, many present day researchers look primarily at the internal processes—and therefore fail to see the cultural and social roots of thinking and learning. In doing so, they fail to understand the roots of literacy as social and functional and cultural behavior. Literacy and cultural development are inextricably bound, and learning a new literacy (i.e., becoming biliterate) therefore requires one to become, in a sense, bicultural. In this sense, it is impossible to consider some kinds of literacy as good and others as less desireable—each reflects the culture (or institution) in which it is learned. The form of literacy that is taught and learned is based upon the ways in which literacy is perceived by that social group, and in this respect all literacies are appropriate to the context in which they are learned. However, it is also necessary to look beyond the literate behaviors of the local community or school to the society at large. While some literacies have local applicability (e.g., decoding Arabic to read the Koran, or reading only for the literal text meaning in classes where that is valued), people also need the opportunity to learn the kinds of literate thinking engaged in by the larger society. And as a society becomes more technological and makes greater interpretive demands on its people, schooling needs to reflect these changes in the kinds of literacy activities that are most valued.

LITERACY IN SCHOOLS: A SOCIOCOGNITIVE VIEW

Let me turn now to consider how well schools in the United States are currently teaching children to become literate, in ways that would make sense from a sociocognitive perspective—involving the literate thinking behaviors called for at this point in time. The National Assessment of Educational Progress (NAEP) has been examining the achievement of American school children in a variety of school subjects since 1969. The areas they assess that are of most interest here are reading and writing—both of which have been assessed relatively regularly since the early years of the assessment. The reports on the 1984 assessment provide an overview of achievement in reading since 1971 (Applebee, Langer, & Mullis, 1985), and achievement in writing since 1974 (Applebee, Langer, & Mullis, 1986)—over a decade of achievement in both subjects in the elementary, middle school, and secondary grades. The NAEP reports indicate that while students were reading somewhat better in 1984 than they were in 1971, and after a decline in 1979 were again writing as well in 1984 as they were in 1974, literacy performance was in general poor. Improvements occurring in reading and writing were due to increased proficiency in the most basic skills. Students failed at activities that required more thoughtful uses of language. Overall, the results indicate that American students are learning to read and write, but they are not learning to become literate thinkers.

Whether by accident or by design, school curricula and the tests that go with them seem to have rewarded relatively simple performance and have undervalued the attainment of more thoughtful literacy behaviors. Further evidence of this is seen in a variety of recent studies.

In a 1978 report to the Ford Foundation, Graves found that elementary school students were seldom asked to write, and what writing they did consisted of workbook exercises and drills emphasizing such subskills as punctuation, vocabulary, and grammar instead of the communication of a message. He also reported there was little emphasis on writing instruction. What passed for writing instruction was talk about finished writing: papers were graded, errors were marked, and suggestions were offered for further improvement—but students rarely had to carry those suggestions to completion. Even teacher–student conferences focused on *what* the writing should look like but not on *how* to do it.

At the secondary school level, Applebee (1981) found that although 44% of class time was devoted to writing, only 3% of class time was devoted to activities in which the students were asked to write a paragraph or more. Writing was used for exercises and for testing what had been learned—for filling in blanks—not as an opportunity for students to develop their own ideas.

More recently, Applebee and I (Langer and Applebee, 1986a; in press) found that even teachers who were deeply committed to using writing for broader purposes, who have sought to learn new instructional approaches, and who were committed to using writing as a way to help their students think and learn, had great difficulty in carrying out these good intentions. We found that their good intentions were undercut by their deeply rooted views of their role as transmitter of knowledge—and with it their overarching concern with diagnosing what their students needed to learn, teaching the missing information, and testing to evaluate the success of that teaching. This pattern of test/teach/retest left even the best-intentioned teachers with little room to encourage students to develop broader literacy skills.

Tests reinforce these emphases. In my own studies of testing, I have shown that not only do standardized tests (the norm-based multiple choice reading achievement tests) focus on small and unrelated items of information, but it is also difficult to know if a student has gotten the right answer for the wrong reason or the wrong answer for the right reason (Langer, 1985a, 1987). Literacy, as I define it, is not helpful to get through this type of test, although it is the sort of test most frequently used to gather data about students' reading and language skills.

These reports are dismaying. They suggest that students are not being encouraged to think broadly and deeply about ideas and content. Their school experiences are not helping them to learn the literate behaviors important to the present day culture. These results are a signal either that the schools have not been teaching what they set out to teach, or that they have not set out to teach the kinds of literacy behaviors that we value. I suspect it is the latter, and that schools are basing their instructional programs on a narrow definition of literacy as reading and writing rather than recognizing that literacy is also a way of thinking and doing.

This is also the kind of education that is curriculum driven, where there is a set of skills or information to be learned, and the teacher tests to see what the students know or don't know, teaches what isn't known, then tests to see if it has been learned. Perhaps more by accident than by design, when instruction is driven by this model, the focus shifts almost inevitably toward discrete skills and items of information that are easy to test, and away from deeper understandings that are more complicated and time-consuming to consider.

This kind of approach to instruction (a) permeates much of school learning today, and (b) inhibits students from becoming the more thoughtful and more literate language users and learners we would like them to become. In such instruction, the teacher rather than the student does the thinking—about the subject matter as a whole as well as about the structure of the particular activity. Rather than learning *how to do something new and thoughtful,* such instruction emphasizes *whether the student has done something right.*

There is, however, another way to think about teaching and learning, what I have called the sociocognitive view. Whereas the old view of instruction focused on content to be transmitted, the sociocognitive view is more concerned with how people learn *how* to do new things. And people learn to do new things most effectively, and perhaps exclusively, in contexts where the learner is engaged with others in carrying out socially meaningful tasks.

Literacy Instruction

The discussion so far provides the base for a sociocognitive view of literacy instruction. This view combines issues of society and schooling, and asserts that: (1) all learning is socially based, (2) literacy learning is an interactive process; and (3) cognitive behaviors are influenced by context, and affect the meanings the learners produce.

1. All learning is socially based.   Literacy learning results from understandings that grow in social settings where reading and writing and talk about language have particular uses for the people involved. It takes place when learners see models of literate behavior as other people engage in literacy activities, and when they talk and ask questions about what is happening, why, and how. For example, Luria (1929/1977-78) describes how young children learn to write by first emulating the writing behaviors of the adults around them—they copy the way the adult writing looks before they fully understand what it means. With time, they begin to understand what writing means to the adults, that the writings represent meanings that the writer wishes to convey in print. They learn to understand what particular literacy activities mean and the rules for completing them through exposure to the social environments in which the activities occur.

The particular uses of literacy to which children are exposed can be broader or narrower. In either case, students come to understand and use literacy in ways that reflect the environments in which they learn—both at home and in school. If the culture of the classroom treats reading and writing as a set of encoding and decoding skills detached from more functional activities, more restricted uses of literacy will be learned, with underlying rules and meanings interpreted and practiced in accordance with the uses to which literacy is put by the teacher and classmates. Alternatively, when reading and writing are treated as purposeful activities that grow out of shared questions and issues within the classroom culture, broader and more varied uses of literacy will be learned. The choice of methods of instruction thus becomes more than a question of *how* to teach children to read and write; it is also a question of *what* children will learn.

2. Literacy learning is an interactive process.   In becoming literate, people assume control over and internalize new skills and understandings—by understanding how the skills and ideas work toward some end in the social context, and by learning to use them toward that end. They develop implicit rules to govern their behavior as they come to understand their new skills in relation to the activity they are engaged in. The understanding they develop is shaped in two ways by their interactions with others: the interactions provide instruction (direct and indirect) in how to complete particular tasks, and they provide reactions that help the student judge how well the task has been accomplished.

In the most productive learning environments, the instructional interactions will be supportive and collaborative: simplifying the situation, clarifying the structure, helping the students accomplish tasks that would otherwise be too difficult for them to do, and providing the framework and rules of procedure that they will gradually learn, so that instructional support will no longer be necessary (Applebee & Langer, 1983; Langer, 1984; Langer & Applebee, 1984, 1986a,b). When people work together to solve a problem and complete an activity, they can pool their group knowledge, each offering what they know to help get the job done. Alternatively, one more knowledgeable person can act as a tutor, helping the others to do what they have set out to do.

However, schools sometimes limit the nature and extent of the interactions that take place during literacy learning. Reading and writing may be taught as exercises and tests of particular skills, and interaction with others about the nature and meaning of the activities may be considered disruptive rather than facilitative. When social interaction is restricted and collaboration is discouraged, children will learn the particular behaviors invoked by those more restricted uses of literacy to which they are exposed.

3. Cognitive behaviors are influenced by context and affect the meanings that learners produce.

People learn to use literacy activities for particular purposes, and they learn particular strategies for completing those activities, based upon the contexts in which the activities take place. Hence the contexts in which literacy is used and learned lead to particular ways of thinking and doing.

Metalinguistic and metacognitive strategies are learned through the interactive events that are at the heart of literacy learning. Like other aspects of literacy learning, these strategies can be broader or narrower, depending upon the context in which they are learned. When instruction is based upon functional uses of literacy within the classroom community, there will be a ready audience to respond to attempts at learning, and to help when needed. Because the purposes of literacy activities will be clear, the learner will be able to tell how well what he or she is doing is contributing to getting the task done. Thus self-awareness in both language and cognition will occur first in the social setting, and can later become internalized as monitoring behaviors that can be carried out alone.

However, many school activities foster more limited interactions, leading to a different set of cognitive strategies and monitoring skills. Rather than encouraging self-questioning and self-appraisal, some classrooms emphasize recitation of previously memorized material or the ability to discover the interpretation preferred by the teacher. In these cases, the interaction within the classroom will foster rote memorization and test taking skills, rather than self-assessment, and may lead to a restricted set of cognitive strategies (see Langer, 1986a, 1986b). Students learn the cognitive strategies and meta-cognitive and metalinguistic behaviors required in their school environment.

These principles derive directly from the notion that literacy learning is a sociocognitive activity, and that higher level thinking is a result of learning social/functional relationships—things that work do so because they make sense in social settings. In becoming literate, learners internalize the structures of these socially meaningful activities, however extensive or limiting they might be.

Learning and Schooling.   It is necessary to tease apart and then bring together again issues of learning and schooling. While it may be possible with expert schooling to teach more and more people to be more broadly literate, it is also possible that many people, particularly members of certain minority groups, won't learn (see Ogbu, this volume). Cressey (1983) suggests that "It may be analogous to teaching fortran to a literature scholar. It is alien and external until a situation arises in which it can be useful (p. 41)." This usefulness grows out of the realities the learners face—at home, in their communities, at work, and in school. Literacy learning begins and continues when people understand its advantages and know it will benefit them; when they take ownership for their ideas and are empowered to use them for their purposes. If the perceived advantages of literacy shift from job success and financial gain (which may be seen as closed to some minority groups) to personal and social uses, *in light of* rather than antagonistic to personal and cultural differences, associations with literacy as part of the majority ideology may begin to diminish.

Literacy cannot be detached from specific sociocultural contexts, yet schools try to do this all the time. Students from a variety of cultures and subcultures are expected to understand and learn many new and complex ideas and to interpret them as the teacher does, even if they are only minimally fluent in English or are being exposed to middle class language and values different from their own. Interpretations and meanings that are contiguous with literacy in the students' first language and first culture are ignored, as are cultural differences in ways of learning and assumptions about learning (Heath, 1983; McDermott, 1977). Approached in this way, literacy instruction fails for too many students.

Since the 1970s, research on literacy and schooling has followed a number of productive paths: it has looked at cultural, social, and linguistic differences between students and the materials of instruction (Steffenson, Joag-dev, & Anderson, 1979; Scollon & Scollon, 1981; Au, 1980); at transitions from home and community to school (Cook-Gumperz & Gumperz, 1981; Heath,

1983; Scollon & Scollon, 1981; Wells, 1982); at communicative interactions among students and between students and teachers in the instructional environment (Cazden, 1979; Green & Wallat, 1981; McDermott, 1977; Schultz & Florio, 1979; Erickson, 1975); at the language of instruction (Cazden, 1979; Heath, 1983; Au, 1980; Michaels & Collins, 1982); and at social aspects of schooling (Philips, 1983; Schieffelin & Cochran-Smith, 1986). The issues have generally been taken separately, and the studies often focus on minority group students who are poor academic achievers in a traditional sense. While the language and social issues that facilitate or impede learning have been frequently studied, the patterns of learning that result have rarely been considered. See Heath (1983) for an exception.

Thus, both literacy researchers and practitioners tend to look at literacy as if reading and writing need to be learned in some pristine and decontextualized sense, detached from the social purposes they serve. This, by its very nature, inhibits both researchers and practitioners from considering literacy as a way of thinking within society. And particularly at this point in time in American society, literate thinking is precisely the goal on which we should be focusing.

The Role of the Teacher and the Role of the Student

A sociocognitive view means two things for instruction: first that more attention is paid to the social purposes to which literacy skills are put—we learn best when we are trying to accomplish something that is personally and socially meaningful. (This does not mean, however, that all class activities need to be group activities, nor that language and literacy learning are incidental.) Second, it means paying more attention to the structure of tasks that students are asked to undertake, so that direct instruction in needed skills will be provided as part of each task at points where it is needed. In this way students will have a better chance of understanding how new skills relate to the activities that are being completed. Rather than simply memorizing isolated rules, they will be able to make sense of how the rules work in completing literacy tasks.

Let me conclude by providing a brief discussion of some of the dimensions that are important to consider when reflecting on instructional interactions from a sociocognitive perspective. Every interaction takes place simultaneously on a number of different levels, ranging from the particular purposes the participants hope the interaction will achieve to the cultural and linguistic functions reflected in the dialogue that results. In considering the instructional implications of particular interactions, three dimensions are particularly important: who controls the course of the interaction, the pedagogical functions served by the interaction, and the form of the contribution that each participant makes. Alternatives within each of these dimensions are summarized in Table 1 and discussed further below.

Table 1. Dimensions of Instructional Interaction

Control of the Interaction
1. non-shared conception of goal
2. teacher regulated
3. shared regulation
4. learner regulated

Pedagogical Function
1. motivation
2. reassurance
3. help
4. extension

Participants' Contributions
1. observing/demonstrating
2. assimilating/direct instruction
3. problem solving/problem setting
4. mutual reflection and task definition

1. Control of the Interaction.   One important dimension of instructional interaction concerns who controls most of the thinking and doing. Are the students passive recipients of the learning or are they knowledge seekers? (The notion of control should not be confused with the issue of ownership [Applebee & Langer, 1983; Langer, 1984; Langer & Applebee, 1984, 1986a,b] for the goals of the activity, but focuses instead on who orchestrates the learning of a particular subgoal.)

At times a student or group of students and teacher lack a shared conception of what they are doing—either the student does not fully understand the teacher's purpose in promoting the activity, or the communicative interaction has broken down (sometimes due to cultural or social differences). In either case, this indicates that for those individuals, the activity is inappropriate and will not support the intended learning.

When students and teacher have a shared conception of what they are doing, students may be involved in varying degrees in regulating the ways in which the interaction proceeds—in deciding what gets done, how, and when. The interaction may be completely regulated by the teacher; teacher and students may share in regulating the interaction; or the interaction may be controlled by the students. Generally, control of the interaction will vary based on the degree of difficulty (and newness) of the skills and knowledge needed to complete the task that is underway. While some instructional interactions begin with teacher regulation, move to shared regulation, and finally to student regulation, the pattern is necessarily task specific and needs to be examined closely. An interaction that appears to be predominantly teacher regulated may signal a task that is too difficult for a student or may be unnecessarily dominated by the teacher, and one that is completely regulated by the student may indicate a task that is too easy for new learning to occur.

2. Pedagogical Function.   Instructional interactions can serve a variety of different pedagogical functions, depending upon the goals of the teacher and the needs of the students. The interaction may be concerned primarily with motivating the participants to engage in the activity in the first place; with providing reassurance and encouraging risk-taking and decision making; with offering help through such strategies as modeling, direct instruction, questioning, or task segmentation; or with extending the task in order to foster new and more complex learning. Each of these represents an important pedagogical function that can be realized in differing ways by the teacher and students, and each is likely to occur some time during any one activity. Less effective instructional interactions may fill only one or two of these pedagogical functions, or may provide motivation, reassurance and help, but fail to extend and generalize newly learned skills and knowledge to other more challenging situations.

3. Participants' Contributions.   The third dimension of the instructional interaction is concerned with the nature of the contribution of each of the participants. What, primarily, do they do to carry the interaction forward? What shape do their contributions take?

Some instructional interactions are organized primarily around demonstration, with students observing while the teacher (or another student) demonstrates how to complete the task. Other interactions are organized around direct instruction, with explicit presentation of information or procedures for the learners to assimilate. A third type of interaction involves the posing of more open-ended problems and a search for appropriate solutions as the students think the issues through. Finally, a fourth type of instructional interaction involves mutual reflection and task definition around shared problems or interests. This may involve evaluation and reassessment of earlier solutions, or a broadening of the topic or problem being addressed. Again, the likelihood of any one of these types of interaction is task dependent, but open-ended questioning is more likely to occur as students' knowledge increases, as is the broadening of the topic or problem being addressed. All four types of instructional interaction have their place, as long as students' own interpretations and understandings are legitimately considered and discussed among the participants.

From a sociocognitive perspective, effective literacy instruction is marked by new roles for teacher and students. Unlike traditional roles as knowledge giver and receiver, the interaction is based in social cooperation. The literacy activities themselves will also be different. They will be content-based, involving purposeful and meaningful goals as opposed to snippets of ideas presented in exercise form. Because the activity is understood by the student, and often even regulated by the student, evaluation of the success of the learning is assumed by the student. Therefore, planning, monitoring, and task evaluation, learning behaviors present in the most successful students, are encouraged. In addition, the content of the activity, the thinking and learning about new ideas and new uses of thought and language, is supported throughout. The students are encouraged in every way to become flexible and independent thinkers.

All this is a far cry from the pretest, assign, and retest view of instruction most of us have gotten so used to. However, it is difficult for teachers to adopt a sociocognitive view. The more traditional paradigm with its pre and post tests too easily identifies points of "success," indicating that the teacher has "taught" and that the students have "learned." Also, it elicits the kinds of responses the students generally need to give when they take standardized tests. But this very same oversimplicity prevents the activities from leading toward higher level learning—because they do not involve the students as active and thoughtful learners in meaningful tasks.

Literacy instruction needs to help students think more deeply and more broadly about language and experience. To achieve this, it will be necessary to look for successful literacy learning not in isolated bits of knowledge, but in students' growing ability to use language and literacy in more and broader activities. It will also be necessary to judge progress in learning by students' ability to successfully complete those activities. When we do this, the nature of instructional activities will change dramatically—from pretend to real tasks, from parts to wholes, from practice to doing, and from recitation to thinking.

CONCLUSION

I have covered a good deal of ground in this presentation of a sociocognitive approach to literacy learning. This was necessary because the view itself is broad-based and simultaneously embraces issues of both society and schooling. It takes a new perspective on literacy, viewing it as a culturally-based *way of thinking* rather than as a simple act of reading and writing. It also maintains that literacy learning is a sociocognitive activity; both social and cognitive factors play a role in the processes individuals go through in becoming literate. *Who the people are* and *how they live* makes all the difference in how they will learn as well as how they will use literacy. Yet through engagement in literate thinking, and within the constraints of the culture, the uses of literacy will change, as will the culture itself.

REFERENCES

Adult functional competency: A report to the Office of Education. (1975). Austin: University of Texas, Division of Extension.

Applebee, A.N. (1981). *Writing in the secondary school* (Research Report No. 21). Urbana, IL: National Council of Teachers of English.

Applebee, A.N. (1984). *Contexts for learning to write: Studies of secondary school instruction.* Norwood, NJ: Ablex.

Applebee, A.N., & Langer, J.A. (1983). Instructional scaffolding: Reading and writing as natural language activities. *Language Arts, 60,* 168-175.

Applebee, A.N., Langer, J.A., & Mullis, I.V.S. (1985). *The reading report card.* Princeton, NJ: Educational Testing Service.

Applebee, A.N., Langer, J.A., & Mullis, I.V.S. (1986). *Writing trends across the decade, 1974-1984.* Princeton, NJ: Educational Testing Service.

Au, K. (1980). Participation structures in a reading lesson with Hawaiian children. *Anthropology in Education Quarterly, 11*(2), 91-115.

Bakhtin, M.M. (1985). *The formal methods in literary scholarship: A critical introduction to sociological poetics.* Cambridge, MA: Harvard University Press.

Bruner, J.S. (1978). The role of dialogue in language acquisition. In A. Sinclair, R.J. Jarvelle, & W.J.M. Levelt (Eds.), *The child's conception of language.* New York: Springer-Verlag.

Bruner, J.S., Olver, R.R., & Greenfield, P.M. (1966). *Studies in cognitive growth: A collaboration at the center for cognitive studies.* New York: Wiley.

Cazden, C. (1979). Peekaboo as an instructional model: Discourse development at home and at school. *Papers and Reports on Child Language Development, 17,* 1-19.

Chafe, W. (1980). *The pear stories: Cultural, cognitive, and linguistic aspects of narrative production.* Norwood, NJ: Ablex.

Clanchy, M.T. (1979). Literact and illiterate; hearing and seeing: England 1066-1307. In H.J. Graff (Ed.), *Literacy and social development in the west.* New York: Cambridge University Press.

Clifford, G.J. (1984). Buch und lesen: Historical perspectives on literacy and schooling. *Review of Educational Research, 54*(4), 472-501.

Cook-Gumperz, J., & Gumperz, J.J. (1981). From oral to written language: The transition to literacy. In M. Farr Whiteman (Ed.), *Variation in writing: Functional and linguistic-cultural differences.* Hillsdale, NJ: Erlbaum.

Cressey, D. (1980). *Literacy and the social order.* New York: Cambridge University Press.

Cressey, D. (1983). The environment for literacy: Accomplishment and context in seventeenth-century England and New England. In D. Resnck (Ed.), *Literacy in historical perspective.* Washington, DC: Library of Congress.

Erickson, F. (1975). Gatekeeping and the melting pot: Interaction in counseling encounters. *Harvard Education Review, 45*(1), 44-70.

Furet, F., & Ozouf, J. (1977). *Reading and writing: Literacy in France from Calvin to Jules Ferry.* New York: Cambridge University Press.

Graves, D. (1978). *Balance the basics: Let them write.* New York: Ford Foundation. (ERIC Document Reproduction Service No. ED 192 364)

Goody, J. (1977). *The domestication of the savage mind.* New York: Cambridge University Press.

Graff, H.J. (1979). *The literacy myth.* New York: Academic Press.

Green, J., & Wallat, C. (1981). Mapping instructional conversations: A sociolinguistic ethnography. In J. Green & C. Wallat (Eds.), *Ethnography and language in educational settings.* Norwood, NJ: Ablex.

Heath, S.B. (1981). Toward an ethnohistory of writing in American education. In M. Farr Whiteman (Ed.), *Variation in writing: Functional and linguistic-cultural differences.* Hillsdale, NJ: Erlbaum.

Heath, S.B. (1983). *Ways with words.* New York: Cambridge University Press.

Kaestle, C.F. (1985). The history of literacy and the history of readers. In *Review of research in education (Vol. 12).* Washington, DC: American Educational Research Association.

Lakoff, R.T. (1982). Some of my favorite writers are literate: The mingling of oral and literate strategies in written communication. In D. Tannen (Ed.), *Spoken and written language: Exploring orality and literacy.* Norwood, NJ: Ablex.

Langer, J.A. (1984). Literacy instruction in American schools. *American Journal of Education, 93*(1), 107–131.

Langer, J.A. (1985a). Levels of questioning: An alternative view. *Reading Research Quarterly, 21*(5), 586–602.

Langer, J.A. (1985b). A sociocognitive view of literacy learning, *Research in the Teaching of English, 19*(4), 235–237.

Langer, J.A. (1986a). A sociocommunicative view of literacy learning. Plenary speech to California Teachers of English to Speakers of Other Languages (CATESOL), 20 April 1986, Oakland, CA.

Langer, J.A. (1986b). Learning through writing: Study skills in the content areas. *Journal of Reading, 29*(5), 400–406.

Langer, J.A. (1987). The construction of meaning and the assessment of comprehension. In R. Freedle & R. Duran (Eds.), *Cognitive and linguistic analyses of test performance.* Norwood, NJ: Ablex.

Langer, J.A. (in preparation). *Literate communication and literary instruction.*

Langer, J.A., & Applebee, A.N. (1984). Language, learning, and interaction: A framework for improving the teaching of writing: In Arthur Applebee (Ed.), *Contexts for learning to write: Studies of secondary school instruction.* Norwood, NJ: Ablex.

Langer, J.A., & Applebee, A.N. (1986a). *Writing and learning in the secondary school* (Final report to the National Institute of Education, Grant No. NIE-G-82-0027). Washington, DC: National Institute of Education.

Langer, J.A., & Applebee, A.N. (1986b). Reading theory and instruction: Toward a theory of teaching and learning. In E. Rothkopf (Ed.), *Review of research in education (Vol. 14).* Washington, DC: American Educational Research Association.

Langer, J.A., & Applebee, A.N. (in press). *The uses of writing in academic classrooms: A study of teaching and learning.* Urbana, IL: National Council of Teachers of English.

Luria, A.R. (1929/1977–78). The development of writing in the child. *Soviet Psychology, 16,* 65–114.

McDermott, R. (1977). Social relations as contexts for learning in school. *Harvard Educational Review, 47*(2), 198–213.

Michaels, S., & Collins, J. (1982). Oral discourse styles, classroom interaction and the acquisition of literacy. In D. Tannen (Ed.), *Coherence in spoken and written discourse.* Norwood, NJ: Ablex.

NAEP. (1986). *Profiles of literacy: An assessment of young adults.* Princeton, NJ: Educational Testing Service.

Ninio, A., & Bruner, J. (1978). The achievement and antecedents of labeling. *Journal of Child Language, 5,* 1–15.

Olson, D.R. (1977). From utterance to text: the bias of language in speech and writing. *Harvard Education Review, 47*(3), 257–282.

Olson, D.R. (1985). *See jumping: Some oral antecedents of literacy.* In H. Goelman, A. Oberg, & F. Smith (Eds.), *Awakening to literacy.* London: Heinemann.

Olson, D.R. (in press). On the cognitive consequences of literacy. *Canadian Psychology.*

Ong, W. (1982). *Orality and literacity: Technologizing of the word,* London: Methuen.

Philips, S. (1983). *The invisible culture: Communication in classroom and community on the Warm Springs Indian Reservation.* New York: Longman.

Resnick, D.P. (1983). *Literacy in social perspective.* Washington, DC: Library of Congress.

Resnick, D.P., & Resnick, L.R. (1977). The nature of literacy: An historical exploration. *Harvard Education Review, 47*(3), 370–385.

Schieffelin, B.B., & Cochran-Smith, M. (1986). Learning to read culturally: Literacy before schooling. In H. Goelman, A. Oberg, & F. Smith (Eds.), *Awakening to literacy.* London: Heinemann.

Schultz, J., & Florio, S. (1979). Stop and freeze: The negotiation of social and physical space in a kindergarten-first grade classroom. *Anthropology in Education Quarterly, 10*(3), 166–181.

Scollon, R., & Scollon, S.B.K. (1981). *Narrative, literacy, and interethnic communication.* Norwood, NJ: Ablex.

Scribner, S., & Cole, M. (1980). *The psychology of literacy.* Cambridge, MA: Harvard University Press.

Smith, A. (1982, Fall). Information teachology and the myth of abundance. *Daedelus,* pp. 1–16.

Steffenson, P., Joag-dev, C., & Anderson, R. (1979). A cross-cultural perspective on reading comprehension. *Reading Research Quarterly, 15,* 10–29.

Stubbs, M. (1980). *Language and literacy.* London: Routledge & Kegan Paul.

Tannen, D. (1982). The oral/literate continuum in discourse. In D. Tannen (Ed.), *Spoken and written language: Exploring orality and literacy.* Norwood, NJ: Ablex.

Vygotsky, L.S. (1962). *Thought and language.* Cambridge, MA: M.I.T. Press.

Vygotsky, L.S. (1978). *Mind in society.* Cambridge, MA: Harvard University Press.

Vygotsky, L.S. (1979). The gensesis of higher mental functions. In J. Wertsch (Ed.), *The concept of activity in Soviet psychology.* New York: Sharpe.

Wells, G. (1982). *Learning through interaction.* London: Cambridge University Press.

Wertsch, J.J.V., McNamee, G.W., McLare, J.B., & Budwig, N.A. (1980). The adult-child dyad as a problem solving system, *Child Development, 51,* 1215–1221.

PART I
PSYCHOLOGICAL ISSUES
IN LITERACY

Chapter Two
Second Game:
A School's-Eye View of Intelligence

ROBERT J. STERNBERG
Yale University

In the science-fiction short story, *Second Game* (De Vet & MacLean, 1958), the Veldians judge the intelligence of the members of their society by their ability to play a rather complicated, chess-like game. One's ability to play this game determines not only the society's evaluation of one's intelligence, but one's position in the society as well. Thus, the society chooses as its leaders those who play the game best, and fills slots at various levels of the job skill hierarchy according to level of game performance. In sum, to be intelligent on Velda is to excel in a particular way.

A starkly contrasting view of intelligence is held on the planet Standard, in Anthony's (1973) science-fiction novel, *Race Against Time.* Standard is actually Earth many centuries after wars, pollution, and plague have wiped out the large majority of the original Earth population. The Standards, having learned the lessons of the past, no longer view traditional kinds of excellence as intelligent. Indeed, those excellences were what brought the decimation of the human population through clever inventions such as bombs, man-made strains of disease for use in germ warfare, and the like. The intelligent person on Standard is the one who conforms to "the standard," who is as average as a person can be. Such a person will adapt perfectly to the standard society, thus fitting the notion of intelligence as adaptation to the environment. In sum, to be intelligent on Standard is to excel in no way at all.

The Veldian and Standard conceptions of intelligence are certainly wrong, or at best, incomplete. In *Second Game,* the protagonist, Robert Lang, a representative of the Galactic Federation, is able to accomplish his goal—to find out why Veldians resist contact with Federation planets—by purposely losing the first game in a two-game set and then winning the second game. He uses the first game successfully to determine the opponent's strengths and weaknesses. Thus, his successful attempt at purposive adaptation actually leads him to lose one game, and this loss, not a win, is intelligent both to find out the opponent's style and to lure the opponent to play him in the first place. In *Race Against Time,* the protagonist, John Smith, is able to discover the sad history of Standard, and how he is different from the Standards, by not conforming to the Standard norms, and by outwitting the Standards and running away from them. Accomplishment of his goals, then, like accomplishment of Lang's goals, requires an action-set that is unintelligent by planetary standards. In short, there is a sense in which intelligence is socio-culturally defined, but also a sense in which it is not. In one aspect, then, intelligence is subjective and subject to society's dictates, and in another aspect, objective and immune to such dictates.

The main thesis of this chapter is that in the world of intelligence, we need to understand the rules of two games, that almost all of the scientists choosing to study intelligence have studied the rules of the first game, and that this exclusive preoccupation with the first game has been a mistake. The rules of the first game are set by nature: The investigator needs to discover the latent mental structures and processes that underlie intelligence in an objective sense. This sense is the one that not only led Robert Lang to win his second game, but to lose his first game, and the one that led John Smith to conform to the Standard in appearance, but not in reality. The rules of the second game are set by society: The investigator needs to discover the manifest behaviors that the society labels as intelligent in various situations and that underlie intelligence in a subjective sense. It will be argued that the rules of the first game are universal, whereas the rules of the second game are socio-culturally specific.

Some might ask: Why study the rules of the second game at all? They might argue that it doesn't matter what people think intelligence is; what matters is what it actually is. To the extent that there is a difference between what intelligence actually is and what it is thought to be, they would say that such a difference merely represents human error. People's conceptions of intelligence, in this view, have no more claims to legitimacy than does phlogiston, an imaginary substance once believed to be responsible for fire. But this point of view is wrong scientifically, and it is not only wrong but also pernicious educationally.

The science-fiction stories described above make clear why it is important to understand intelligence in both its objective and subjective aspects. Each aspect addresses a different question with relation to the individual. The objective aspect addresses the question of the relation between intelligence and the internal world of the individual: What goes on "inside a person's head" that renders the mental functioning of that person more or less intelligent? The subjective aspect addresses the question of the relation between intelligence and the external world of the individual: What goes on in the society that renders the behavior of an individual to be judged as more or less intelligent? To the extent that intelligence is defined in terms of adaptation to one's environment, both aspects of intelligence are important: The Veldians and the Standards might have been dead wrong in their conceptions of intelligence, but these conceptions had an extremely powerful influence upon a person's adaptation to the environment. A person who is thought by society and the schools to be intelligent—or unintelligent—will be treated in certain ways, regardless of their "actual" intelligence. In principle, the correlation between the behaviors that might emanate from intelligence, objectively defined, and intelligence, subjectively defined, might range anywhere from -1 to $+1$. In practice, the correlation will probably be positive, but almost certainly less than 1.

To the extent one is interested in education, the subjective aspect of intelligence is of paramount importance, because the conceptions of intelligence held and inculcated by the school—the school's-eye view of intelligence—will determine what is rewarded and what is punished, and ultimately, who garners society's rewards and who does not. People have long recognized the differences between the objective and subjective aspects of intelligence, and their importance for schooling. Indeed, Binet was commissioned to devise the first major intelligence test because teachers were not distinguishing between maladaptive performance resulting from mental retardation (in the objective sense) and maladaptive performance resulting from behavior problems, with the result that students from both groups were being lumped together in classes for the retarded. Even then, the prevailing subjective view of intelligence resulted in many students being placed in classes in which they did not belong, and potentially, in their being deprived of the kind of station in life they might have had, had they been perceived differently. Then, as today, the school's-eye view of intelligence played a major role in determining who succeeds and who fails, not only in school, but also in later life.

There is not, truly, any one school's-eye view of intelligence. The view can vary depending upon the age of the children involved, the point of view (e.g., children, parents of school children, teachers, administrators), and the time and place of the school under consideration. The remainder of this chapter will be devoted to elaborating what these various views are; how they coexist and, in some cases, clash with each other; and how they matter in the schooling and later life of the child.

THREE PROFILES OF INTELLIGENCE:
ALICE, BARBARA, AND CELIA

Consider three students—Alice, Barbara, and Celia—who are or have been genuine students in our psychology graduate program at Yale (with their names changed to protect the innocent!). In analyzing the profiles of these students, two questions need to be addressed: Which students, if any, are intelligent in the objective sense, and which are intelligent in the subjective sense?

Alice was the admissions officer's dream. She was an easy admit to our graduate program at Yale. She came with stellar aptitude test scores, outstanding college grades, excellent letters of recommendation, and overall, pretty close to a perfect record. Alice proved to be, more or less, what her record promised. She had excellent critical, analytical abilities, and these abilities helped her earn outstanding grades in her course work during her first two years at Yale. When it came to taking tests and writing course term papers, she had no peer among her classmates. During her first couple of years in the graduate program, she was an outstanding success. But after the first two years, Alice no longer looked quite so outstanding. In our graduate program, as well as in other programs, there is a shift in emphasis after the first couple of years. This shift reflects a change in emphasis in many endeavors in human lives. In standard course work, the emphasis is upon critical, analytical ability, just the kinds of things that standard intelligence tests measure fairly well. But after the first two years, there is a shift in emphasis toward more creative, synthetic aspects of intelligence. It is not enough just to be able to criticize other people's ideas, or to learn and understand concepts that other people have proposed. One must start coming up with one's own ideas, and figuring out ways of implementing these ideas. Alice's synthetic abilities were far interior to her analytic ones, but there would have been no good way of knowing this fact from the kinds of evidence available in the admissions folder. For although conventional measures can give us a fairly good reading on analytic abilities, they give virtually no reading on synthetic abilities. Thus, Alice was "IQ-test" smart, but she was not equally intelligent in all senses of the word, and in particular, in the synthetic side of intelligence.

Barbara was the admissions officer's nightmare. When she applied to Yale, she had good grades, but abysmal aptitude test scores, at least by Yale standards. Despite these low scores, she had superlative letters of recommendation. Her recommenders described her as an exceptionally creative young woman, someone who had designed and implemented creative research with only the most minimal guidance. Moreover, her resume showed her to have been actively involved in important and publishable research. Her referees assured us that this research was a sign of her own ability to generate and to follow through on creative ideas, and that it was not merely a sign of the ability of her advisors. The first time Barbara applied to Yale, her case was discussed at length, but she was rejected. The long discussions she received in the admissions committee meeting seemed almost an attempt by the committee members to salve their collective conscience, with their knowing that ultimately they would reject her. The vote was five to one against her admission. Unfortunately, most people like Barbara are rejected not only from our program, but from other competitive programs as well. As a result, they either have to enter a program that is much less competitive or else enter a different field altogether.

   This pattern of events is not limited to graduate school. There are thousands of people like Barbara (although perhaps not quite so gifted on the synthetic side) who are rejected in a similar way from law schools, business schools, education schools, medical schools, and the like (including jobs requiring selection tests). Some of them never even get to the point of applying, having been rejected earlier from competitive colleges. But in Barbara's case, an unusual thing happened. The one person who voted for her admission (myself, of course) was so convinced of her talents that he hired her as a full-time research associate. At the same time that she was a research associate, she also took two courses, two-thirds of the standard load of regular first-year graduate students. Her accomplishments during her initial year at Yale should have been an embarrassment to the admissions committee. She was one of the best students in both her classes, despite her working full time. She was not as good in classes as was Alice, but was certainly way above the average. Moreover, she showed herself to have the outstanding research abilities that her referees had promised: She independently involved herself in creative, enterprising research. The next year, Barbara reapplied to Yale, as well as to other graduate programs. This time around, the vote for her admission was unanimous, and she was also admitted to other equally competitive programs. We were most pleased when she decided to come to Yale. Although Barbara was never quite so excellent as Alice in her course performance, she was ready for the change in demands of the graduate program. When these demands shifted from an emphasis on analytic abilities to an emphasis on synthetic abilities, Barbara was ready: Indeed, she was in her element. Barbara did not have Alice's analytic abilities, but she greatly surpassed Alice in synthetic abilities.

   Celia, on paper, appeared to be somewhere between Alice and Barbara in terms of her suitability for admission to the graduate program. She was very good on almost every measure of ability to succeed in graduate school, but not truly outstanding on any of them. We admitted her, expecting her to come out near the middle of the class. This did not happen. Rather, Celia proved to be outstanding, although in a way that is quite different from Alice or Barbara. Celia's expertise proved to be in figuring out and in adapting to the demands of a complex environment in which what is required for success is not always what would seem to be required, on paper. Placed in a new kind of setting, Celia can figure out what is required of her, and then go ahead and do it just right. She knows exactly how to get ahead. In conventional parlance, Celia is "street-smart." She excels in practical intelligence. It is not that Celia never made mistakes. But she made relatively few of them, and corrected them quickly. Moreover, she put herself in a position in which everyone was convinced that she had exactly the abilities it would take to obtain a good academic job and then do well in it. Although she had neither Alice's analytic abilities nor Barbara's synthetic ones, she was better able to take what abilities she had and apply them to the everyday environment of academia than practically anyone else who had come along within the recent past. For example, she made sure that she would have three excellent letters of recommendation (the number customarily required for job applications), whereas neither Alice nor Barbara, despite their outstanding accomplishments, had quite assured themselves that three recommenders were so well aware of their work that they could be counted on for strong letters.

The vignettes of Alice, Barbara, and Celia, informal though they may be, tell us something about intelligence, both as it is objectively defined and as it is subjectively defined.

First, the perceived nature of intelligence can change with level of schooling. Through college, analytic abilities weigh heavily in teachers' evaluations of intelligence. These abilities are important in standardized ability and achievement tests, in some teacher-made tests, in classroom discussions, and the like. Later on, whether in school or on the job, synthetic abilities become more important—the ability to come up with one's own new ideas and ways of implementing these ideas. There is a transition from particular valuing of Alices to particular valuing of Barbaras that, although not complete, is nevertheless quite noticeable.

Second, conventional standardized tests measure analytic abilities fairly well, but scarcely measure synthetic abilities at all. Nor is it clear, at the present time, how synthetic abilities can be measured in a nontrivial way. But, for lack of adequate predictor measures, teachers and administrators use measures of analytic ability to predict success, even when they are inappropriate. Alices almost always have the edge on prediction.

Third, conventional standardized tests do not measure very well the student's ability both to make the most of his or her latent abilities, and to implement these abilities in everyday settings, whether inside or outside the school. This ability to make the most of one's abilities in practical and social settings is important to intelligence as it is manifested in behavior, and can itself be a kind of practical intelligence, or "street-smarts." Without at least some of Celia's skills, one's intelligence can simply get lost and have little or no impact upon the world.

Fourth, schools may be rewarding ability patterns that pay off a great deal in the short-run, especially in early schooling, but not ability patterns that pay off in the long-run, especially in later schooling and in adulthood. The great contributions to the arts, sciences, and other fields are probably made by the Barbaras of the world, not by the Alices. There are many Alices who do extremely well in school and then disappear into the woodwork, never to be heard from again.

Fifth, this pattern of rewards may ultimately have pernicious effects on society and the contributions that can be made to it. The reason for this derives from reinforcement theory. Through the early years of advanced

graduate education (in whatever field), students like Alice tend to be contin-
ually reinforced for their analytic abilities, because these are the abilities the
school values. As a result, such individuals develop a pattern of use and
capitalization upon these abilities. When the reward system changes, as it
eventually does, the Alices come to be intermittently, rather than continu-
ally, reinforced for their analytic abilities. After all, such abilities continue
to matter—they just don't matter quite so much. But reinforcement theory
predicts that intermittent reinforcement will sustain a given pattern of functioning more, rather than less, than continual reinforcement. As a result,
the Alices of the world may well not seek other abilities in themselves that
would lead to greater success in later life, even if they have these abilities
within them to develop. The Barbaras and Celias, on the other hand, will be
only modestly reinforced for their abstract analytic abilities early in their
schooling. As a result, they may realize that they need to find other abilities
within themselves upon which to capitalize. When the reinforcement pattern changes later in life, therefore, they may be more prepared than the
Alices to capitalize upon their synthetic or practical abilities. The sad part
of this story is that Alice might potentially have the synthetic or practical
abilities of Barbara and Celia, but never find, develop, and capitalize upon
these abilities because of the pattern of reinforcement she has received in
her schooling.

Finally, there is a danger that students such as Barbara and Celia may
come to perceive themselves as not particularly intelligent because of their
lesser test scores and the lesser reinforcement they receive in school. When,
later on, they do start to succeed, they are potentially at risk for perceiving
themselves as imposters, that is, people who succeed despite the fact that
they are not very capable. They may view themselves as "putting one over"
on the world rather than as capable people in their own right.

In sum, the vignettes show that the subjective side of intelligence *does*
matter, having substantial effects upon the way in which rewards are distributed by the schools and, ultimately, by the students, both to themselves
and to others.

IMPLICIT THEORIES OF INTELLIGENCE AND SCHOOLING

In recounting the above vignettes, I have argued that intelligence in the objective sense can manifest itself in different forms, and that the form in
which it manifests itself can have substantial effects both upon the way a
student is perceived by others and upon the way the student perceives himself or herself. Is there any evidence beyond the anecdotal that people have
"implicit theories" of intelligence, that these theories affect their judgments
of their own and others' intelligence, and that these effects extend to the

classroom? I believe that there is fairly strong evidence in the affirmative with respect to all three of these issues.

INTELLIGENCE AS PERCEIVED BY ADULTS

The Structure of Implicit Theories

In a first series of studies on these issues, Sternberg, Conway, Ketron, and Bernstein (1981) sought to determine the structure and use of people's implicit theories of intelligence. In a first study, laypersons entering a supermarket, commuters in a train station, and students in a college library were asked to list behaviors that they believed characterized an extremely intelligent, academically intelligent, or everyday intelligent individual. We then compiled a master list of behaviors, and asked new samples of subjects to rate how characteristic each behavior was of an ideally "intelligent person," "academically intelligent person," and "everyday intelligent person." A separate set of samples was asked to rate how important each behavior was to defining intelligence, academic intelligence, and everyday intelligence. We were particularly interested in two particular samples: laypersons and experts (renowned university professors) in the field of intelligence, broadly defined. From these studies, we learned some interesting facts about people's implicit theories of intelligence.

First, laypersons have quite well-defined implicit theories of intelligence. Three factors emerged clearly from their rating data: practical problem solving ability (e.g., reasons logically and well, identifies connections among ideas, sees all aspects of a problem, gets to the heart of problems), verbal ability (e.g., speaks clearly and articulately, is verbally fluent, converses well, reads with high comprehension), and social competence (e.g., accepts others for what they are, admits mistakes, displays interest in the world at large, is on time for appointments).

Second, there is a high correlation between lay and expert views of intelligence: The median correlation between the response patterns of university professors specializing in the study of intelligence and those of laypersons was .82. There were two main differences between the two groups, however. The first was that experts considered motivation to be an important ingredient in academic intelligence, whereas no motivation factor emerged for the laypersons. Behaviors central to the motivation factor for experts included, for example, displays dedication and motivation in chosen pursuits, gets involved in what he or she is doing, studies hard, and is persistent. The second difference was that experts placed somewhat less emphasis on the social–cultural aspects of intelligence than did the laypersons. Behaviors such as sensitivity to other people's needs and desires, and frankness and honesty with self and others, showed up in the social competence factor for laypersons but not for experts.

In order to get a better sense of just how experts and laypersons differ in their views of intelligence, I went back to the original ratings of the importance of the various behaviors to people's conceptions of intelligence. I was particularly interested in those kinds of behaviors that received higher ratings from laypersons than from experts, and in those that received higher ratings from experts than from laypersons. The pattern was clear. Consider first some of the behaviors that laypersons emphasized more than did experts in defining intelligence: acts politely, displays patience with self and others, gets along well with others, is frank and honest with self and others, and emotions are appropriate to situations. These behaviors, which are typical of those rated higher by laypersons, clearly show an emphasis on *inter*personal competence in a social context. Consider next some of the behaviors that the professors typically emphasized more than did laypersons in defining intelligence: reads with high comprehension, shows flexibility in thought and action, reasons logically and well, displays curiosity, learns rapidly, thinks deeply, and solves problems well. These behaviors clearly show an emphasis on *intra*personal competence in an individual context. To the extent that there is a difference, therefore, it is clearly in the greater emphasis among the laypersons than among the professors on intelligence as an interpersonal and social construct.

Third, the three kinds of intelligence are correlated, but differentially. For laypersons, the correlations between ratings of characteristicness were .75 between intelligence and academic intelligence, .86 between intelligence and everyday intelligence, and .45 between academic intelligence and everyday inteligence. For experts, the correlations were .83 between intelligence and academic intelligence, .84 between intelligence and everyday intelligence, and .46 between academic intelligence and everyday intelligence. Two conclusions emerge from these correlations. First, the professors view intelligence as closer to academic intelligence than do laypersons. Second, academic and everyday intelligence are viewed as related but clearly distinct constructs.

Fourth, a fine-grained analysis of our data reveals not only distinguishable differences between experts and laypersons, but also distinguishable subpopulations among laypersons. Students, we found, gave greater weight to academic ability as a component of general intelligence than commuters did. Commuters, on the other hand, considered everyday intelligence—the ability to function well in daily life—more important.

The experts in our initial studies were all college professors, but their fields were almost exclusively psychology and education. These professors had clear notions of what they looked for when they looked for intelligence in their students. But would these notions be the same across fields? Would professors of philosophy, for example, look for the same kinds of attributes as would professors of, say, physics, in evaluating the intelligence of a student? In order to address this question, I conducted a separate set of studies in which professors of art, business, philosophy, and physics were asked to list behaviors that were characteristic of highly intelligent individuals in their fields. Once the behaviors were compiled, new samples of professors in the same fields were asked to rate the characteristicness of each behavior in the repertoire of an extremely intelligent person (Sternberg, 1985b). We found differences in emphasis across fields.

Whereas the professors of art emphasized knowledge and the ability to use that knowledge in weighing alternative possibilities and in seeing analogies, the business professors emphasized the ability to think logically, to focus on essential aspects of a problem, and both to follow others' arguments easily and see where these arguments lead. The emphasis on assessment of argumentation in the business professors' implicit theories is far weaker in the artists' implicit theories. The philosophy professors emphasized critical and logical abilities very heavily, and especially the abilities to follow complex arguments, to find subtle mistakes in these arguments, and to generate counter-examples to invalid arguments. The philosophers' view very clearly emphasizes those aspects of logic and rationality that are essential in analyzing and creating philosophical arguments. The physicist, in contrast, places more emphasis on precise mathematical thinking, the ability to grasp quickly the laws of nature. In short, professors in different fields had a core view of the nature of intelligence, but there were also important and intuitively plausible differences among the fields in what kinds of behaviors were emphasized in the assessment of intelligence.

The studies described above queried teachers regarding their conceptions of intelligence, but of course, all of the teachers were at the undergraduate and graduate levels. One might well wonder how teachers of younger students conceive of intelligence, and whether there are differences as a function of the grade level of the students whom the teachers teach. Fry (1984) addressed this question in a series of studies in which she used the Sternberg et al. (1981) procedures with teachers at different levels of schooling ranging from the elementary to the college level. Her results generally replicated those of Sternberg et al. (1981), but she found clear differences in emphasis as a function of the grade level at which the teachers taught. At the elementary level, teachers emphasized the social competence aspects of intelligence in their evaluations. At the secondary level, teachers emphasized verbal skills. And at the college level, teachers emphasized problem solving skills. These results have potentially important implications for understanding what is valued in the schools at different levels. In particular, they suggest that in the elementary school grades, noncognitive factors carry a large weight in teachers' conceptions of intelligence. (My own experiences with the teachers of my own children are quite consistent with this finding, and have often resulted in my great frustration as my discussions of cognitive progress with these teachers seemed always to turn to discussions of social skills, whether I wanted this turn in the discussions or not!)

In sum, both laypersons and teachers at all levels have rather well-defined notions of intelligence. These notions display a common core, but are shaded according to the individual's walk of life. In particular, teachers' conceptions of intelligence vary as a function of the level of teaching and as a function of the field of teaching at the upper levels. There is not one "school's-eye" view of intelligence, but several such views, and these views color the ways in which teachers perceive the intelligence of their students.

Use of Implicit Theories

Clearly, people have well-defined implicit theories of intelligence. But do they actually use these implicit theories in evaluating themselves and others? We sought to address these questions in our research.

To find out whether or not what people say intelligence is actually has any relation to their judgments of the intelligence of others, we sent lay subjects a series of personal sketches of fictitious people, employing behaviors taken from the master list. These sketches in some ways resembled brief and telegraphic letters of recommendation one might get if one sought written evaluations of people's intelligence. Consider two typical sketches:

Susan:

She keeps an open mind.
She is knowledgeable about a particular field.
She converses well.
She shows a lack of independence.
She is on time for appointments.

Adam:

He deals effectively with people.
He thinks he knows everything.
He shows a lack of independence.
He lacks interest in solving problems.
He speaks clearly and articulately.
He fails to ask questions.
He is on time for appointments.

The respondents' task was to rate the intelligence of each person on a scale from 1 (low) to 9 (high). Our task was to find out whether or not respondents' ratings were consistent with laypersons' conceptions of intelligence. If they were, then behaviors that received higher characisticness ratings for intelligence should lead to lower ratings of the intelligence of the fictitious persons. "Keeps an open mind," for example, had been rated 7.7, whereas "shows a lack of independence" had been rated just 2.7. Averaging the characteristicness ratings for each of the fictitious persons, we came up with a score of 6.0 for Susan and of 4.3 for Adam. By comparison, our respondents rated Susan's intelligence at 5.8 and Adam's at 4.3. Overall, when we calculated the correlation between the two sets of ratings (expected values on the basis of the average characteristicsness ratings for the described persons, on the one hand, and actual ratings of the described persons, on the other), we obtained a coeffficient of .96. In other words, laypersons' ratings of other people's intelligence were indeed firmly grounded in their implicit theories about intelligence.

We also used multiple-regression techniques in order to determine the weights for each of the three factors in laypersons' implicit theories. As independent variables, we used approximation factor scores of each of the described individuals on each of the factors of the implicit theory (as well as on unintelligence). The multiple correlation was .97. The standardized regression (beta) weights for each of the three factors were .32 for problem solving ability, .33 for verbal ability, and .19 for social competence. (There was also a weight for unintelligent behaviors of $-.48$.) These weights indicate the psychological importance assigned to each of these factors by the subjects in the study. All weights were statistically significant and all signs were in the predicted directions, with only unintelligent behaviors showing a negative weight. As expected, the unintelligent behaviors had the highest regression weight, because there was only one independent variable for such behaviors, as opposed to three for intelligent behaviors. Moreover, as anyone who has read letters of recommendation knows, even one negative comment can carry quite a bit of weight. Of the three kinds of intelligent behaviors, the two cognitive kinds (problem solving and verbal ability) carried about equal weight, and the noncognitive kind (social competence) carried less weight.

Do people use their implicit theories of intelligence in evaluating their own intelligence? Sternberg et al. (1981) had one group of subjects rate themselves on each of the behaviors in the master list, and also had these subjects rate themselves on intelligence, academic intelligence, and everyday intelligence. In order to get a score from the behavioral ratings, we correlated each individual response pattern with the prototypical response pattern for the ideally intelligent person (obtained from the subjects described earlier). One might view the correlation between the individuals' self-descriptions and the prototypical response pattern as measuring the degree to which a given subject resembles the prototype of an intelligent person. Higher scores represent closer resemblance between the individual and the prototype.

The mean correlation of subjects' response patterns for themselves compared to the prototypical response pattern was .40 for intelligence, .31 for academic intelligence, and .41 for everyday intelligence. On the average, then, people saw themselves as having a moderate degree of resemblance to each of the prototypes. The range in degree of resemblance was quite large, though. For intelligence, for example, the range of correlations for individual subjects was from − .05 to .65.

These prototype scores were then correlated with both self-ratings of intelligence, academic intelligence, and everyday intelligence, and with IQ. The respective former correlations were .36, .42, and .17 for intelligence, academic intelligence, and everyday intelligence, and the latter correlations were .52 for the intelligence prototype score, .56 for the academic intelligence prototype score, and .41 for the everyday intelligence prototype score. Thus, IQ tests come closest to measuring what people conceive of as academic intelligence, and least close to measuring what people conceive of as everyday intelligence.

To conclude, people not only have, but use their implicit theories of intelligence in evaluating others. These implicit theories are important in the judgments of both laypersons and teachers. But how about the students? Do they have implicit theories, and if so, how do these theories match up with those of the schools? This question is addressed in the next section.

CHILDREN'S CONCEPTIONS OF INTELLIGENCE

Several studies have also been done on children's conceptions of the nature of intelligence. Three sets of studies are particularly relevant.

Yussen and Kane (1983) conducted a series of studies on children's conceptions of intelligence. In the first study, they conducted interviews with children in the first, third, and sixth grades. All were lower-middle to middle-middle class. They found that younger children's conceptions of intelligence were less differentiated than older children's conceptions. Older children were also more likely to characterize intelligence as an internalized quality of the individual. In other words, the younger children were more likely to believe that a person's level of intelligence could be assessed by things the person does or says than were the older children. There was also a monotonically decreasing trend in levels of self-ratings with grade level.

In a second study, Yussen and Kane asked first and sixth graders to imagine either of two children, one of whom is smart and one of whom is not smart. The task was then to assess the performance of the children on various tasks. For example, suppose the hypothetical target child is Alice. She may be imagined to be either smart or not smart. Subjects would be asked questions such as: "Suppose Alice is having a jumping contest with her friends. How often will she jump the farthest and win the contest?" or "Suppose Alice hears a new song. How much of it will she remember the next day?" The questions were divided into four categories: physical, social, academic, and cognitive. The two sample questions above are physical and cognitive, respectively. In this second study, three clearcut findings emerged. First, in all descriptive categories, smart children were judged as better than children who are not smart. Second, the gap between smart and not smart children is relatively small for the physical behaviors, but relatively large for each of the other kinds of behaviors. Third, the gaps are about the same for both first and sixth graders.

In a last study, children in grades three and six, as well as college-age adults, were asked to characterize an intelligent individual who was either an infant, 10 years old, an adult, or an older adult. The results of this study were complex, and can only be presented here in barest outline.

Consider first the infant. Everyone agreed that gross and fine sensori-motor control, the tendency to do things without help, and precocious language acquisition are important to intelligence. Both groups of grade school children, but not the adults, also emphasized the importance of the infants' knowing what they should and should not do under particular circumstances. But only the adults mentioned motivation and curiosity as signaling infant intelligence.

Consider next the 10-year-old. All age groups agreed that superior school performance is typical of the intelligent child. But whereas everyone mentioned general kinds of knowledge and performance indicators, only the children emphasized the importance of excellence in the specific pursuits of reading and mathematics. All of the groups mentioned certain social skills, such as being helpful to others and being an adaptable member of a group. But only the children mentioned physical skills, such as in sports, as typifying the intelligent individual, whereas only the adults mentioned motivation, learning, thinking abstractly, showing interest and affiliation with peers, exhibiting independence, and creativity.

The greatest divergence between the children's and adults' characterizations were for their conceptions of the intelligent adult. The children emphasized the importance of performance on specific tasks, such as managing the household, excelling at a job, earning money, and teaching children. They also valued the adult's ability to drive, perform in sports events, and show manual skill. In contrast, adults stressed abstract qualities in their characterizations, such as independence, social adjustment, general cognitive abilities, open-mindedness, and so on.

Finally, there were both similarities and differences between age groups in their characterizations of older adults. Children emphasized protecting oneself from and dealing with physical infirmities. They also emphasized amount of knowledge and the older adults' ability to find recreational outlets for themselves. The comments of the adults, on the other hand, stressed the importance of wisdom—including both its accumulation and its sharing with others.

To conclude, both children and adults have definable conceptions of intelligence for people of different ages. Although these conceptions overlap, there are notable differences in the conceptions as well. These differences may lead to children's performing in ways that they believe distinguish themselves as intelligent, but that are not necessarily perceived in this way by adults. For example, the school-age children, but not the adults, viewed distinction in sports as typifying the intelligent 10-year-old. A study yet to be done is one of children's views of adults' perceptions of intelligence, and of adults' views of children's perceptions of intelligence. Such a study might directly indicate just how children and adults miscommunicate in attempting to show their intelligence to each other.

An interesting follow-up to the Yussen and Kane work was done by Alexander (1985), who compared gifted versus nongifted children's perceptions of intelligence. Children in the sample ranged in age from 12 to 17 years. In general, gifted children tended to emphasize cognitive attributes such as understanding, reasoning, and problem solving in their conceptions. Nongifted students, on the other hand, more emphasized social and academic attributes. Nongifted students were more likely to weigh physical attributes as important than were the gifted students. Thus, the gifted students seem to come closer to the adults' conceptions of intelligence, based on the findings of Yussen and Kane, whereas the nongifted students have perceptions more similar to those of Yussen and Kane's children.

Some of the most interesting work on children's conceptions of intelligence has been done by Dweck (see, e.g., Dweck & Elliott, 1983). Dweck has suggested that children can be classified in one of two ways, depending upon their implicit theory of intelligence. "Incremental theorists" view intelligence as a repertoire of skills that leads to increases in performance through effort, and believe that effort is an investment that leads to increases in intelligence, In contrast, "entity theorists" view intelligence as a global, stable entity whose adequacy is judged through performance. Hence, they view effort as a risk that may reveal low intelligence. Thus, incremental theorists tend to stress learning and increasing competence through learning. Entity theorists tend to stress performance and the judgment of their competence through performance. For the incremental theorist, the optimal task is one that maximizes their learning, thus making them smarter. For the entity theorist, the the optimal task is one that maximizes their looking smart. Dweck and Elliott outline a whole range of cognitions and behaviors that separate the two kinds of children, showing differing world views whose implications may go far beyond alternate conceptions of intelligence. The authors note that by late grade school, virtually all children understand aspects of both of these two views, but that, independent of their actual level of intelligence, they tend to favor one view or the other. Dweck's work suggests that studies of children's conceptions of intelligence need to focus upon individual differences as well as group commonalities, as there can be practically meaningful differences in conceptions of intelligence across children. Incremental and entity theorists have very different views of just what they should do in school to maximize their intelligence, and the appearance of it. In the short-run, entity theorists may be benefited by their engagement in activities that make them "look smart." In the long-run, however, they may be penalized by their reluctance to engage in tasks that, ultimately, will make them smarter.

ETHNOGRAPHIC STUDIES OF THE SCHOOL'S-EYE VIEW OF INTELLIGENCE[1]

We have seen how laypersons, teachers, and students have views of intelligence that correspond in some ways but not in others. Moreover, there are differences within as well as between groups. What happens when a child goes to school, having been raised with one view of intelligence and then being confronted in the school with another? The confrontation can be a receipe for disaster, as shown in the brilliant work of Shirley Heath (1983) on language development in three U.S. subcultures.

Heath studied language development in three communities in the Piedmont Carolinas, Trackton (lower class black), Roadville (lower class white), and Gateway (middle class white). It is possible to present here only a fraction of the observations she has made on the effects of match and mismatch between what constitutes intelligent behavior from the point of view of the school and from the point of view of the community in which a given child was raised.

Children in Trackton start off on the wrong foot by not being able to answer even so simple a question as whether they are present in the class. They have grown up with nicknames different from those on their birth certificate—hence, their failure to respond when asked their name (Heath, p. 278). Moreover, even having found out this name, they object to being called by it, and are reluctant to answer to it. Teachers, however, protest using names like "Frog" and "Red Girl," and hence often insist on using the formal name.

Moreover, in Trackton, questions for which the questioner has or expects the specific information needed for an answer are rare. A question such as, "What's my name?" or "What's your name?" is not expected to yield a literal answer, but rather, recognition of a social relationship. The name given will depend on who asks it, and on why the question is asked (Heath, p. 111). In even so simple a situation as responding to one's name, there-

---

[1] This section of the chapter is based upon and condensed from Sternberg and Suben (in press), which discusses, among other things, the implication of Shirley Brice Heath's work for understanding the socialization of intelligence.

fore, the Trackton children appear stupid because of their unwillingness or inability to respond appropriately.

Roadville children also confront a problem in naming, although a very different kind of problem. In Roadville, a very small number of first names —such as Robert, Betty, and Elizabeth—tend to be favored for children. The result is that there will be many children of the same age with the same name. In school, as a result, multiple Roadville children may respond to a given name. The obvious solution, to use additional initials (such as the middle or last ones), is resisted by the children, causing frustration for both teachers and students alike.

The problem of Trackton children goes beyond mere naming. Trackton children do not expect adults to ask them questions, in general, because in Trackton, children are not seen as information-givers or as question-answerers (Heath, p. 103). As a result, the very act of being asked a question is strange to them. When Heath asked Trackton children to do tasks she gave them or to do jobs she assigned them, the children often protested, seeing no reason why they should do these tasks (Heath, p. 108). Trackton children particularly have trouble dealing with indirect requests, such as, "It's time to put our paints away now," because such unfamiliar kinds of statements may not even be perceived as requests (Heath, p. 280). These children have particular difficulty with "Why?" questions, because adults in Trackton do not engage children in conversations in which such questions are asked (Heath, p. 109), in stark contrast to typical middle class upbringing.

In Roadville, as in Gateway, the situation young children confront is very different. Adults see themselves as teachers, and thus ask and answer questions, including "Why?" questions (Heath, p. 129). By the time they go to school, these children have had considerable experience with both direct and indirect requests. Unfortunately, parents in Roadville do not persist in this attitude. Once their children start school, they more or less abdicate their role as teachers, leaving it to the school to do the job. From their point of view, their days as teachers are now over (Heath, p. 138).

Heath suggests that there is an implicit conflict in means of resource allocation across the three communities she has studied. One of the ways American schools prepare children for a schedule-dominated adulthood is through the expectation that the schools' fairly strict schedules will be observed. Place constraints are equally important. Things are expected to go in their proper place at the proper time. In Trackton, the flow of time is casual. There are no timed tasks at home, and few tasks that are even time-linked (Heath, p. 275). For example, people eat when they are hungry, and there are few constraints on which parts of the meal come before or after which other parts (Heath, p. 276). There are few scheduled activities, and routines, such as going to bed, may happen at very different times on different days (Heath, p. 167). The children are used to a flow of time in which their wants and needs are met as a function of whether there is someone there to meet them, and whether the provisions needed are available (Heath, p. 275). It is, thus, odd for the Trackton child to adhere to a schedule that appears to the child as essentially arbitrary and capricious. Timed tests, of course, seem even stranger than school schedules: Before entering school, the child may have had literally no experience with being timed in the performance of a cognitive task. In Trackton, things get done, basically, when they get done!

The Trackton child has similar difficulties with space allocation. Being told to put things in a certain place has little or no meaning to the Trackton child (Heath, p. 273). He or she is used to putting things down when done, but the place may vary from time to time. The child has so few possessions that it will generally not be a problem finding the object later. The Trackton child's relatively poor handling of time and space becomes a basis for teachers' unfavorable judgments almost from the start of school.

Children from Roadville and Gateway have a very different sense of time and place. Roadville parents want their children to grow up with a very strict sense of everything having its time and place (Heath, p. 137). In Roadville, even the stories maintain a strict chronological order, emphasizing sequences of events (Heath, p. 185). In Gateway, life is strictly scheduled, and even babies are expected to adhere to this fairly strict scheduling (Heath, p. 243). Things have a time and a place, and children are expected to learn what these are, just as they will later be expected to do so in school.

Trackton children are at a disadvantage when they start school from the standpoint of understanding similarities and differences between objects and skills that are important in school and critical on typical intelligence tests.

Trackton children never spontaneously volunteer to list the attributes of two objects that are similar to or different from each other. Instead, they seem to view objects holistically, comparing the objects as wholes rather than attribute-by-attribute (Heath, p. 107). Although they may be sensitive to shape, color, size, and so on, they do not use these attributes to make judgments as to how the two objects are similar or different. This unfamiliarity with abstraction, and their viewing of things in holistic contexts, impedes progress in reading as well as in reasoning. The Trackton child experiences a holistic coherence with respect to printed words such that if the print style, type font, or even the context of a given word changes, the child notices the change and may become upset. At the same time, the child fails to realize the symbolic equivalence of the print under these transformations, which, although relevant to the child, are irrelevant to the meaning of the printed word (Heath, p. 192). Each new appearance of a word in a new context results in a perception of a different word (Heath, p. 223).

The holistic perceptual and conceptual style of the Trackton child also interferes with the child's progress in mathematics, where one object plus one object may be perceived as yielding one object, in that the two objects are viewed as a new whole rather than as composed of two discrete parts resulting from the summation. Rather than carrying rules over from one problem to another, children may see each problem as a distinct whole, needing new rules rather than transfer of old ones (Heath, p. 291).

The situation is quite different in Roadville. Adults encourage children to label things, and they talk to the children about the attributes of these things (Heath, p. 127). A primary goal in adults' play with children is to encourage them to define the attributes of the play stimuli, and the toys the adults give the children encourage them to match attributes such as color, shape, size, and so on (Heath, p. 136). Gateway parents, too, give their children educational toys from an early age. Children are encouraged to note points of similarity and difference between objects, and to label these differences as they are encountered (Heath, p. 351). Gateway parents talk to children about names of things in books as well as in the world, discussing matters of size, shape, and color as they arise.

Like the Trackton children who sometimes suffer from a holistic perspective, the Kpelle tribe in Africa seem to view certain kinds of problems holistically, which inhibits the transfer of problem solving skills to other contexts that appear to be dissimilar. Cole and his associates showed that the Kpelle were completely stymied by a problem in inferential combination that utilized an unfamiliar apparatus, but successfully solved an analogous problem that involved familiar objects (Cole, Gay, Glick, & Sharp, 1971). The American apparatus consisted of a box with three compartments. When a button was pushed on one of the compartment doors, a marble would be released. Pushing a button on a second door resulted in the release of a ball bearing. Insertion of a marble into a hole in the third door led to the release of a piece of candy. Even though the Kpelle learned how to obtain the item from each compartment individually, they were almost always unable to figure out how to start with nothing and end up with a piece of candy (i.e., by pushing the botton to get the marble and then inserting the marble into the hole in the other door). The second version of the problem was constructed so as to require the identical steps for its solution. In this case, the candy was in a box locked with a red key. Each of two nearby matchboxes contained a key; one key was red, the other, black. To solve this problem, the red key had to be removed from its matchbox and used to unlock the box containing the candy. After learning what the individual containers held, nearly all the Kpelle subjects solved this problem spontaneously. The lack of transfer to the American version of the problem can be attributed to the subjects' failure to compare the problems on a point-by-point basis. Holistically viewed, the American version seemed to be a totally new and different problem.

Trackton children are disadvantaged in reading as much by attitudes toward reading as they are by their perception of the reading material. In

Trackton, reading is strictly a group affair. An individual who chooses to read on his or her own is viewed as antisocial. Solitary reading is for those who are unable to make it in the Trackton social milieu (Heath, p. 191). Moreover, there are few magazines, books, or other reading materials in Trackton, so that children have little opportunity to practice reading, or to be read to. Whereas Roadville parents frequently read to their children, especially at night (Heath, p. 223), such a practice would be most unusual in Trackton (Heath, p. 167).

McDermott (1974) has noted that reading is an act that aligns the black child with the wrong forces in the universe of socialization. Whereas reading is a part of the teacher's agenda and a game the teacher wishes the students to play, it is not a part of the black students' agenda and the games they wish to play. Not reading is accepting the peer group's games over the teachers' games, and Trackton children are likely to make just this choice.

Attitudes toward reading are different in Roadville and Gateway, but the attitudes of these two communities also differ between themselves. Once children start school, parents in Roadville generally stop reading to their children, expecting the school to take on this task. Adults encourage children to watch Sesame Street, one means for the children to pick up reading (p. 134), but the adults themselves scarcely set examples to model. Heath notes that the two outstanding features of reading habits in Roadville are, first, that everyone talks about it but that few people do it, and second, that few take any follow-up action on the reading they do (Heath, p. 220). Unlike in Trackton, Roadville homes do have reading matter, such as magazines. But the magazines usually pile up unread, and are then thrown away in periodic cleanings of the house (Heath, p. 221).

Attitudes toward reading are different, yet again, in Gateway. There, children are coached before they enter school in both reading and listening behaviors (Heath, p. 253). Children are encouraged to read, to learn the structures of stories, and to use what they learn in their lives.

Cross-cultural studies of classification, categorization, and problem solving behavior illustrate the effects of three processes I have labeled selective encoding, combination, and comparison (see Davidson & Sternberg, 1984; Sternberg, 1985a). *Selective encoding* is at issue in studies of attribute preference in classification tasks. In these tasks, a subject may be shown a red triangle, a blue triangle, and a red square, and asked which two things belong together. Western literature shows a consistent developmental trend, such that very young children choose color as the decisive (or relevant) stimulus attribute, whereas older children shift their preference to form by about age 5 (cf. Suchmann & Trabasso, 1966). Cross-cultural studies, on the other hand, often fail to show this color-to-form shift (Cole et al., 1971). Cole and Scribner (1974) suggest that the preference for form versus color may be linked to the development of literacy (where alphabetic forms acquire tremendous importance), which differs widely across cultures.

Luria (1976) provides an illustration of *selective combination* in a categorization task. Shown a hammer, a saw, a log, and a hatchet, an illiterate Central Asian peasant was asked which three items were similar. He insisted that all four fit together, even when the interviewer suggested that the concept "tool" could be used for the hammer, saw, and hatchet, but not for the log. The subject in this instance combined the features of the four items that were relevant in terms of his culture, and arrived at a functional or situational concept (perhaps one of "things you need to build a hut"). In his failure to combine the "instrumental" features of the tools selectively into a concept that excluded the log, however, the subject was not performing intelligently—at least, from the perspective of the experimenter's culture.

In many of Luria's studies, the unschooled peasants have great difficulty in solving the problem given them. Often, they appear to be thrown off by an apparent discrepancy between the terms of the problem and what they know to be true. For example, take one of the math problems: "From Shakimardan to Vuadil it is three hours on foot, while to Fergana it is six hours. How much time does it take to go on foot from Vuadil to Fergana?" The subject's response to this problem was, "No, it's six hours from Vuadil to Fergana. You're wrong...it's far and you wouldn't get there in three hours." (Luria, 1976, p. 129). In terms of *selective comparison,* performance suffered precisely because the subject was comparing incoming data to what he knew about his world, which was irrelevant to the solution of the problem. As Luria put it, the computation could readily have been performed, but the condition of the problem was not accepted.

A major difference between communities is in preferred mode of communication. In Trackton, there is a heavy emphasis upon nonverbal, as opposed to verbal, forms of transmission of knowledge. Adults pay little or no attention to a baby's words. Even sounds that are clearly linked to objects are ignored. In contrast, adults pay careful attention to babies' nonverbal responses, and praise responses such as coos and smiles that seem appropriate to a situation (Heath, p. 75). People talk about babies, but rarely to them. During the first six months to a year of life, babies are not even directly addressed verbally by adults (Heath, p. 77). Signs of aggressive play in children are acknowledged, and generally encouraged (Heath, p. 79). Babies sit in the laps of mothers and other adults frequently during the first year, and during that time, the child literally feels the nonverbal interaction of the conversationalist (Heath, p. 82). Children are expected to pay close attention to nonverbal signals about the consequences of their actions, and to act accordingly (Heath, p. 81). When older children show younger children how to do things, they do not generally describe the required actions in words. Rather, they exhibit the behavior, and simply tell the younger child to do it in the way he or she is seeing it be done. Watching and feeling how to do things are viewed as more important than talking about how to do them (Heath, p. 85).

In Roadville, there is much more stress on verbal interaction and development. When babies respond to stimuli verbally, adults notice these responses, and ask questions and make statements in response that are directed at the baby (Heath, p. 122). When the children start to combine words, usually between 18 and 22 months, adults respond with expansions of these combinations (Heath, p. 124). Children are encouraged to label things, and as importantly, to communicate their needs and desires verbally (Heath, p. 127).

Habits of verbal learning in Roadville, despite these desirable features, do not very closely match up with what will later be expected in school. Home teaching and learning are modeled not upon modes of knowledge transmission in the schools, but rather upon modes of knowledge transmission in the church. Children are expected to answer questions with prescribed routines. The measure of a child's understanding of things is his or her ability to recite back knowledge verbatim. The style of learning is passive: One listens, repeats back, and thereby is expected to learn (Heath, p. 226). The sign of learning is memorization, not understanding (Heath, p. 140). Even in their play, Roadville children use language in the same way as in more serious endeavors: They tell stories in strict chronological order, and do not embellish them either with evaluations or creative fictions.

In Gateway, modes of learning are different, yet again. As in Roadville, early language use is encouraged and reinforced. Mothers talk to babies, and assume that the babies are listening to them and will want to respond (Heath, p. 248). Parents believe that a child's success in school will depend, in part, upon the amount of verbal communication directed to the child, and received from the child (Heath, p. 350). But whereas Roadville parents discourage fantasy, Gateway parents encourage it, and praise children's imaginary tales. When children ask questions, adults answer at some length, and probe the children's knowledge in order to assess just what is known and what needs to be known (Heath, p. 253). The goal is to encourage understanding rather than verbatim recall.

When the goal of learning is verbatim recall, on the other hand, the techniques used by Roadville mothers are extremely effective. In Islamic cultures, for example, memorization of lengthy passages from the Koran is a goal unto itself. According to Cole and Scribner (1974), Nigerian children in Koranic schools are trained to memorize the Koran in Arabic, a language they do not speak or understand. In Nigeria, as in Roadville, the mode of learning is geared to what is to be learned; the result is perfectly acceptable in its immediate context, but may not be ideal in other situations.

In school and in later life, children will encounter many novel situations. A measure of their intelligence will be their ability to cope with these novelties. Children in all three environments—Trackton, Roadville, and Gateway —learn to deal with novelties, but novelties of very different kinds.

Children in Trackton need to acquire flexibility from an early age. Indeed, flexibility is a key element of success in Trackton (Heath, p. 111). As their first year of life comes to an end, Trackton children learn to play out roles on a community stage, and it is crucial for them to learn to gauge audience reactions to their actions (Heath, p. 79). They have to interpret cues, know what to say when, and to adjust their behavior as needed. As boy toddlers become a part of the Trackton milieu, they are teased and challenged, both verbally and nonverbally. Clever put-downs win praise, and successful responses to challenges are taken as a sign of intelligence (Heath, p. 80). Heath (p. 176) notes that by the age of 4, a child is usually able to come up with the right level and content of ridicule in one-liner responses to aggressive challenges. Use of insult, and especially rhyming insult, is strongly reinforced by peers right through early adolescence. Because preschoolers are physically unable to meet aggressive challenges of new and varied kinds, they must learn to outwit their aggressors, dealing with novel challenges as they go along (Heath, p. 84). Later on, they will be very quick at besting teachers in verbal combat, but this skill in coming up with novel and quick retorts will probably not elicit the same admiration from the teachers that it does from one's peers and even from elders in Trackton. In sum, the Trackton child acquires considerable flexibility and ability to deal with novelty, but in a domain that will not be reinforced, or negatively reinforced, in later schooling.

Children in Trackton engage in other forms of novelty as well. Storytelling is an important aspect of Trackton life. A good story is one that is creatively fictionalized in a way that expands upon real events. The story may be fictionalized to the extent that the outcome has little resemblance to what actually happened. All that is required is that the story have some seminal basis in fact (Heath, p. 166). The best stories are "junk," which consists of highly exaggerated and fictionalized narrative. Stories are not intended to convey actual events, but to promote social interaction, and to enhance the reputation of the storyteller (Heath, p. 166). Stories emphasize one's accomplishments, victories over adversity, cleverness, and personal power (Heath, p. 170). The audience gladly accepts the fictive characteristics of the stories and the expansions upon reality in the stories without any need for acknowledgement of what actually happened or of what was embellished. Unfortunately, the audience of the teacher in school does not react the same way at all. Accounts of Trackton children that would be accepted in Trackton may well be perceived as deliberate lies, and as attempts to deceive the teacher or other school authorities. Again, the creative abilities that are developed in Trackton do not provide the Trackton student with a needed edge in school, because of the very thin line that is drawn between truth and fiction.

The situation in Roadville is entirely different. Stories are intended to recount actual events as they actually happened (Heath, p. 149). There are rigid rules of chronicity and factuality in stories, and children are thus discouraged from exercising creativity in invention of narrative, or from exploring alternative ways of creating stories (Heath, p. 144). Children are not expected to evaluate the actions of characters, nor to elaborate on the inner emotions of characters. It is considered inappropriate for the child to introduce fictive characters or fancy into his or her story (Heath, p. 160).

As a result, by the time they enter nursery school, Roadville children have had little or no experience with creative story telling. When the children are asked to tell stories, they do not create or repeat fictional or fanciful stories. In order for Roadville children to accept such stories, a distinct frame of mind must be created where departures from reality are to be allowed (Heath, p. 162). Even when such departures are allowed, the Roadville child's fictional stories often fail to set the scene, to introduce characters, or even to have any particular point. The child is simply unable to form coherent stories of the kind that the school expects. This situation is scarcely surprising, as the stories that are requested in schools would be received at home as lies, and would be likely to bring upon the children immediate punishment (Heath, p. 296).

The attitude of the Roadville child toward stories also emerges in their play. Although these children are very conscientious about following rules, the children have trouble following rules when the play turns from realistic play to fantasy play. These children simply do not know how to engage in fantasy play. Eventually, Roadville children were observed to stop playing in those areas of the classroom where they could not bring to bear their play habits from home (Heath, p. 274). Because the schools do not follow the norms of Roadville any more than they follow the norms of Trackton, and whereas a child from Trackton may easily be perceived as a liar, a child from Roadville may easily be perceived as utterly lacking in spontaneous creativity. Thus, the encouragement of creativity in Trackton and the discouragement of it in Roadville both lead to unfortunate ends when the child from either community enters school.

The situation in Gateway is quite different from that in either Trackton or Roadville. Children's imaginary tales are acknowledged and praised, so long as they take the form of fantasy and are clearly introduced with the signals appropriate for fictional stories (Heath, p. 250). Children are encouraged to mix fact and fiction, but only so long as it is clear both to child and to listerner which is which. Children learn the difference between expository and fictional accounts, and later will be able to generate each with relative ease. Stories by Gateway children do not have the exaggerated characteristics of the stories by Trackton children, but neither do they have the extremely literal and formulaic character of stories by Roadville children. The Gateway children learn to balance their synthetic and creative abilities with their analytic and critical ones in a way that will later be praised and rewarded in the schools.

CONCLUSIONS

Students of intelligence have focused the lion's share of their efforts upon discovering the nature of intelligence as it exists, somehow, within the head, independent of the context in which it is manifested. I have argued in this chapter that these efforts need to be complemented by efforts to understand how intelligence is perceived. Our efforts to understand and predict school success will always be limited if we fail to take into account the complex interaction between intelligence, as an objective construct *inside* the head, and intelligence as a subjective, social construct *outside* the head.

The ways in which people define intelligence are important in all aspects of living, and particularly in schools. We need to understand how the view of intelligence held by the school interacts with the view of intelligence held by both parents and children. To the extent that these views match, both teachers and students will be playing the "second game" of understanding intelligent behavior in the same way. To the extent that these views mismatch, however, teachers and students will be playing the same game with different rules, and will encounter mutual frustration, and potentially, mutual disrespect. Evidence from a variety of sources suggests that there are multiple conceptions of intelligence, that people use these conceptions in their evaluations of themselves and of each other, and that to the extent that their conceptions are discrepant from each others', they will undervalue the intelligence of the others from whom their views differ. All of our efforts to understand, measure, and even train intelligence will be of limited value unless we take into account the subjective as well as the objective side of intelligence.

There is resistance among many of those psychologists who study intelligence to studying the subjective side of it. Typical reactions I have gotten from such psychologists are: "that stuff is social psychology, not cognitive psychology"; "what difference do people's conceptions of intelligence make?" "people's conceptions of intelligence tell you nothing about what intelligence is." All of these reactions are understandable, in some degree, especially coming, as they do, from those who emphasize the cognitive approach to studying intelligence. But these reactions also close the eyes of those who matter most to the field to the important interaction between the objective and subjective aspects of intelligence, and ultimately, will limit both the understanding we can have of intelligence and the prediction we can get of how people will use their intelligence. Whereas many schools may value the skills that IQ tests test, certain individuals may not. There is a need for schools to make explicit what is often now implicit—their conception of what constitutes intelligent functioning on the part of the student. It is clear that their conception may well not match up to the conceptions of many of their students.

Schools that value IQ-like skills must open their eyes to the broader set of skills that intelligence comprises beyond what the tests test. By looking at the subjective as well as the objective aspects of intelligence, and by seeking to understand the "school's-eye view" of intelligence, we come a step further toward a full understanding of an elusive but highly significant psychological construct. Moreover, we open the possibility of better methods of understanding, assessing, and training it.

REFERENCES

Alexander, P. (1985). Gifted and nongifted students' perceptions of intelligence. *Gifted Child Quarterly, 29,* 137–143.

Anthony, P. (1973). *Race against time.* New York: Tom Doherty Associates.

Cole, M., Gay, J., Glick, J., & Sharp, D.W. (1971). *The cultural context of learning and thinking.* New York: Basic Books.

Cole, M., & Scribner, S. (1974). *Culture and thought: A psychological introduction.* New York: Wiley.

Davidson, J.E., & Sternberg, R.J. (1984). The role of insight in intellectual giftedness. *Gifted Child Quarterly, 28,* 58–64.

DeVet, C.V., & MacLean, K. (1958). *Second game.* New York: Street and Smith.

Dweck, C.S., & Elliott, E.S. (1983). Achievement motivation. In P.H. Mussen (Ed.), *Handbook of Child Psychology* (pp. 643–691). New York: Wiley.

Fry, P.S. (1984). Teachers' conceptions of students' intelligence and intelligent functioning: A cross-sectional study of elementary, secondary, and tertiary level teachers. In P.S. Fry (Ed.), *Changing conceptions of intelligence and intellectual functioning: Current theory and research* (pp. 157–174). New York: North-Holland.

Heath, S.B. (1983). *Ways with words.* New York: Cambridge University Press.

Luria, A.R. (1976). *Cognitive development: Its cultural and social foundations.* Cambridge: Harvard University Press.

McDermott, R.P. (1974). Achieving school failure: An anthropological approach to illiteracy and social stratification. In G. Spindler (Ed.), *Education and the cultural process.* New York: Holt, Rinehart, and Winston.

Sternberg, R.J. (1985a). *Beyond IQ: A triarchic theory of human intelligence.* New York: Cambridge University Press.

Sternberg, R.J. (1985b). Implicit theories of intelligence, creativity, and wisdom. *Journal of Personality and Social Psychology, 49,* 607–627.

Sternberg, R.J., Conway, B.E., Ketron, J.L., & Bernstein, M. (1981). People's conceptions of intelligence. *Journal of Personality and Social Psychology, 41,* 37–55.

Sternberg, R.J., & Suben, J.G. (in press). The socialization of intelligence.

Suchmann, R.G., & Trabasso, T. (1966). Color and form preference in young children. *Journal of Experimental Child Psychology, 3,* 177–187.

Yussen, S.R., & Kane, P.T. (1983). Children's ideas about intellectual ability. In R. Leahy (Ed.), *The child's construction of social inequality* (pp. 109–133). New York: Academic Press.

Chapter Three
Metacognition in Second Language Behavior

RICHARD P. DURAN
University of California, Santa Barbara

This chapter will discuss some trends in research on bilingualism and second language learning, calling attention to executive processes in second language behavior. It will also review some relevant research in the areas of language proficiency assessment, discourse behavior, and cognitive functioning in bilinguals. Examples of language and cognitive processing behaviors will call attention to ways in which a learner's plans may guide the production and recognition of discourse in a second language.

METACOGNITION AND SECOND LANGUAGE LEARNING

Executive processes in second language behavior will be labeled "metacognitive," and related to Flavell's (1981) development of this concept and to Sternberg's (1985, this volume) more recent triarchic theory of intelligence. According to Flavell, thinking and language behaviors are ultimately problem solving behaviors, while metacognition includes both knowledge about knowing and strategic knowledge that governs problem solving and coming to know. Metacognitive behaviors are instances in which individuals experience a conscious awareness of metacognitive knowledge. Because metacognition calls attention to the context of communication and to language form and modality—speaking, reading, writing, and oral comprehension—as well as to other problem solving activities not accompanied by overt language behavior, it is especially pertinent in understanding ways in which people learn and use a second language.

Two conjectures drawn by Flavell which deal with metacognition and communication are worth noting for second language research. First, he suggests that it does not make good theoretical sense to consider cognitive processes governing communication as totally distinct from other forms of cognitive behavior. This claim seems reasonable. The conduct of communication is embedded in problem solving contexts which draw from other forms of knowledge that individuals possess. Further, information processing skills and capacities constrain behavior in a general sense. Accordingly, it may be useful to analyze communication skills by taking into account selected characteristics of the cognitive system which individuals bring to play when they communicate. For example, we might improve our understanding of reading comprehension processes in a second language by taking into account how readers allocate attention while reading a text and how they organize their use of short-term memory to extract meaning from the text at various levels of semantic processing. A basic question that emerges immediately in considering such issues involves the individual's familiarity with the language system and the discourse genre required by problem solving and attendant language processing.

A related point raised by Flavell concerns the value of fostering metacognitive experiences as children develop communicative skills—in helping children to (a) contrast the role of speaker and listener, (b) recognize interaction cues that signal recognition of meaning and uncertainty about meaning, and (c) develop strategies for eliciting clarifications of meaning. These concerns have received increasing attention among cognitive researchers. Paris and Schmidt (1984), for example, survey developmental research investigating children's ability to:

- gain and hold the attention of an audience
- adapt messages to the context of communication
- provide relevant responses to the listener's message
- provide feedback from the perspective of a listener

Issues of metacognition in communication are important to adult communication as well as to children's communication, and are of special importance to understanding how communication skills are acquired and learned in a second language. Later in this chapter, we will see that these issues are receiving intensive attention in language proficiency testing, communication, and problem solving of bilinguals.

Sternberg's (1985, this volume) triarchic theory of intelligence offers an overview of intelligent behavior which is useful to consider in second language research. His theory considers the individual's ability to shape and seek whole environments, to respond to environmental contingencies in an innovative or increasingly automated fashion, and to execute explicit cognitive processes—termed "cognitive components"—in carrying out specific problem solving tasks. When extended to populations of second language users, such a view implies that analyses of skill in second language functioning should take into account the underlying nature of the problem solving contexts faced by individuals. Approaches should consider the extent to which an individual is attending to general sociocultural contingencies, coping with real world but possibly unfamiliar problem solving tasks, or marshaling specific cognitive skills to solve relatively familiar problems. Any extended account of metacognition in second language functioning will need to be sensitive to distinctions of this sort. The general issue remains: How do bilinguals regulate their performance in a second language, given that such functioning is likely to require active planning and monitoring behavior that is influenced by a less than native communicative proficiency in the second language?

Research on metacognitive processes in a second language is needed to improve our understanding of how bilingual persons function in educational contexts. It can help explain the cognitive factors underlying bilinguals' ability to learn from instruction and to study in their second language. At present, instructional research has not drawn sufficiently from the findings of cognitive research, from related research on communicative proficiency assessment, or from studies of communicative competence.

DEVELOPMENTS IN LANGUAGE PROFICIENCY
ASSESSMENT THEORY

Historically, the term "language proficiency" has been used most commonly to describe knowledge of and ability to use a non-native language system. The meaning of the term in second language learning research has been influenced by the attempts of language testing researchers to operationalize its definition in terms of tests of language proficiency. Most testing approaches have presumed that language proficiency is a unitary construct, reflecting realized mastery of a (standard variety) language along some unidimensional scale. From this perspective, individual learners of a second language, at any point in time, possess a degree of overall skill in the second language which can be measured by means of a test. As Spolsky (1979) has noted, until the recent past, psychometric approaches to the definition of "language proficiency" have been heavily influenced by several successive movements in linguistic, psychological, and testing research. These movements include the development of transformational grammar (and other theories of grammar), the development of psycholinguistics as a field, and the development of mathematical and statistical models of mental test performance. The thrust of these movements, until recently, has held a widespread assumption that tests of global language proficiency could be constructed from collections of test items, each item measuring a discrete skill. From this perspective the items making up language proficiency tests have content and construct validity because they are presumed to contain points of linguistic knowledge reflective of our current notions of how language is organized and processed (particularly at the sentence level).

In recent years, however, this view has been challenged by language testing researchers such as Oller (1983), Canale and Swain (1979), Canale (1983), and Bachman and Palmer (in press), among others. Oller (1983) has contended that language proficiency is best conceived of as a generalized integrated complex of skills closely linked to general intelligence. The other investigators mentioned have taken a different stand, based on current research on discourse analysis and the ethnography of communication. They argue that language skills assessment must be developed from a more comprehensive model of language proficiency based on the notion of "communicative competence," and that language assessment ought be sensitive to different forms of communicative competence. Canale (Duran, et al. 1985, p. 7) outlines the following four classes of communicative competence useful for this purpose:

Grammatical competence: Mastery of the language code (e.g., vocabulary and rules of word formation, sentence formation, pronunciation, and spelling).

Sociolinguistic competence: Mastery of appropriate use (comprehension and production) of language in different sociolinguistic contexts, with an emphasis on appropriateness of (a) meanings (e.g., topics, attitudes, and functions) and (b) forms (e.g., register, formulaic expressions).

Discourse competence: Mastery of how to combine meanings and forms to achieve unified text in different genres—such as casual conversation, an argumentative essay, or a business letter—by using both (a) cohesion devices to relate forms (e.g., use of pronouns, transition expressions, parallel structures) and (b) coherence principles to organize meanings (e.g., concerning the development, consistency, and balance of ideas).

Strategic competence: Mastery of verbal and nonverbal strategies both (a) to compensate for breakdowns in communication due to insufficient competence or to performance limitations (e.g., use of paraphrase, dictionaries) and (b) to enhance the rhetorical effect of language (e.g., use of slow and soft speech, use of literary devices).

While communicative competence taxonomies have an intuitive appeal, they can be criticized on theoretical grounds. Such taxonomies grossly oversimplify the problem of describing categories of linguistic and pragmatic phenomena and their interaction. The potential for such criticism is evident even to novice students of language. However, they enable second language researchers to examine the limitations inherent in existing language proficiency testing practices. They are especially effective in evaluating the content and construct validity of existing proficiency tests and in documenting specific classes of skills which are and are not included in such tests. The Test of Teaching of English as a Foreign Language (TOEFL) study (Duran, Canale, Penfield, Stansfield, & Liskin-Giasparro, 1985) for example, has helped TOEFL program staff in evaluating the range of communicative skills assessed by the test and it has also aided them in refining procedures for the development of test items.

Another advantage in evaluating existing proficiency tests using communicative frameworks is that the outcome of such analyses, when made publicly available, can help test users evaluate the soundness of educational decisions made on the basis of test scores.

Some investigators adopting taxonomic views of communicative competence believe it is possible to construct tests of the communicative competence dimensions they identify. In this regard, they probably diverge radically from researchers in the areas of discourse analysis and ethnography of communication (e.g., Hymes, 1974; Gumperz & Hymes, 1972), who would be likely to emphasize the context-embeddedness of communicative competence and its socially negotiated realization, and to feel these cannot be evaluated in the less-than-natural testing situation.

These reservations aside, the taxonomic communicative competence approach to description of second language skills is of potential value in guiding the design of new forms of second language proficiency tests which have limited and well-defined purposes. Indeed, new forms of assessment might be designed to probe specific kinds of metacognitive skills guiding high level comprehension and language production skills. For example, one of the more important metacognitive comprehension skills which college-aged second language learners must acquire is the ability to recognize discourse markers signalling interconnections among ideas distributed across clauses and sentences of an academic text. In developing academic reading skills in English, students need to become skillful at recognizing and interpreting the significance of logical connectors such as "in conclusion," "as was mentioned above," "provided that," "in order that," "regardless of the fact that," etc. Taxonomic trait approaches to the description of communicative competence developed from grammars such as those proposed by Quirk, Greenbaum, Leech, and Svartvig (1985) can help English as a Second Language specialists and second language researchers in identifying such structures in relating them to other classes of skills. Such identification and systematic description of structures could lead to development of diagnostic assessments of specific classes of skills not targeted for assessment by existing tests of language proficiency.

CONVERSATIONAL INFERENCE AND METACOGNITION

The notions of discourse, sociolinguistic, and strategic competence referred to in Canale's taxonomic approach to communicative competence were, in large part, adopted from research in the fields of ethnography of communication and micro-sociolinguistics. Gumperz (1982a, 1984) addresses discourse phenomena which are related to metacognitive processes guiding oral interaction. His work is especially relevant here because it explicitly considers the discourse strategies of interlocutors communicating in a second language.

Gumperz utilizes the notion of "conversational inference" to characterize the processes by which interlocutors govern their exchange of meaning in face-to-face oral discourse. From this perspective, discourse production and discourse understanding are inherently on-line dynamic processes. These on-line processes are influenced by socially negotiated perceptions of communicative circumstances as well as by language form occurring in speech, and by accompanying paralinguistic cues which convey and embellish meaning. A central tenet in the theory of conversational inference is that speakers deliberately enact linguistic and paralinguistic strategies which sustain interaction and contribute to the thematic development of the information to be shared. In order for conversation to proceed and for meaning to develop, speakers must negotiate or assume conventions for interaction. The term "contextualization conventions" is applied to these shared conventions for oral interaction. Contextualization conventions are based on shared background knowledge about the grammatical, lexical, and phonological cuing systems of a language. And in addition, they are based on shared knowledge about norms for social interaction, given a purpose and setting for communication.

Gumperz gives a good deal of attention to the role in communication played by contextualization cues pertaining to prosody. Prosodic cues involve use of rhythm and pausing in speech, modulation of intonation and stress, vowel elongation, etc. Other forms of non-linguistic cues are also important in that they also serve to guide oral communication and the receipt of meaning. Examples of such non-linguistic cues include use of facial expressions, eye contact, and gestures, and vocalized backchannel cues signifying receipt of meaning or the monitoring of meaning. While Gumperz himself does not refer to metacognition per se, the relevance of this concept to the description of conversational inference strategies is implied in the following by Gumperz (1984, p. 1):

> When we look at problems of understanding from a participant's perspective, we see that what we must explain are on-line processing strategies. Conversationalists employ strategies in inferring the contextual presuppositions about what is expected in an encounter. Related strategies are also used in segmenting the stream of talk into information or idea units, in determining the transition-relevant points for turn taking and in integrating what is said at various points in time into coherent themes. Empirical investigations of conversational exchanges have led to the discovery that in making judgments relevant to these tasks, participants depend on their own perception of stylistic and prosodic signalling cues that have heretofore not been seen as having semantic import and that are thus not ordinarily covered in sentence level linguistic analysis. These features of speech performance are processed in accordance with contextualization conventions that retrieve schematic information from and make it available as an input into the interpretive process.

Subsequently, Gumperz (1984, p. 1) stated his views on cognition and conversational inference strategies more explicitly:

> My claim is that the capacity to contextualize and thus make sense of what is heard in terms of what is already known is governed by cognitive abilities that

share many of the same characteristics of grammatical competence. They are conventional in nature, learned as part of the everyday language socialization process, and once internalized are usually employed automatically without conscious reflection.

Gumperz's notion of conversational inference becomes especially useful for the study of second language discourse behavior when we add to it concern about second language learners' perceptions of the structure of speech events (Hymes, 1974). Given a social setting for interaction and speech events of recognized purpose and structure within such settings, it becomes possible to interpret how well language learners utilize language and contextualization cues to meet communicative ends.

A former colleague, Elsa Guerra, and I conducted an ethnographic study of four 7- and 8-year-old bilingual children's oral narratives at home exploring these issues (Duran, 1983). We visited the homes of families and videotaped children reading storybooks and telling stories at home. In reviewing our field notes and videotapes we were very much impressed by one child's enactment of oral story reading during our very first session with her. Lili demonstrated a virtuosity and fluency in oral behavior which was astonishing to us. As she read aloud from the storybook "Runaway Bunny" in English, we found her to shift rapidly and fluently between oral reading of the story and managing her audience's attention. English oral story reading was an unknown activity previously in Lili's home. Our "experiment" had introduced oral reading in English at home. Thus, of course, we had influenced the activity we observed.

Probably, we charged it with affection for the family and child, and also with a concern for the importance of reading. It seems in retrospect that reinforcers of this sort could serve to motivate literacy activities at school— for Lili and other children. We were aware that Lili's English and Spanish skills and progress in reading achievement were slightly above her grade level as judged by her teacher. Nonetheless, we were surprised by Lili's performance.

The variety and form of organizing and regulating behaviors we observed in Lili was considerable. Regardless of how motivation and personal aptitudes affected Lili, we sensed dimensions of literary competence in Lili which could not be explained based on Lili's teacher's evaluation of her school performance and based on our own periodic observations of Lili at school.

Many of Lili's behaviors can be interpreted as metacognitive in origin. These clearly indicated the attention that Lili was paying to her reading task —reacting to the social context of communication, and monitoring and coordinating her reading activity. Her metacognitive strategies included:

- Using a different set of contextualization cues when reading from the omniscient perspective of the text as opposed to the "quoted" perspective of story characters.

- Interrupting story text reading to comment on relevant knowledge not stated explicitly in the text or to display and interpret storybook illustrations.
- Interrupting reading of a story text to request the help of adult audience members in the pronunciation of difficult storybook words.
- Stepping outside of the role of story reader to manage the inattention and disruptive behavior of her audience.
- Keeping track of the next storybook portion to be read following activities interrupting the reading of text.

Guerra and I interpreted Lili's behavior in terms of enactment of cognitive scripts (Duran & Guerra, 1982). We hypothesized that the literacy behavior we had observed stemmed in large part from Lili's memory for how her bilingual teacher and librarian read stories to her class. We had no way of proving that such a script existed as a schema in Lili's memory. Nonetheless, it still seems plausible for us to hypothesize that the reading behavior we observed Lili undertake was based upon a plan for performing the story reading activity, and that this plan was based on knowledge acquired through previous experience. Lili's reading behavior was clearly purposeful and it showed order and closure in its execution. At times Lili needed to leave reading of the story per se to attend to other needs—such as asking for help in pronouncing a word—but she returned inevitably to her reading of the story.

A difficulty in proposing cognitive script models of speech behavior is that we know so little about how individuals might cognitively represent and negotiate participation in speech events. It is interesting to note, however, that sociolinguists' descriptions of speech event parameters show a remarkable similarity to the knowledge structures which cognitive psychologists have ascribed to scripts (Freedle & Duran, 1979). Purposive, and often ritualized, forms of everyday interaction lend themselves more readily to script-theory-based accounts. Under such circumstances (e.g., ordering a McDonald's hamburger), the bundling of speech activity with interaction follows a routinized course with minimal need for interlocutors to negotiate the social basis and course of interaction.

However, interaction in more socially diverse contexts may have an intrinsic, unpredictable character. As Cole (1985), Hymes (1972), Mehan (1983), Winograd and Flores (1986), and others have commented, communicative and other social behaviors may not be reducible to *cognitive* accounts of interaction and negotiation of interaction. There may be social and contextual influences on individuals' behavior which cannot be understood in purely cognitive terms—though cognition may always prove critical to the regulation of behavior. The dynamics of situations, their embeddedness in the real world, and the flow of interaction and information arising in communicative contexts might create the need for interactive acts and for interpretations of meaning that simply are not predictable based on cognitive accounts of individual knowledge alone. If such a viewpoint holds, then psychological approaches to second language learning would not be adequate, in and of themselves, to deal with factors affecting the acquisition and learning of a second language system. Added concern would be needed for how social factors and social dynamics—outside of the individual—create affordances which predispose second language learning.

Wong-Fillmore's (1979) research on effective strategies for children's learning of English is interesting in this regard. She found that children's attempts to show familiarity with social situations and with the purposes for communication were instrumental in children's acquisition of English. The strategies she cited are intrinsically of a metacognitive nature. They involved children's ability to carry out some of the very same communicative strategies cited earlier in the work of Paris and Schmidt (1984) and Flavell (1981). Recall that such strategies included gaining and holding the attention of an audience, adapting messages to the context of communication, providing relevant responses to listener's messages, and providing feedback from the perspective of a listener. Children's enactment of strategies such as these, when enacted with fluent language speakers, would accomplish two things simultaneously. First, children would be exposed to fluent models of second language behavior, and second, this exposure would be coupled with the opportunity to learn appropriate behaviors instrumental to carrying out the social business embedded within situations. The nature of a communicative activity and the forms of social relations possible within it themselves become an object of learning, and in turn this knowledge can act as a scaffold for learning how second language form is tied to instrumental behaviors in an activity.

This idea, of course, is familiar to persons who try to learn a language in the course of travel in a foreign country. In this case, for example, individuals begin to learn a language by picking up language use appropriate to interactions structured around scriptal activities such as purchasing food or other items, asking for directions, etc.

BILINGUALISM AND COGNITION

Attention to metacognition in studies of bilingualism is not new, though it has not been until recently that studies have begun to draw intensively on methods of contemporary cognitive psychology. In the past, second language research in metacognition was largely concerned with comparisons between or among fluent bilinguals, and bilinguals with unbalanced development of first and second language skills. The main issue had been whether bilinguals acquire a heightened ability to analyze and manipulate languages by virtue of their mastery of more than one language system.

A recurrent research finding over the past 25 years has been that bilingual persons with high proficiency in two languages outperform comparison groups of other bilinguals or of monolinguals on cognitive tasks requiring conscious attention to language form, and unusual manipulations of language. Many of these studies attempted to control for background differences which might account for fluent bilinguals' superior performance on metalinguistic tasks. Reviews of this research and methodological critiques are provided by Cummins (1978), Diaz (1983), and Hakuta and Diaz (1985). In general, the studies have found fluent bilinguals to show higher performance on problem solving tasks requiring temporary transformation of the usual meaning of words to suit a task (Ben Zeev, 1977; Feldman & Shen, 1971), use of invented word meanings (Cummins, 1978), and sensitivity to alternative word meanings (Feldman & Shen, 1971). In addition, some studies have reported the higher performance of fluent bilinguals on measures of general intelligence, cognitive development, and field independence as measured by verbal and nonverbal tests (Diaz, 1983; Hakuta & Diaz, 1985; DeAvilla & Duncan, 1981).

More recently, investigators have begun to address the question of metacognition and related cognitive processes in bilinguals. For example, Goldman, Reyes, and Varnhagen (1984) have found evidence that bilingual children interpret and recall fables in a similar fashion regardless of the input language for fables. While children's understanding and recall of stories is affected by their language proficiency, the same general set of comprehension strategies seem to guide understanding in each language. Duran and Enright (in preparation), similarly, have found that adult Spanish–English bilinguals are likely to interpret syllogism problems in the same fashion regardless of language of input, though performance on problems is slower in the less proficient language. Dornic (1980) provides an extensive review of cognitive research showing that bilinguals' performance on simple cognitive processing tasks is strongly related across two languages, though it is less efficient in the more unfamiliar language. Research such as this suggests that the metacognitive orientation which bilinguals rely on in interpreting problem solving tasks, and the cognitive processes which are used in solving problems, *can be* similar across well-defined problem solving tasks in the two languages, though proficiency in a language may moderate the accuracy of problem interpretation and problem solving efficiency. It is important to note that this hypothesis is restricted to well-defined and familiar problem solving tasks. Sternberg's triarchic view of intelligence would suggest that a broader analysis of cognitive processing may be needed to account for bilinguals' real world problem solving and their adjustment to less familiar cultural and social environments—an issue discussed earlier in this chapter.

Bialystock and Ryan (1985) have recently called attention to the concept of metacognition in the development of first and second language skills. They argue that the notion of metacognition is necessary in order to understand the fuller range of literate and oral uses of languages which second language learners must acquire and which extend beyond mastery of language form in isolation. Following Flavell and Wellman (1977), they suggest that language learners vary in their ability to analyze language form as they acquire a language. At the unanalyzed end of the analyzed–unanalyzed language continuum, there is acquisition and highly automatic use of formulaic routines. In contrast, at the analyzed pole of the continuum, there is acquisition of articulated representations of how language form may be treated as an object and structured to meet communicative ends. Bialystock and Ryan note that the amount of real world context relevant to language use affects the need for more analyzed versus less analyzed processing of language. Language use with limited connections to immediate real world contexts relies more heavily on explicit analysis of language form. In contrast, language use with immediate connections to ongoing activities and sources of information is less likely to require extensive analysis of language form.

A second dimension of metacognitive awareness mentioned by Bialystock and Ryan concerns the cognitive control of executive functioning during language processing. For second language learners, the issue is the selection of language information for analysis and the coordination of strategies for language processing given the demands of communicative settings. Allocation of attention and depth of processing are important considerations in the description of cognitive control (McLaughlin, Rossman, & McLeod, 1983).

In reading in a second language, for example, it is important to consider how word decoding, syntax recognition, and comprehension processes are coordinated and how manipulations of attention support this coordination. As with monolingual readers, one would hypothesize that readers with high proficiency in a second language should be better able to concentrate their attention on the extraction of meaning from a text. Such persons are capable of enacting automated, analytic word recognition and syntax recognition reading strategies. The attention of these proficient readers is more likely to be focused on extracting meaning from a text and on the execution of inferences supporting additional interpretations of a text.

In contrast, it can be hypothesized that poor readers in a second language need to allocate a good deal of attention to word and sentence syntax recognition. Such readers would be more likely to juggle back and forth between effortful word decoding and syntax recognition, and extraction of the extended meaning of a text.

NEW DIRECTIONS FOR METACOGNITIVE RESEARCH

Clearly, not all research need strive for ecological validity in order to be a contribution to knowledge, but attaining this goal would demonstrate the utility of the underlying theoretical perspectives, and as well be useful for second language pedagogy.

The reading and reasoning comprehension tasks faced by students learning in a second language represent one real world arena which would benefit from such investigation. In collaboration with a research team at the University of California at Santa Barbara, I am currently embarked on a program of research which has this aim. Our target population is non-English background students enrolled in undergraduate classes at our university.

Two separate studies are underway. One study, under sponsorship of the Center for Language Education and Research of the University of California at Los Angeles, is investigating students' ability to recognize valid versus invalid conclusions which might be drawn from everyday and academic text passages. The aim of this work is to discover how subjects' ability to comprehend the discourse structure and linguistic characteristics of passages affects their ability to judge the validity of putative conclusions drawn from passages. We are investigating the way in which the characteristics of texts interact with the language of conclusions, and further, how well subjects are able to recognize these underlying correspondences. We also wish to learn the extent to which the propensity to commit reasoning fallacies of various types is or is not connected to language processing difficulties. Finally, we are interested in learning whether subjects show a propensity to commit similar reasoning fallacies across a variety of passage content areas.

A second research study, in collaboration with Susan Goldman and under the sponsorship of the Office of Naval Research, is investigating non-English background students' reading and reasoning strategies in answering questions based on passages presented during experimental sessions. Passages are drawn from actual readings required of students in their classwork or from other sources relevant to students' classwork. The research study is investigating how students' question answering strategies are related to their level of expertise in the subject matter (student vs. teaching assistant) and their ability to recognize and process the necessary linguistic characteristics of passages.

Both lines of research described above are drawing from metacognitive accounts of reading comprehension processes. Following on the research of Fillmore (1983), Langer (1985, 1987), and Kay (1987), reading is conceived of in terms of levels of understanding which guide reading strategies and which can be used to describe various depths of comprehension processing engaged in by students. Five levels of comprehension are hypothesized. When functioning at the lowest level, students would focus on comprehension of words in isolation, while at the next higher level they would focus attention on understanding isolated clauses and sentences. At the third level, students would focus on semantic relationships explicitly signalled across clause and sentence units, but would not be engaged in extensive reasoning about the whole topic or situation depicted in a passage; this latter form of reasoning would be supported at the next higher level of comprehension. The fifth and final level of comprehension would entail going beyond the immediate world described in a text being comprehended. It would involve reading in a manner supporting reasoning about hypothetical situations which might be related to the contents of the text being read.

Collins and Smith (1982, pp. 176–177) complement the above perspective. They outline a series of comprehension monitoring strategies which readers engage in when comprehension fails at levels suggestive of those outlined above. They suggest that when readers detect comprehension failure at any level, they adopt specific strategies to sustain comprehension. Strategies cited include:

- Ignoring an uncomprehended word or segment with the expectation that the information not comprehended was of little importance.
- Suspending judgment about meaning with the expectation that later materials would lead to clarifications about meaning.
- Forming a tentative hypothesis about the meaning of a word or segment based on a partial comprehension. Rereading of a segment just read in order to extract further meaning.
- Jumping back to reread previous material in order to improve current understanding of material.
- Going to an expert source (teacher, dictionary, etc.) in order to get help in comprehending material.

The foregoing sorts of processes are important. They identify units of language and thinking behavior which are likely to occur in real world academic situations encountered by second language learners. Our current challenge is to devise innovative research methods for investigating such processes. Beyond these concerns, there is also the challenge of devising training principles and training methods which might be used to improve comprehension skills among second language learners. This latter goal ought to be pursued with the collaboration of teachers engaged in the teaching of particular subjects as well as in the teaching of a second language itself (Snow & Brinton, 1985).

REFERENCES

Ben Zeev, S. (1977). The influence of bilingualism on cognitive development and cognitive strategy. *Child Development, 48,* 1009–1018.

Bachman, L., & Palmer, A. (In press). *Fundamental considerations in the measurement of language abilities.* Reading, MA: Addison-Wesley.

Bialystock, E., & Ryan, E. (1985). A metacognitive framework for the development of first and second language skills. In D.L. Forrest-Pressley, G.E. MacKinnon, & T. Gary Waller (Eds.), *Metacognition, cognition, and human performance. Theoretical Perspectives* (Vol. 1). New York: Academic Press.

Canale, M., & Swain, M. (1979). Communicative approaches to second language teaching and testing. In *Review & Evaluation Bulletins, 1, 5.*

Cole, M. (1985). The zone of proximal development: Where culture and cognition create each other. In J. Wertsch (Ed.), *Culture, communication, and cognition: Vygotskian perspectives.* New York: Cambridge University Press.

Collins, A., & Smith, E. (1982). Teaching the process of reading comprehension. In D. Detterman & R. Sternberg (Eds.), *How and how much can intelligence be increased.* Norwood, NJ: Ablex.

Cummins, J. (1978). Bilingualism and the development of metalinguistic awareness. *Journal of Cross-Cultural Psychology, 9*(2), 131–149.

De Avila, E., & Duncan, S.H. (1981). Bilingualism and the metaset. In R. Duran (Ed.), *Latino language and communicative behavior.* Norwood, NJ: Ablex.

Diaz, R. (1983). Thought and two languages: The impact of bilingualism on cognitive development. In E. Gordon (Ed.), *Review of research in education, Vol. 10.* Washington: AERA.

Duran, R., & Guerra, E. (1982). Chicano children's literacy learning at home. Paper presented at the American Anthropological Association Annual Meeting, Washington, DC.

Duran, R. (1983). Cognitive theory and Chicano children's oral reading behavior. *Quarterly Newsletter of the Laboratory of Comparative Human Cognition, 5*(4).

Duran, R., Canale, M., Penfield, J., Stansfield, C.H., & Liskin-Gasparro, E. (1985). *TOEFL from a communicative viewpoint on language proficiency: A working paper* (Report No. 17 R 85-8). Princeton, NJ: Educational Testing Service.

Feldman, C., & Shen, M. (1971). Some language-related cognitive advantages of bilingual five-year-olds. *Journal of Genetic Psychology, 118,* 235–244.

Fillmore, C.J. (1983). *Ideal readers and real readers.* Berkeley, CA: Cognitive Science Program, Institute of Human Learning.

Flavell, C.J. (1981). Cognitive monitoring. In W.P. Dickson (Ed.), *Children's oral communication skills.* New York: Academic Press.

Flavell, C.J., & Wellman, H. (1977). Metamemory. In R. Kail, & J. Hagen (Eds.), *Perspectives on the development of memory and cognition.* Hillsdale, NJ: Erlbaum.

Freedle, R., & Duran, R. (1979). Sociolinguistic approaches to dialogue with suggested applications to cognitive science. In R.O. Freedle (Ed.), *New directions in discourse processing.* Norwood, NJ: Ablex.

Goldman, S. (1985). *Goals, plans and outcomes in teaching and learning reading.* Paper presented by the XX Congress of Psychology, Caracas, Venezuela.

Goldman, S., Reyes, M., & Varnhagen, C.K. (1984). Understanding fables in first and second language. *Journal of the National Association for Bilingual Education, 3*(2), 35–66.

Gumperz, J.J. (1982a). *Discourse strategies: Studies in international sociolinguistics.* New York: Cambridge University Press.

Gumperz, J.J. (Ed.) (1982b). *Language and social identity: Studies in international sociolinguistics.* New York: Cambridge University Press.

Gumperz, J.J. (1984). *Communicative competence revisited* (Report No. 24). Berkeley, CA: Cognitive Science Program.

Gumperz, J.J., & Hymes, D. (Eds.) (1972). *Directions in sociolinguistics: The ethnography of communication.* New York: Holt.

Hakuta, K., & Diaz, R. (1985). The relationship between degree of bilingualism and cognitive ability. In K.E. Nelson (Ed.), *Children's language* (Vol. 5). Hillsdale, NJ: Erlbaum.

Hymes, D. (1972). Models of language and social life. In J. Gumperz & D. Hymes (Eds.), *Directions in sociolinguistics: The ethnography of communication.* New York: Holt, Rinehart, and Winston.

Hymes, D. (1974). *Foundations in sociolinguistics: An ethnographic approach.* Philadelphia: University of Pennsylvania Press.

Kay, P. (1987). Three properties of the ideal reader. In R. Freedle & R.P. Duran (Eds.), *Cognitive and linguistics analyses of test performance*. Norwood, NJ: Ablex.

Lambert, W.E. (1967). A social psychology of bilingualism. *Journal of Social Issues, 23*, 91–109.

Langer, J.A. (1985). Levels of questioning: An alternative view. *Reading Research Quarterly, 2*(5), 586–602.

Langer, J.A. (1987). The construction of meaning and the assessment of comprehension: Analysis of reader performance on standardized test items. In R. Freedle & R. Duran (Eds.), *Cognitive and linguistic analyses of test performance*. Norwood, NJ: Ablex.

McLaughlin, B., Rossman, T., & McLeod, B. (1983). Second language learning: An information-processing perspective. *Language Learning, 33*(2), 135–158.

Mehan, H. (1983). The role of language and the language of role in institutional decision making. *Language in Society, 12*, 187–211.

Oller, J. (1983). Reading skills of non-native speakers of English. *IRAL, 11*(1).

Paris, S.G., & Schmidt, C.R. (1984). The development of verbal communicative skills in children. *Advances in Child Development and Behavior, 18*, 1–47.

Quirk, R., Greenbaun, S., Leech, G., & Svartvik, J. (1985). *A comprehensive grammar of contemporary English*. London: Longman.

Snow, A.M., & Brinton, D.M. (1985). *Linking ESL courses with university content courses: The adjunct model*. Los Angeles: University of California. (ERIC Document Reproduction Service 244515).

Spolsky, B. (1979). Linguistics and language testers. In B. Spolsky (Ed.), *Advances in language testing* (Vol. 1). Washington, DC: Center for Applied Linguistics.

Sternberg, R. (1985). *Beyond IQ. A triarchic theory of human intelligence*. New York: Cambridge University Press.

Winograd, T., & Flores, F. (1986). *Understanding computers and cognition*. Norwood, NJ: Ablex.

Wong Fillmore, L. (1979). Individual differences in second language acquisition. In C. Fillmore, W. Wang, & D. Kempler (Eds.), *Individual differences in language behavior*. New York: Academic Press.

REFERENCE NOTE

Duran, R., & Enright, M. (In preparation). Syllogistic reasoning in bilingual subjects.

PART II
LITERACY AND THE
LITERARY EXPERIENCE

Chapter Four
The Orality of Literature and the Literacy of Conversation[1]

DEBORAH TANNEN
Georgetown University

In a paper entitled "Reconceiving Literacy," Bleich (in press) observes that, in light of growing concern with what he calls intersubjectivity (in the terms of classroom ethnographers, meaning as an interactional achievement), two elements not usually found in purely cognitive approaches to language, *affect* and *dialogue,* become central.[2] These two elements are central to the present chapter as well.

I have been arguing in a number of recent papers and books that orality and literacy, and spoken and written language, are not dichotomous but rather complex and intertwined. Therefore, we, as researchers, in addition to analyzing the discourse types that in some way typify spoken and written language respectively—that is, casual conversation on the one hand and written expository prose on the other—should be thinking in terms of understanding the dimensions and patterns underlying, connecting, and distinguishing a variety of discourse types.

Research on orality and literacy (most often cited are Goody and Watt, 1963; Havelock, 1963; Olson, 1977; and Ong, 1967; see Tannen, 1982a for summary and discussion) has provided significant insight into some of these patterns. I have benefited from such insight in my own analysis of discourse. However, in some ways the orality-literacy paradigm has led us astray. As Becker (1984a) eloquently reminds us, theories blind our vision, obscuring aspects of the world that do not fit into their frame at the same time that they illuminate those aspects that do.

[1] Research on the material presented here was begun with the support of a Rockefeller Humanities Fellowship, for which I am grateful. Discussion of dialogue in conversation is drawn from Tannen (1986a). A different version of this material was presented at the 1985 LSA/TESOL Institute at Georgetown University and will appear as "Hearing Voices in Conversation, Fiction and Mixed Genres," in *Linguistics in Context: Connecting Observation and Understanding Lectures from the 1985 LSA/TESOL and NEH Institutes,* edited by Deborah Tannen, to be published by Ablex Publishing Corporation.

[2] Bleich (in press) amasses and integrates a staggeringly diverse range of sources to illustrate his notion of intersubjectivity. These include, among others, George Herbert Mead, Vygotsky, Derrida, Ong, Levi-Strauss, and researchers in the fields of feminist epistemology and child language acquisition, as well as two authors represented in this volume: Heath and Tannen.

Many educators, picking up on what has been called "literacy theory" (that is, research in anthropology, psychology, and rhetoric on orality and literacy or oral and literate traditions), argue that minority children do poorly in school because they come from an oral culture. For example, D'Angelo (1983, p. 104) writes:

> Many students come from what Walter Ong would call a "residually oral" culture, a stratum within the mainstream of society where oral modes of expression permeate thinking. They come from homes where speech is more widespread than reading or writing....
>
> The thinking of preliterate and nonliterate people is concrete, syncretic, diffuse, perceptual, affective, situation-bound, additive, and digressive, concerned with everyday events, actions, and happenings rather than with abstract ideas. The thinking of literate people tends to be more abstract, discrete, definite, and articulated, consisting of generalizations, deductions, and inferences. Without writing, according to some scholars, the mind cannot participate in the kinds of analytical, sequential thinking necessary to develop even a single magazine article. Writing may be artificial, but it is also an artifice and an art that seems to be essential for the development of consciousness.
>
> What I am suggesting is that one possible reason for the decline in literacy might be related to the incipient or undeveloped forms of literate thinking in some of our students.

D'Angelo thus sees orality and literacy as not only dichotomous but mutually exclusive.

Ogbu (this volume) shows that this hypothesis cannot be valid. Elsewhere (Tannen, 1985) I have demonstrated a similar point on different grounds. Drawing on my conversational analysis of what I then called (but would now rather not call) oral and literate strategies in casual conversation (Tannen, 1984), I have shown that New York Jewish conversational style uses highly oral strategies. Nonetheless, children of this cultural group do very well, not very poorly, in school. Jewish culture is both highly oral *and* highly literate. Hence the argument that orality precludes literacy must fall.

In the present paper, I continue this line of argument by drawing on an ongoing research project comparing conversational and literary discourse. The thrust of this research is to demonstrate that ordinary conversation and literary discourse have more in common than has been commonly thought.[3]

---

[3] Christopher Ricks (1981, p. 42), in a review of Goffman's *Forms of Talk,* reports feeling "what everybody always feels about the main contentions which issue from somebody else's discipline: that it is odd that certain things need to be said." Just so, it will seem odd to some, in particular to creative writers, that I feel it needs to be said that literary language is made of the same stuff as ordinary conversation. W.H. Auden, for example, is said to have commented that "poetry is memorable speech"; similar observations are reported by Heath (this volume) based on her ethnographic interviews with contemporary writers. Such insight notwithstanding, the relationship between conversation and written literature does need to be articulated, as witness the excerpt from D'Angelo cited above and conventional wisdom cited below.

Whereas conversation is generally thought to be messy, pedestrian and error-ridden (many would even adduce here the list of adjectives D'Angelo (1983) used to describe "the thinking of preliterate and nonliterate people"), literary discourse is thought to be an exalted use of language. I seek to show that both operate on the same linguistic dimensions—means of contributing to interpersonal involvement.

In this research, I am examining closely a variety of spoken and written discourse types in order to compare the linguistic means by which they create involvement. I group these linguistic patterns in two categories: first, uses of language that sweep the audience along through their rhythm, sound, and shape; and second, those that require audience participation in sense-making, such as indirectness, tropes, imagery and detail, and constructed dialogue (with many of these intertwined in storytelling). (For more discussion of this theoretical framework see the last chapter of Tannen, 1984 and Tannen, in press).

Among these numerous linguistic patterns I believe contribute to involvement, I have begun investigation of repetition, detail, figures of speech, storytelling, and constructed dialogue. The present paper draws on my analysis of constructed dialogue (Tannen, 1986a) and builds on it to include analysis of dialogue in three different discourse types produced by junior high school students: a school writing assignment, a story told in conversation, and notes written to friends.

WHY CONSTRUCTED DIALOGUE?

Many researchers (for example, Chafe, 1982; Labov, 1972; Ochs, 1979; Schiffrin, 1981; Tannen, 1982b) have observed that narration is more vivid when speech is presented as first-person dialogue ("direct quotation") rather than third-person exposition ("indirect quotation"), and that the former is more commonly found in conversational narrative (sometimes generally referred to as spoken discourse) than written expository discourse (but not of course in written literary discourse, precisely, I would suggest, because fiction and poetry are akin to conversation in workings and effect). But there is more to it than that. The creation of voices occasions the imagination of alternative and distant worlds that is the stuff of dreams and art.

Friedrich (1979, p. 473) suggests that "it is the more poetic levels and processes of language, however defined, that massively model, constrain, trigger, and otherwise affect the individual imagination." I see constructing dialogue as one such poetic process. Constructed dialogue in conversation and in fiction is a means by which experience surpasses story to become drama. Moreover, the creation of drama from personal experience and hearsay contributes to the emotional component that is crucial for cognition to be effected.

I have compared constructed dialogue in two genres of two languages: stories told in conversation in American English and Athenian Greek, and excerpts from an American and a Greek novel (Tannen, 1986a). Here I will cite examples from the American conversation and fiction samples, referring only briefly to the Greek samples. I will first present evidence to support my claim that dialogue in conversational storytelling is constructed rather than reported, by examining the dialogue in a single conversational narrative. After this I demonstrate that constructing dialogue is part of a pattern of vivid storytelling by reference to a study of dialogue in Brazilian and American narration. I then move to discussion of the spoken and written discourse of junior high school students, in and out of school. Finally, I present an excerpt of an unusual and unusually effective document: a conference proceedings which is written like a novel.

To begin, I want to place the phenomenon of dialogue in the context of storytelling.

STORYTELLING AS AN ACT OF MIND

I cannot here recapitulate his entire argument (though I would like to), but I shall refer cryptically to an eloquent essay by Rosen (1984) showing that storytelling in literature is a refinement of storytelling in everyday life—and that storytelling is at the heart of everyday life. Citing Barbara Hardy, Bakhtin, Genette, Eagleton, and others, Rosen argues that storytelling is "an explicit resource in all intellectual activity," "a disposition of the mind," a "meaning-making strategy" which represents the mind's "eternal rummaging in the past and its daring, scandalous rehearsal of scripts of the future."

I would add that inseparable from this cognitive function of stories—the creation of meaning in personal lives—is an interactive function. The telling and hearing of experience as stories is made possible by, and simultaneously creates, interpersonal involvement which carries a metamessage (G. Bateson, 1972) of rapport.[4] That is, hearers can understand and appreciate a story because they recognize its details and can imagine a possible life to account for such events. That the hearer's experience thus matches the storyteller's, creates a sense of a shared universe—of experience and of discourse. When this occurs in interpersonal interaction, rapport is drawn on and established. When it occurs in literature, the sense of rapport is broadened to include a wide audience and a published author—a community of rapport.

Thus storytelling is a means by which humans organize and understand the world, and feel connected to it and to each other. Giving voice to the

---

[4] The overriding importance of language use to create rapport is a repeated theme of R. Lakoff (1979). Building on her work, I discuss this phenomenon at length in an academic (Tannen, 1984) and in a popular (Tannen, 1986b) mode.

speech of the people in a story—and we shall see presently that such voice-giving can be quite literal—creates a play peopled by characters who take on life and breath.

The casting of thoughts and speech in dialogue creates particular scenes and characters, and it is the particular which moves readers by establishing and building on a sense of identification between speaker or writer and audience.[5] As teachers of creative writing exhort neophyte writers, the accurate representation of the particular communicates universality, whereas attempts to represent universality directly often communicate nothing—a seeming paradox which may underly Becker's (1984b) call, following Pike, for the "substitution of particularity for the pursuit of generality or universality as the goal of our craft".

STORYTELLING AS DRAMA

The great American writer Eudora Welty (1984) locates her beginnings as a writer in the magic of everyday storytelling. She was first exposed to this magic when her family acquired a car, and a storytelling (that is, gossipy) neighbor was invited along on family outings. It was the sound of dialogue that cast a spell on the child Eudora:

> My mother sat in the back with her friend, and I'm told that as a small child I would ask to sit in the middle, and say as we started off, "Now *talk*."
>
> There was dialogue throughout this lady's accounts to my mother. "I said" ..."He said"..."And I'm told she very plainly said"..."It was midnight before they finally heard, and what do you think it *was*?"
>
> What I loved about her stories was that everything happened in *scenes*. I might not catch on to what the root of the trouble was in all that happened, but my ear told me it was dramatic. (pp. 12–13)

Note that in this telling, Welty herself creates a scene (the child nestled between two adults in the back of a car), an inextricable part of which is constructed dialogue:

> "Now *talk*."
> "I said"...
> "He said"...
> "And I'm told she very plainly said"...
> "It was midnight before they finally heard, and what do you think it *was*?"

Welty knows that narratives in ordinary conversation are artistic creations. This assumption is seen again in her recollection of (or, more pre-

---

[5] Havelock (1963) discusses this sense of identification as the basis for cognition in literary modes—for him, oral literature—which he calls "subjective knowing." I am eager, however, to avoid the dichotomy between subjective and objective knowing which Havelock constructs, a dichotomy that parallels the oral/literate one. I am grateful to A.L. Becker for patiently prodding me to avoid this terminology and attendant imaging.

cisely, her artful reconstruction of) Fannie, a woman who came to the Welty house to sew. Like the gossipy friend who was invited on car trips, Fannie delighted Eudora with her stories about other people, which the child did not understand but nonetheless loved to hear:

> The gist of her tale would be lost on me, but Fannie didn't bother about the ear she was telling it to: she just like telling. She was like an author. In fact, for a good deal of what she said, I daresay she *was* the author. (p. 14)

Welty does not, by this observation, criticize Fannie; rather, she places her among the ranks of talented storytellers.

The parallel between gossip and literature, though not unprecedented (it is drawn, for example, by Britton, 1982), is not generally accepted. Popular opinion lionizes literary storytelling but scorns gossip. This view of gossip is voiced in Welty's account in the character of her mother. A native of West Virginia, the elder Welty considered the Mississippi practice of social visiting to be "idling". And she was exasperated by the chatter that so delighted her daughter:

> "What did she say?" I asked.
> "She wasn't *saying* a thing in this world," sighed my mother. "She was just ready to talk, that's all." (p. 13)

Accordingly, her mother tried to prevent Fannie from telling stories in her child's presence:

> "I don't want her exposed to gossip"—as if gossip were measles and I could catch it. (p. 14)

The suggestion that oral stories are created rather than reported was made by another professional storyteller: a medicine show pitchman, Fred "Doc" Bloodgood. In answer to my query about the accuracy of parts of his sample pitches (Bloodgood, 1982), he responded: "Anyway, as my dad always told me, 'Never let a grain of truth interfere with the story'." I doubt that Bloodgood's dad ever said this; in any case it doesn't matter whether or not he did. What matters is that "as my dad always told me" is an apt particular way to introduce a general maxim.

Given this perspective of the creative act of storytelling in any genre, and of the centrality of dialogue in making stories dramatic, I will move to the examination of dialogue in narrative.

REPORTED SPEECH IS CONSTRUCTED DIALOGUE

The conversational discourse I have analyzed consists of stories told in conversation either in dyads or in small groups, recorded by someone who happened to be there.[6] The literary discourse examined consists of excerpts from novels. The American novel used is *Household Words* by Joan Silber (1976), an enormously moving and beautifully written novel which won the Hemingway Award for first novels.

I will begin by demonstrating that dialogue presented in oral storytelling is constructed, not reported, by looking closely at the dialogue in a conversational story. The point is to show that the lines of dialogue in the narrative were not actually spoken by the characters to which they are attributed. What, then, are they doing in the story? The speaker uses the animation of voices to make his story into drama.

The narrative was told by a young man who came home from his work as a resident in the emergency ward of a hospital, to find a group of his friends gathered in his home, hosted by his wife.[7] Asked whether anything interesting had happened at the emergency room, he responded by telling this story.

1   We had three guys come in,
2   one guy had a cut right here.
3   On his arm? [Listener: uhuh]
4   Bled all over the place, right? [Listener: Yeah]
5   These three guys were hysterical.
6   They come bustin' through the door.
7   Yknow you're not supposed to come in to the emergency room.

---

[6] The American stories were recorded, chosen, and initially transcribed by students in my Discourse Analysis class, Fall 1983. Terry Waldspurger helped identify constructed dialogue and count words. I recorded the Greek stories in Athens; Fileni Kalou transcribed them; Maria Spanos checked transcriptions and helped with identification of constructed dialogue as well as translation.

[7] Kimberly Murphy recorded and initially transcribed this story. I am grateful to her for finding it, and to her and the speaker for permission to use it. In this and a later example, the transcription of speech is presented in lines and verses in order to capture in print the rhythmic chunking of oral discourse and consequently to facilitate comprehension. See Tannen (in press) for discussion of this transcription practice, its precedents and theoretical implications. The following transcription conventions are used:

Punctuation reflects intonation not grammar. Hence,

.   period indicates sentence final falling intonation.
,   comma indicates phrase-final intonation ("more to come").
?   question mark indicates rising intonation.
:   colon indicates elongation of preceding vowel sound.
    CAPITALIZATION indicates emphatic stress.
...   three dots indicate pause of at least half second.
..   two dots indicate perceptible pause of less than half second.
/?/   question mark in slashes indicates unintelligible utterance.
-   dash indicates abrupt cutting off of sound.
" "   quotation marks are inserted to mark dialogue.
    Lines drawn over dialogue show intonation contours.

 8   You're supposed to go to the registration desk, yknow?
 9   and fill out all the forms before you get called back.
10   They come bustin' through the door,
11   blood is everywhere.
12   It's on the walls, on the floor, everywhere.
13   [sobbing] "It's okay Billy, we're gonna make it /?/."
14   [normal voice] "What the hell's wrong with you."
15   W-we-we look at him.
16   He's covered with blood, yknow?
17   All they had to do was take a washcloth at home
18   and go like this...
19   and there'd be no blood. There'd be no blood.
20   [listener: You put pressure on it]
21   Three drunk guys came bustin' in,
22   all the other patients are like, "Ugh Ugh".
23   They're bleedin' everywhere yknow.
24   People are passin' out just lookin' at this guy's blood here.
25   [Listener: Like "We're okay"]
26   "Get the hell outta here!"
27   [Listener: Yknow he's got stories like this to tell every night, don't you.]
28   Yeah [Listener: Mhm]
29   "Get the hell outta here!" yknow?
30   These three guys-
31   "What the hell's wrong with you guys!
32   You don't know anything about first aid?
33   Hold onto his arm."
34   ["Innocent" voice] "We raised it above his head."
35   "Oh yeah" shh shh [Listener: So it bled up]
36   Yknow they're whimmin' his arm around
37   [voice change] "Come here Billy. No, come here Billy."
38   Two guys yankin' him from both sides.
39   [sobbing] "Am I gonna die? Am I gonna die?"
40   He's passed out on the cot.
41   Anyway so...[sobbing] "Am I gonna die."
42   "How old are you."
43   "Nineteen"
44   "Shit. Can't call his parents."
45   [voice change] "Don't tell my parents.
46   Please don't tell my parents.
47   You're not gonna tell my parents, are you?"
48   [Listener: /?/ "We're going to wrap you in bandages"]
49   What happened. Then the cops were there too, the cops.
50   [voice change] "Who stabbed dja."
51   "I didn't get stabbed. I fell on a bottle."...
52   "Come o::n, looks like a stab wound to me."
53   [Listener A: Well this is Alexandria, what do you think?]
54   [Listener C: Really no shit.]

There are at least five different voices animated in this narrative, and each of these voices is realized in a paralinguistically distinct representation: literally, a different voice.

Billy's two friends are represented by one voice, and the quality of that voice creates the persona that the speaker is developing for them. In line (13) they are presented as trying to reassure Billy, but the quality of the voice representing them shows that they are themselves emotionally distraught:

13 [sobbing] "It's okay Billy, we're gonna make it /?/."
   **

37 [voice change] "Come here Billy. No, come here Billy."

When the friends protest, in (34), that

34 ["Innocent" voice] "We raised it above his head."

the quality of the voice suggests belabored innocence that is really stupidity.

Another example of more than one person animated in the story as a single voice is the speaker himself, merged with the rest of the hospital staff. The quality of this voice suggests frustration and impatience but also reasonableness and clam. Dialogue uttered by this persona is the closest to normal conversational intonation and prosody.

14 [normal voice] "What the hell's wrong with you."
   **

29 "Get the hell outta here!"
   **

31 "What the hell's wrong with you guys!

32 You don't know anything about first aid?

33 Hold onto his arm."
   **

35 "Oh yeah"
   **

42 "How old are you."
   **

44 "Shit. Can't call his parents."
   **

48 [Listener: /?/ "We're going to wrap you in bandages"]

In line (48) a line of dialogue is animated by a listener, one who self-evidently was not present to hear it uttered by those to whom it is attributed.

Billy himself is animated in the most paralinguistically marked role-play. The voice representing his speech is animated as sobbing, gasping, desperate, out of control:

39   [sobbing] "Am I gonna die? Am I gonna die?"
     **
41   [sobbing] "Am I gonna die?"
     **
43   "Nineteen"
     **
45   [voice change] "Don't tell my parents.
     **
46   Please don't tell my parents.
47   You're not gonna tell my parents, are you?"
     **
51   "I didn't get stabbed. I fell on a bottle."...

The paralinguistically exaggerated role-play of Billy's voice, and the slightly less marked animation of the single voice of his friends, contrast sharply with the relatively ordinary quality in which the speaker/hospital staff voice is represented. These contrasting voices reflect and create the dramatic tension between the unreasonable behavior of "these three drunk guys" and the reasonable behavior of the speaker/staff.

Marked in a different direction is the stereotypically flat voice of the policeman:

50   [voice change] "Who stabbed dja."
     **
52   "Come o::n, looks like a stab wound to me."

Finally, the other emergency room patients are animated in a single voice:

22   all the other patients are like, "Ugh Ugh".
     **
25   [Listener: Like "We're okay"]

It is clear in all these examples that the lines of dialogue in this story are not reported, but rather constructed by the speaker, like lines in fiction or drama, and to similar effect. Through the quality of the voices created as much as (or more than) what they say, a drama is constructed. The animation of voices breathes life into the characters and their story—and the conversational interaction for which the story was created.

CONSTRUCTED DIALOGUE AS INVOLVEMENT

Of the 25 stories told by American women about being molested which I compared with 25 stories told by Greek women about the same subject, the American women's stories included one instance of constructed dialogue. The Greek women's stories included 119. Constructed dialogue is one of a range of features which made the Greek women's stories vivid and involving.[8] (See Tannen, 1983 for presentation and discussion of this range of features). It seems that the use of constructed dialogue is associated not only with Greek but with other ethnic styles as well—all those that come across as particularly "vivid." Kirshenblatt-Gimblett (1974) and Tannen (1984) show this for East European Jews, Labov (1972) for American blacks.

There is evidence that Brazilian speech falls into this category as well, and that constructed dialogue is a dimension of that effectiveness. In a pilot study comparing how Brazilian and American speakers told the story of Little Red Riding Hood, Ott (1983) found that Brazilian speakers used far more constructed dialogue. The American man in the study used six such instances, all formulaic for this fairy tale:

"Grandma, what a big nose you have."
"All the better to smell you my dear."
"Grandma, what big ears you have."
"All the better it is to hear you my dear."
"Grandma, what a big mouth and big teeth you have."
"All the better to eat you with my dear."

The American woman in the study used 15 instances of dialogue, including the formulas found in the American man's story, but also including some improvised variations on them ("What long whiskers you have"; "The better to wiggle them at you my dear") and the casting of other parts of the story in dialogue. For example, she has the mother tell Little Red Riding Hood, "Go to your grandmother's house..." The Brazilian woman who told the same story used 20 instances of dialogue, and the Brazilian man used 43!

The Brazilian man's version of Little Red Riding Hood represents almost all action in dialogue, thus making the story rich in particularity. For example, at the beginning: (Brazilian excerpts were translated from the Portugese by Ott)

One time on a beautiful afternoon, in her city, her mother called her and said:
"Little Red Riding Hood, come here."
"What is it, mother? I am playing with my dolls, can I continue?"

Long segments are composed only of dialogue. For example, when she is accosted by the wolf on her way to her grandmother's house:

"Little Red Riding Hood, Little Red Riding Hood".
And Little Red Riding Hood stopped and looked: "Who is there?"

---

[8] This is not to suggest that Americans never tell effective stories nor that they never construct dialogue extensively in their storytelling. The narratives analyzed here make clear that they do. It is simply to say that in the corpus of stories I collected by women about being molested, the stories told by Greeks were more vivid. I want to stress, too, that there is no way of knowing whether there was in fact more talk in the experiences of the Greek women; I know only that in telling these stories, they presented themselves as having engaged in more talk.

"Ah, who is talking here is the spirit of the forest."
"Spirit? But I don't know you."
"No, but I am invisible, you can't see me."
"But what do you want?" (imitating child's voice)
"Where are you going, Little Red Riding Hood?"
"Ah, I'm going to my granny's house."
"What are you going to do there, Little Red Riding Hood?"
"Ah, I'm going to take some sweets that my mother prepared for her."
"Ah, very good...the sweets are delicious, they are, they are, they are,
they are..." (licking his lips)
"Do you want one?"
"No, no, no, no. (Accelerated) Spirits don't eat.
Okay, okay. Then, now, yes, yes, you are going to take it to your granny
...remember me to her, okay?"
"Okay, bye."

Thus, through constructed dialogue and other linguistic means (such as repetition and colloquial interjections), this speaker created a vivid new story out of a standard fairy tale.

GRAPHIC VOCABULARY IN LITERARY NARRATIVE

The vividness of the foregoing story samples comes in part from the ordinariness of the diction, the familiarity of colloquial linguistic patterns. The effectiveness of some literary writing seems to derive from an opposite phenomenon: the choice of relatively unfamiliar (from the point of view of daily parlance) graphic lexical items.

A major part of my study of dialogue in conversational and fictional narrative focused on how the dialogue was introduced. The most frequent introducers in all four types of discourse studied—American and Greek conversation and fiction—were forms of the verb "say" (most frequently, in English, "s/he said" or "s/he says"). When the spoken English dialogue was not introduced by a form of "said," it was usually introduced by no verb at all (accounting for 26% of dialogue; as in the example above, dialogue was identified as such by its voice quality) or by a form of "go" ("so he goes") or "be" + "like" ("and I'm like"). "Go" and "like" accounted for 19% of the English introducers. The characteristic that set the novel *Household Words* off most noticeably from the other three discourse types studied is the use of graphic lexical items to introduce dialogue, accounting for 27% of introducers in a single chapter studied.

In this single chapter, the author of the novel used the following verbs to introduce dialogue: explain, complain, croon, coo, demand, call, call down, call out, wheeze, cry out, mutter, bellow, murmur, go on, titter, grumble, gasp, whisper, hiss, sob, scream, suggest, groan, intone, grimace, yip, warn, sniff, want to know, shout, wail, repeat, supply, yelp, snap. Of these, only five are repeated, once each (explain, whisper, scream, shout, and suggest).

It might seem, reading these verbs in a list, that the writing of this novel is overwrought. (The author herself, on reading the list, had that impression —a regrettable but signficant piece of evidence for the distortion involved in microanalysis of any type: Wrenching phenomena out of context falsifies their nature.) However, this is not the case. When the words appear in the text, they are effective, as seen in the following excerpt. In this passage, the heroine, Rhoda, serves lunch to her fifth-grade daughter Suzanne and Suzanne's classmate Ina Mae. (Verbs introducing dialogue are underlined.)

Suzanne...reached out to give Ina Mae a "feeny bird," a rap on the skull with flicked fingers, as Ina ducked away, screaming, "Get away from me!"

"How about," Rhoda suggested, "clearing off the kitchen table so you can have some good old peanut butter and jelly sandwiches?"

"Oh boy," Suzanne groaned sarcastically. "Oh boy, oh boy, oh boy."

"*The boy,*" Rhoda intoned, beating time with a spoon at the kitchen sink, "*stood by the burning deck,/His feet were full of blisters./He tore his pants on a red-hot nail/So now he wears his sister's.*" The girls, unfamiliar with the original poem (a staple of recitations in Rhoda's childhood) failed to find this wickedly amusing. "Oh, Mother," Suzanne grimaced. "Ina, for Christ's sake, would you please pass the jelly? I'm starving, you know."

"You poor old thing," Rhoda said. "You're so hungry you could dydee-dydee-dydee-die." Ina giggled. Rhoda poured a glass of milk for the guest. "Say when," she suggested.

"I HATE milk," Ina yipped.

"Oh, we never serve milk in this house. This is cow juice. Don't be fooled by the carton." Rhoda smiled mysteriously.

"She thinks she's funny," Suzanne said. (p. 104)

Graphic introducers are evaluative devices, to use a term coined by Labov (1972) to describe the elements in oral narrative that contribute to its point. The author uses them to hone her description of the characters, their personalities and states of mind, and their relationships to each other—and to make that description more particular.

IN-SCHOOL WRITING

Given the centrality of dialogue in creating vivid narration, and the evidence that at least some styles of written literary narrative use more graphic introducers in addition to the introducer "said,"[9] it is not surprising that a junior high school teacher gave her class the assignment of writing a story in which dialogue is introduced with words other than "said". The following is the

---

[9] The same would not be true of other writers, for example Hemingway and such contemporary "minimalist" writers as Raymond Carver.

story produced in fulfillment of this assignment by Michelle Lange:[10] (Verbs introducing dialogue are underlined.)

> Bob, Susie, and Lisa were walking in the park when suddenly Bob shrieked, "Look!"
> "What?" Susie and Lisa inquired.
> "I can't believe it!" Bob again shrieked.
> "What is it? Tell us," Susie insisted.
> "Look, on the sidewalk, sixty-dollars!" Bob exclaimed.
> "Oh my gosh," Lisa mumbled as she sighed.
> "This couldn't possibly be true," Susie theorized.
> "Maybe it's counterfeit," Lisa suggested.
> "No," Bill confidently stated, "It's real, all right."
> They reached their hands out and grabbed the money off the sidewalk. "Touch it," Bob suggested, "We have real money in our hands."
> "What should we do with it?" Susie asked.
> "I know one thing for sure, "Lisa warned us, "we can't let our parents know we have this money!"
> "Why not?" Bob questioned.
> "Because if our parents find we have this money, they'll either keep it, or make us turn it in to the police department," Lisa pointed out.
> "There's twenty dollars for each of us!" Susie busted out.
> The children each took their share of the money.
> "What are we going to do with our money?" Bill inquired.
> "I have an idea," Susie replied. "Why don't we make a club house!"
> Lisa and Bob chorused, "Great Idea!"
> "Maybe we can make it in the woods behind my yard," Bob offered.
> "O.K.," Susie and Lisa agreed.
> "Let's go to Bill's house now to start planning the materials needed for the club house," Lisa ordered.
> "O.K.!" Bob and Susie enthusiastically exclaimed.

Michelle fulfilled her assignment admirably. But the assignment frame aside, the accretion of verbs introducing dialogue other than "said" gives the very impression that the fiction writer feared when she read a list of verbs she had used in her chapter. But in the novel the graphic introducers were interspersed with "said," which still accounted for the majority of instances, and the connotations and associations of the graphic verbs contributed effectively to the evaluation, in other words, the story world. In Michelle's composition, total avoidance of "said" gives the narrative as a whole a forced quality, and the formal register represented by the verbs she

---

[10] I am grateful to Deborah Lange for identifying and bringing to my attention this and the following discourse samples produced by her daughter Michelle and her friends. I am grateful to her and to Michelle for allowing me to use them. The samples are presented exactly as they were produced, except that names other than Michelle's have been changed.

chose is often at odds with the nature of the actions in the story; for example, "theorized" is too lofty for the thought it introduces.

DIALOGUE IN FRIENDLY CONVERSATION

Lest the impression be left that junior high school students are not adept at constructing dialogue and introducing it fluently, I will present another story, one created when Michelle's friend told her about having accidentally run into their mutual friend Stacy.[11]

1   We saw her huge big truck, yknow?
2   That new scu- that new car?
3   It's such a scandal, that car!
     [Listener: I think its so tacky.]
4   I KNOW. And so I SAW it.
5   And then, I didn't see STACY.
6   I'm like c- trying to cruise after the car,
7   because I see the car, yknow run. .like. .driving?
8   And so I go "Oh my God,
9   I have to go run after it
10 and say hi to Stacy,
11 and go "What's up?"
12 'n I look, to the left.
13 Is that scandalous?!
14 Stacy's look- going [screaming] "Michelle, what's up?"
15 I swear she said that.
16 I swear she said that.

17 And then we we had the biggest cow in front of everyone.
18 They were all staring at us
19 cause we're like hugging,
20 and she said, "What are you doing here?"
21 And I'm like "Nothing much" yknow
22 I explained the whole. .weird story
23 and she's like "um. . .well that's cool."

24 And so then we had to crank over to Safeway?
25 Because her mom was gonna be there?
26 Cause she was like doing groceries and stuff?

The very point of this story is the dialogue: the irony that just as Michelle was looking for Stacy and planning to greet her by saying, "What's up?", she heard Stacy's voice saying to her, "What's up?" Note that I could, in the preceding sentence, have replaced the second "What's up?" with the

---

[11] To accommodate her sociolinguist mother, Michelle taped her private conversation with her friend.

phrase, "the same words." I chose to repeat the phrase "What's up," in order to create the effect of the repetition for the reader rather than simply describing it. This is inteneded to illustrate the function of dialogue in creating involvment. This main point is highlighted by Michelle's repetition:

15   I swear she said that.
16   I swear she said that.

What happened to all those terrific, graphic words for saying "said," which were found in the written assignment? These words, which were marshalled when required by a school assignment, were not appropriate to the social situation in which the preceding sample story was created. The lack of such words may make the spoken story—when transcribed—seem impoverished. But the written story seems impoverished, in comparison to the spoken one, in just the way that doesn't show up in writing: voice quality. Perhaps one of the reasons that graphic vocabulary emerges in some forms of writing is to make up for the loss of expressive potential in the human voice.

The spoken story, in contrast with the written one, is vivid and fluent. One might be tempted therefore to conclude that junior high school students are more comfortable speaking than writing. This, however, would be hasty and very likely incorrect. The main difference between these two verbal productions is not that one is spoken and the other written, but rather that one was an outgrowth of a familiar communicative situation. The oddness of the written assignment was not that it was written but that it asked Michelle to do something she does not often do, and to use a register she does not often use, though she has clearly encountered it in the writing of others. Is there, then, a written genre that arises spontaneously out of the communicative needs of Michelle and her friends? The answer is yes—writing notes to each other.

WRITTEN CONVERSATION: PASSING NOTES

For an example of a written register in which Michelle and her friends are comfortable and which they use as a natural outgrowth of their social life, I will present some brief excerpts of seventh graders' verbal productions in yet another discourse type: one that, to my knowledge, has not yet been studied, a form of written conversation: notes that Michelle's friends wrote to her and each other—the same friends they talk to every day, in person and on the telephone. Yet there are contexts in which they choose to write rather than speak. And the diction, vocabulary, and fluency are far more reminiscent of the story told in conversation than of the one written in fulfillment of a class assignment:

High! What's up? I'm kool! I'm cranking in science with Norm N. & Nate Noster. Party train up the butt!

**

You would look so good /w the one and only Tom Baxter! So go for it! He loves you yeah yeah yeah!

**

[about a friend who got into trouble with a teacher] Karen is dead. Shams! DIES! Dead meat all over the street!

Involving, or poetic, aspects of this discourse abound: formulaic phrases which echo songs, including repetition ("He loves you yeah yeah yeah"); sayings ("Go for it!", "one and only"); common parlance (the now-familiar "What's up?"); rhyming ("Dead meat all over the street!"); repetition (as above, plus "dead" repeated in the last excerpt); paraphrase with increasing intensity ("shams, dies"); visual punning ("High!", "kool"); and stylized vocabulary ("cranking," "Party train up the butt!"). The point I wish to emphasize here is that it is not the writtenness of the written assignment that accounts for its linguisitic form but the context in which it was produced, and the special requirements of that context. The notes written by Michelle to her friends provide an example of a written genre that shares many of the features of Michelle's spoken language production.

EMOTION AND COGNITION: MINGLING LITERATE AND LITERARY STRATEGIES

In her memoir of her parents Gregory Bateson and Margaret Mead, anthropologist and linguist Mary Catherine Bateson (1980, p. 180) recalls her efforts to take into account the centrality of emotion in cognition in confronting the task of communicating information that evolved in interaction. Her discussion of this process sheds light on the (as she shows, faulty) assumption that information-laden academic discourse should be emotion-free, emotion being appropriate only to fictional writing. Appointed rapporteur for a conference her father organized on cybernetics at Burg Wartenstein, Bateson "reached the conclusion that my book would be true to the event only if it followed some of the conventions of fiction" because the "conventions of academic reporting...would mean editing out emotions that seemed to me essential to the process."

Bateson contrasts this with the approach taken by Arthur Koestler, who happened to organize a conference on a similar topic at the same time, at Alpbach. Koestler, Bateson reports, tried to separate ideas and emotions and produced two books, a conventional conference proceedings and a novel: "The emotion was edited out of the formal proceedings of the Alpbach

Symposium, which came out dry and academic, and resurfaced in the novel as rage.'' In contrast, Bateson continues,

> There is a sense in which the emotion was edited into [my] book, for I used my own introspective responses of dismay or illumination to bring the reader into the room, and worked with the tape-recorded discussions so that the emotionally pivotal comments would be brought out rather than buried in verbiage.

The successful result of Bateson's effort is a book entitled *Our Own Metaphor* (1972), a document which recreates rather than reports the proceedings of the conference, using, as she noted, linguistic means commonly found in literary writing. The result, I suggest, makes the evolving insights that emerged in the conference available to readers in a way more closely paralleling the way conference participants were able to perceive them. I would like to show how she does this by presenting an excerpt from that book, one which begins in the middle of an exposition presented as the dialogue of a speaker named Tolly:

> I want to show, on the blackboard, a technique for writing, and I want to associate that technique with sentences.
>
> "I'll begin with an extremely simple picture, by way of introduction, and then elaborate it. This will be like those initial minutes in the movies when you see the introductory pictures which give you an idea of the kind of movie it's going to be while telling you who the main characters are, and so on.
>
> "Let's imagine a pendulum swinging back and forth." Tolly hunted around for chalk and then he drew this picture. "This means that for some interval of time the pendulum swings to the right, shown by the arrow labeled R. Here's an occurrence, shown by a point, and then the pendulum swings to the left for some other interval, shown by the arrow labeled L. The occurrence is the end of the swing. You can think of the same picture as representing a billiard ball rolling back and forth on a frictionless table between two reflecting boundaries. Left, right, left, right, and the occurrences are the bounces."
>
> Horst did a double-take. "You mean the *point* indicates the moment it changes from right to left?"
>
> Tolly nodded gleefully. "Yeah. That's right. Unconventional." Once Horst had called my attention to it, I realized that this was indeed unconventional. The minute I stopped thinking that the arrow indicated the direction of the pendulum (which it did not, because the diagram of a light changing from red to green to red would have looked exactly the same), I realized that Tolly was doing the strange thing of using an *arrow* to represent something stable (an "interval of condition-holding" he called it) and a *point* to represent change, the occurrence that initiates new conditions. This was the exact opposite of the convention Barry had used in his diagram, where arrows had represented the transition from, say, organic to non-organic nitrogen compounds, or Fred,

who had used arrows to represent causation. It was not yet clear whether these conventions were simply freakish or arbitrary, or whether this choice of symbols was a first step toward new kinds of meanings (pp. 166–67).

It would be possible to double the length of this chapter in analyzing the many ways that this passage is written like fiction (and also the many ways it is not like a transcript of speech). I will refer briefly to a few. Bateson uses first names for participants, bringing us closer to them than we would feel if they were referred to by last name only or title and last name. She presents Tolly's ideas as dialogue rather than paraphrasing them—with attendant interjections and colloquial diction ("say," "Yeah,"), contractions ("I'll," "it's," "let's"), and fragmented syntax ("Unconventional."). The possible responses of readers are represented and prefigured by the dramatized responses of the audience-participants ("Horst did a double-take"). Note, too, that this response is described as a picture of nonverbal behavior, not merely as a verbal response. The paralinguistic features which frame speech by letting us know how speakers mean what they say—tone of voice, rhythm, intonation, and nonverbal components such as laughter—are described and aided by adverbs ("Tolly nodded gleefully"). Moreover, the importance of the ideas is highlighted by representing the narrator's own developing cognitive state ("I realized..."), as well as by prefiguring future cognition ("It was not yet clear..."). This last device simultaneously builds suspense.

Suspense is also created by the scenically graphic but otherwise puzzling description of apparently irrelevant behavior such as "Tolly hunted around for chalk and then drew this picture." What is added by telling us he hunted for chalk? To answer, contrast this with the conventional academic-writing locution, "See Figure 1." In the latter case we see only the figure. In Bateson's description, we see not only the figure (or, rather, the "picture"), but also the human interaction that gave rise to it. Furthermore, the interruption in exposition gives readers time to prepare to focus attention on the figure/picture, much as the conference participants gained time as Tolly hunted for chalk and then drew. Finally, Tolly is represented as using a simile in his opening lines, likening the figure he is about to draw to a movie lead-in.

CONCLUSION

I am suggesting in this chapter that orality and literacy, speaking and writing, are not dichotomous but rather complex, overlapping, and intertwined. In order to illustrate this, I have shown how both spoken and written storytelling —conversational and literary—make use of constructed dialogue which, by its particularity, occasions the imagination of alternative, distant, and other worlds. By this act of imagination, the hearer or reader participates in sense-making and is thus moved to a sense of rapport that is the means to meaning in both conversation and fiction. I further illustrated the overlapping of discourse patterns in spoken and written discourse types by presenting samples of speech and writing produced by a junior high school student in three different contexts. The final section demonstrates how one writer used literary linguistic means to enhance an academic writing task, means which make use of, rather than exclude, emotional involvement.

Such mixing of genres reflects the mixing of spoken and written modes, of orality and literacy, in our lives. I would like to dramatize this by ending with an excerpt from a long essay in The New Yorker about Lubavitcher Hasidim—an orthodox Jewish sect living in Brooklyn, New York (Harris, 1985). In this excerpt, the writer constructs (I shall not, for now-obvious reasons, use the verb "reports") her conversation with a Hasidic man:

> "Thanks," I said. "By the way, are there any books about Hasidism that you think might be helpful?"
> "There are no books."
> "No books! Why, what do you mean? You must know that hundreds of books have been written about Hasidism."
> "Books about Hasidic matters always misrepresent things. They twist and change the truth in casual ways. I trust Lubavitcher books, like the 'Tanya' [a work written by the movement's founder] and the collections of the rebbes' discourses, because our rebbe got the information in them from the rebbe before him, and so on, in an unbroken chain. I trust scholars I can talk to, face to face."

The effectiveness of presenting this interchange of ideas as a dialogue is by now evident. Harris presents herself as naive to the point of rudeness ("You must know..."), so that the Hasidic man can be shown to explain his view in detail. The excerpt dramatizes, at the same time, the intertwining of oral and literate modes in the passing down of a written text—the Tanya—inextricably intertwined with people, the great religious leaders (rebbes) who are also seen as great scholars—interpreters of that text. The text, in other words, is meaningless apart from its interpretation, which is found in people, not in print—and, moreover, the interaction among people ("scholars I can talk to, face to face"). It is for this very reason that contemporary academics are forever holding meetings, conferences, and lectures—wanting to see scholars face to face rather than encountering them only through their written productions. Nonetheless, producing written texts before and after is a prerequisite of appearing in person as a "scholar."

I am suggesting, then, that we enlarge our field of study beyond the prototypical spoken and written genres of spoken casual conversation and written expository prose, which has been typical of studies of spoken and written discourse in order to understand the overlapping and contrasting linguistic patterns which reflect and create feeling and thinking in discourse in human interaction.

REFERENCES

Bateson, G. (1972). *Steps to an ecology of mind*. New York: Ballantine.

Bateson, M.C. (1972). *Our own metaphor: A personal account of a conference on conscious purpose and human adaptation*. New York: Knopf.

Bateson, M.C. (1984). *With a daughter's eye: A memoir of Margaret Mead and Gregory Bateson*. New York: William Morrow.

Becker, A.L. (1984a). Biography of a sentence: A Burmese Proverb. In E.M. Bruner (Ed.), *Text, play, and story: The construction and reconstruction of self and society* (pp. 135–155). Washington, DC: American Ethnological Society.

Becker, A.L. (1984b). The linguistics of particularity: Interpreting superordination in a Javanese text. *Proceedings of the Tenth Annual Meeting of the Berkeley Linguistics Society* (pp. 425–436). Berkeley: Linguistics Department, University of California.

Bleich, D. (in press). *Reconceiving literacy*. In C. Anson (Ed.), Responding to student writing. Urbana, Illinois: National Council of Teachers of English.

Bloodgood, F. "Doc" (1982). The medicine and sideshow pitches. In D. Tannen (Ed.), *Analyzing discourse: Text and talk. Georgetown University Round Table on Languages and Linguistics 1981* (pp. 371–382). Washington: DC: Georgetown University Press.

Britton, J. (1982). Spectator role and the beginnings of writing. In M. Nystrand (Ed.), *What writers know: The language, process, and structure of written discourse* (pp. 149–169). New York: Academic Press.

Chafe, W. (1982). *Integration and involvement in speaking, writing, and oral literature*. In D. Tannen (Ed.), *Spoken and written language*. Norwood, NJ: Ablex.

D'Angelo, F.J. (1983). Literacy and cognition: A developmental perspective. In R.M. Bailey & R.M. Fosheim (Eds.), *Literacy for life: The demand for reading and writing* (pp. 97–114). New York: Modern Language Association.

Friedrich, P. (1979). Poetic langauge and the imagination: A reformulation of the Sapir Hypothesis. In *Language, context, and the imagination* (pp. 441–512). Stanford, CA: Stanford University Press.

Goody, J., & Watt, I. (1963). The consequences of literacy. *Comparative studies in society and history, 5*, 304–345.

Harris, L. (1985, September 16). Lubavitcher Hasidim, Part I. *The New Yorker*, pp. 4–10.

Havelock, E. (1963). *Preface to Plato*. Cambridge, MA: Harvard University Press.

Kirshenblatt-Gimblett, B. (1974). The concept and varieties of narrative performance in East European Jewish Culture. In R. Bauman & J. Sherzer (Eds.), *Explorations in the ethnography of speaking* (pp. 283–308). Cambridge, MA: Cambridge University Press.

Labov, W. (1972). The transformation of experience into narrative syntax. *Language in the inner city* (pp. 354–396). Philadelphia: University of Pennsylvania Press.

Lakoff, R.T. (1979). Stylistic strategies within a grammar of style. In J. Orasanu, M. Slater, & L.L. Adler (Eds.), *Language, sex, and gender: Annals of the New York Academy of Science, 327*, 53–78.

Ochs, E. (1979). Planned and unplanned discourse. In T. Givon (Ed.), *Discourse and syntax* (pp. 51–80). New York: Academic Press.

Olson, D. (1977). From utterance to text: The bias of language in speech and writing. *Harvard Educational Review, 47*(3), 257–281.

Ong, W.J., S.J. (1967). *The presence of the word*. New Haven, CT: Yale University Press.

Ott, M.M.B. (1983). *Orality and literacy in Brazilian and American storytelling: A comparative study*. Unpublished manuscript. Georgetown University.

Ricks, C. (1981, July 16). Phew! Oops! Oof!: A review of Erving Goffman, *Forms of talk*. *New York Review of Books*, pp. 42–44.

Rosen, H. (1984). *Stories and meanings*. Kettering, England: National Association for the Teaching of English.

Schiffrin, D. (1981). *Tense variation in narrative. Language, 57*(1), 45–62.

Silber, J. (1976). *Household words.* New York: Viking.

Tannen, D. (1982a). The oral/literate continuum in discourse. In D. Tannen (Ed.), *Spoken and written language.* Norwood, NJ: Ablex.

Tannen, D. (1982b). Oral and literate strategies in spoken and written narratives. *Language, 58*(1), 1–21.

Tannen, D. (1983, Fall). "I take out the rock—dok!": How Greek women tell about being molested (and create involvement). *Anthropological Linguistics,* pp. 359–374.

Tannen, D. (1984). *Conversational style: Analyzing talk among friends.* Norwood, NJ: Ablex.

Tannen, D. (1985). Relative focus on involvement in oral and written discourse. In D.R. Olson, N. Torrance, & A. Hildyard (Eds.), *Literacy, language, and learning: The nature and consequences of reading and writing* (pp. 124–147). Cambridge: Cambridge University Press.

Tannen, D. (1986a). Introducing constructed dialogue in Greek and American conversational and literary narrative. In F. Coulmas (Ed.), *Direct and indirect speech* (pp. 311–332). Berlin: Mouton-de Gruyter.

Tannen, D. (1986b). *That's not what I meant!: How conversational style makes or breaks your relations with others.* New York: William Morrow.

Tannen, D. (in press). Ordinary conversation and literary discourse: Coherence and the poetics of repetition. In E.H. Bendix (Ed.), The uses of linguistics. *Annals of the New York Academy of Science.*

Welty, E. (1984). *One writer's beginnings.* Cambridge, MA: Harvard University Press.

Chapter Five
The Literate Essay: Using Ethnography to Explode Myths

SHIRLEY BRICE HEATH
Stanford University

THE ESSAY AS EXAMPLE

The essay, a written genre shrouded in myths and mystery, lies at the heart of academic performance. Beyond asserting general rhetorical principles of persuasion and argumentation, relatively few critical analyses explain the internal structuring of essays and how their composition is revealed to authors and readers. The goal of this chapter is to bring members of the reading audience—most especially teachers—into the composition and reception of the essay form so that they may feel they have stepped *inside a literate essay*. Reading this essay and following its argument should lead readers to experience something of the role of participant that students and teachers in a learning community can create as they explore their own language forms and uses.

It is somewhat surprising that within the current mood of deconstructing literature, so few language scholars have tried to understand what makes each essay that English teachers might regard as "well constructed" or "literate" an instance of the genre *essay*. It may well be that of all the literary forms, the essay has suffered most from an unwillingness on the part of scholars to make strange such a familiar form; academics are, after all, forced to reveal the results of their examination of the essay in that very form. Structural studies of the essay carry the same drawbacks as research on language or the brain. We are forced to transmit our studies of language through the linguistic medium; we must use the brain to study the brain. We resist researching the essay when the reporting instrument is the object of the inquiry.

Thus, instead of turning intense and closely argued analyses on the essay as a genre, we create and perpetuate myths and common-sense theories, such as the "five-paragraph essay formula" and prescriptive rules about teaching outlines and observing rules for choice of voice, person, and organization. This essay attempts to break open some of these myths and to look at ways in which the essay seduces the reader by pulling the reader *inside* its structure to ensure that the reader becomes a co-participant in the recomposition of the piece. What follows here is then both a programmatic display of ways that students across different writing backgrounds and cultural experiences can come to *know* an essay and a firsthand experience for the readers of this essay to be "inside the essay." We look at myths and the role of ethnography in reconsidering how certain myths may hold us back from membership in a learning community.

FINDING MYTHS

William Carlos Williams, an American poet, novelist, and essayist, as well as a full-time physician, probably knew more about the writing of essays than most teachers of composition or academics whose professional reputation depends on their essay writing abilities. Williams wrote numerous essays, but it is not from his essays as models that we learn about how to write essays. It is from his exposure of some of the myths about writing. He came to know about writing through acting as an early ethnographer of communication—an anthropologist within the tribe of the American literary elite who reveled in telling as much as possible about the ways of believing, valuing, and behaving that members of his literary community shared. He knew that other writers would not agree with him; they preferred to maintain myths not only about themselves as authors but about writing in general. Williams levied the same charge against academics, members of English Departments especially, who were, in his view, conspirators who placed knowledge "before a man as if it were a stair at the top of which a DEGREE is obtained..." (1970, p. 139).

If we examine some of the myths that Williams identified, we can consider how those who write essays might benefit from turning an ethnographic eye as participant–observers on the genre. For students learning to write, such practices may be especially helpful for removing some of the fear and paralysis which can result from the myths and mystification that currently surround essays in school. Williams is a good model, because he was at once a writer, critic of the teaching of writing, celebrator of those who wanted to learn to write, and a man that anthropologists who study methods of communication today are happy to embrace as a kindred soul.

Four myths to explode—or at the very least—to consider with a new perspective:

First: teachers of composition can teach students to write.

Second: the classroom is a place in which we can merely practice writing; real writing is almost impossible to accomplish there.

Third: thinking about one's writing is something apart from talking about one's writing.

Fourth: the direction of influence is from oral language habits to written and not the reverse.

Offered in place of these are not four replacement statements which will themselves become myths, but four thought-starters—points for consideration in our definitions of ourselves as members of the writing profession.

1. No one teaches anyone else to write. The process of composition in written form is far too complicated for any individual to be able to articulate the rules so that another individual can learn to write simply by following the given rules. For the same reason we cannot teach young children to talk by devising rules to describe how to talk, so we cannot teach writing by devising and transmitting rules for how it is done. Those rules will always be inadequate for capturing the actual process through which novices *learn* by intuiting rules, trying them, and finally fixing on what works in written communication.

2. The English classroom can be one of the most dynamic communication centers of any individual's life experiences.

3. Learning to write is fundamentally based on multiple, redundant occasions for certain kinds of talk about language as well as extended opportunities for talking about what is written and read.

4. The influence of oral and written language on each other is bidirectional—learning to write influences how one talks, and an individual's ways of talking strongly influence the process of learning to write.

ETHNOGRAPHY AND THE LEARNING COMMUNITY

Myth #1. The myth: Teachers of composition can teach others to write; the replacement thought-starter: no one ever teaches anyone else to write. We can only enable others to learn by providing adequate modeling, opportunity for trials, and chances for having successful communication in writing (cf. Freedman, 1985). My argument here is based not only on an endorsement of William's thoughts about the essay, but also on my long-term research on children learning their first language (Heath, 1983). Williams wrote of the essay: "To essay...is to establish trial. The essay is the most human literary form in that it is always sure, it remains from first to last fixed....Whatever passes through it, it is never that thing. It remains itself and continues so, pure motion." (1970, p. 322). The analogue here is language: To use language is to establish trial. Language is always sure in that its structures—phonemes, morphemes, lexicon, and syntax—are fixed, arbitrary, and systematic, yet infinitely capable of creation within and through it.

Children learn their mother tongue in all its complexities not by imitation or by having someone spell out the grammar rules for them. Indeed such a proposition is impossible, because our analytical powers do not begin to extend far enough for us to be able to explain how our language works. Linguists spend decades simply trying to explain *if-then* clauses or case endings in a single language. Thus in the past two decades, we have had to admit that every neurologically normal individual has a human bioprogram that provides the language-making capacity that takes its ultimate shape through societal influences. With our abilities to learn, and our desire to be socially accepted, we observe, listen, associate, and generate rules that we then test and refine, all the while making judgments about the appropriateness of our applications of these rules. Hence, we come to learn to speak without being taught; what we need are models who communicate with us and meet our social and physical needs through language.

Learning written language is fundamentally very similar to learning oral language. What is needed to learn written language are models who communicate with us through writing and who expect us to transmit our knowledge, needs, and plans for the future through the written channel. Given sufficient opportunity to have such communicative exchange, we can internally generate and test rules for writing to meet satisfactorily the goals we set for ourselves.

However, beyond these fundamental similarities are two critical differences: learning to write requires tools, and the process involves internalizing conventions that are counterintuitive and in contrast to the rules of use of oral language. In most parts of the world, a single institution—the school—enshrines these differences in a nexus of value-laden expectations that give off the strong message that writers and readers should be highly self-conscious about written language. The symbolic power of "correct," "complex," and "comprehensible" written language lies behind educators' convictions of the importance of learning literate behaviors, and thus schools feel compelled to generate fixed rules for written language as well as labels to explain deficiencies in reading and writing. As a result, the internal motivation and self-defined goals for communicating which drive us to be successful oral language learners become displaced by externally established goals and criteria. Thus learning written language casts from the outset an identity-threatening rather than an identiy-enhancing aura.

In addition, written language depends on certain artifacts; to obtain the repetitive, multiple, and reiterative opportunities to read and write which ensure academic success, the learner needs adequate tools of a certain quantity, developmental sequence, and level of complexity. Learners with access to only a few primers and charcoal and parchment cannot match in achievement those who have a variety of printed materials, some of which hold the most complex ideas of the society, and a multiplicity of supplies for writing.

Perhaps the most essential difference between learning written language and acquiring spoken language rests in the fact that learning to read and write requires exclusive attention and some isolation from other activities. Speaking naturally embeds itself in the normal flow of daily life. In contrast, learning to use written language demands blocks of time in which the learner does nothing else. One can talk while one eats, works, travels, and plays; reading and writing demand a certain amount of attention to these accomplishments alone. Moreover, in most societies of the world, the pace of daily life and fundamental human needs can be met without written language, and even in societies where writeen language seems essential, one can solve most problems by oral language. If human beings can accomplish what they want and need by doing one thing which they already know how to do, they usually resist learning a parallel skill. Golfers, cooks, and auto mechanics generally have one way of swinging a club, putting together a souffle, and cleaning a carburetor; only if for some reason the usual way does not work, will any of these individuals turn to a back-up or parallel method.

Ironically, schools, the major locale for providing exclusive attention to reading and writing needed for societally-defined mastery, set aside these essential differences between learning to speak and learning to read and write. The goals and the organization of time and activities in most formal education in societies around the world limit the extent to which individuals can depend on the school as the place for learning to read and write. Schools have the goal of not only teaching writing, but also transmitting content knowledge. If reduced sufficiently in scope and complexity, knowledge can be tested through only a few words; hence, the majority of testing of knowledge does not call for much writing—only single words or brief phrases, as Arthur Applebee's research on writing in American secondary schools has shown (1981). Demands for efficiency of evaluation and predictability of responses force teachers to limit students' opportunities for writing in classrooms. Teaching for "the answer" precludes using written language to explore how and why answers evolve and how they might change. Such limited models and opportunities for productive writing circumscribe the productive written language one can learn in school. If adults spoke with children in only simple straightforward language without affective elaboration or questioning expansion, and expected only one-word utterances or brief phrases of oral language in response, children could not learn to speak beyond the level of the model. Similarly, when the writing which is expected of students is always brief and when students are regarded as remedial or needing "special education," they are deprived of productive opportunities to write—or in Williams' words, they have no opportunity to "try." But are there ways in which classrooms can enable them to have the trials Williams sees as necessary for learning to write essays?

Myth #2. "Real" writing is nearly impossible in classrooms. The thought replacement: classrooms can create for the learning of writing an environment similar to that in which children learn to speak—situations of multiple, redundant, and meaningful opportunities to communicate out of children's felt needs. The classroom can be one of the liveliest communication dens of our life. However, the liveliness to which I refer comes from turning the language arts or English classroom into the place in which we explore language. Proust has told us in *Remembrance of Things Past* that "We are attracted by every form of life which represents to us something unknown and strange, by a last illusion still unshattered" (1934: p. 1120). It is this attraction to making strange that with which we think we are so familiar that can draw students into studying their language—oral and written.

We can for the purposes of illustration think of this study as the ethnography of communication, but it must be ethnography which is grounded in some understanding of the role of this type of work in anthropology (Saville-Troike, 1984). Ethnography is not—as far too much of the current craze for qualitative research makes it out to be—a method; it is instead the genre which results from a set of methods which include long-term residence within a group, knowledge of the language of the group, and selection of methods of data collection which include participant observation, artifact collection, interviewing, and considerable quantitative work. The researcher who collects data in these ways must analyze them through a variety of conceptual frameworks; interpretations of these meanings come not only through the data collected, but also through returning to those from whom the data were collected and discussing interpretations which the researcher has reached (Ellen, 1984).

In numerous collaborative efforts in classrooms across the country, teachers and students have collected language data as ethnographers of communication (Heath, 1983; Heath & Branscombe, 1985; Heath, 1985). Students go out into their own homes and communities, taking fieldnotes on the contexts of the talk they hear, the reading and writing they see others doing, and the actions which result from such communications. Accompanying these fieldnotes may be audiotapes of conversations, sermons, songs, jokes, riddles, or any of a variety of types of language uses. These materials become the data for much of the initial work on language in these classrooms. Necessary to making these collections of language data useful in classrooms is a teacher ready to engage students in language study. Such teachers are not now abundant, since most training programs for language arts or English teachers offer limited opportunities to study forms and uses of language apart from a prescriptivist environment. But for those who have either had such opportunities or are willing to immerse themselves in a collaborative effort with language researchers (see Heath & Branscombe, 1985, for example), the rewards can be unlimited. Students and teachers become involved in producing theories about how language accomplishes actions, relationships, and ideas; such theories generate practices, carried along by the need to test hypotheses and to shatter illusions.

Once accomplished in examining the language of everyday life around them, students can apply their newfound skills of analysis to their own writings and to the language of literary authors. Students can pose questions: who was talking, for how long, about what topic, with what goals? They must then figure out ways to answer these questions. What is countable, and what is to be gained by counting? If one is to count, one must identify the units to be counted—words, sentences, turns in a conversation, etc. This early analysis turns students' attention to the units of language for which they have to discover names and definitions—they can either turn to a book for these terms or devise terms of their own. Often, students from fifth grade on simply remember at this point that their teachers have already given them terms which now become relevant for something the students want to do; hence, they name the units they are identifying with such familiar terms as verbs, nouns, etc. But to count nouns or verbs, there must be agreement about what each of these is. Hence one must decide on definitions and try them out on the real language data the students have collected. Teachers must, in these circumstances, be prepared to acknowledge that most textbook definitions are entirely too limited to cover all the possible circumstances that occur in actual language use, and students will have to make informed decisions about entities that fall in border areas.

To collect more data, students can move out from their own homes to workplaces, analyzing the relatedness of talking to writing or reading and then retelling information gained from written materials to others or reworking such knowledge into actions which one must take. These data require more in-depth analysis—how do thoughts become connected so that people who hear them expressed realize that one thing comes before another, one thing is causally related to another? Students who begin to ask such questions of their data have to find grammatical items or components of language which accomplish these ends. Thus students find that when mainstream middle class native English speakers tell stories about events they have experienced, they use many *ands* to string the elements of the action together. However, when individuals give directions about how to accomplish an action, they tend to relate single actions to each other by using temporal or causal rather than coordinate conjunctions. Students become aware of their own ways of beginning and ending pieces of communication: a joke is known by its opening before it is told; a professor's turn from one topic to another is signalled by the use of "OK" or (in Great Britain) "Right."

A love affair can (and often does) develop with language—oral and written—as students and teacher collect, analyze, and finally interpret their data from oral and written sources. Written texts—from bills to speeding tickets, conversations, and courtroom transcripts—prepare students as experts to move on to short stories, novels, and poems. As they analyze these literary pieces, they apply the same strategies they have applied to the data they collected in their daily world of language use. But such collection and analysis of the familiar helps students begin to act as experts over language, and they can recognize works of literature as creative language uses which are ultimately dependent on ordinary language reworked by nonordinary means. Imagination determines the limits to which teachers and students can explore and find unknowns in the familiar patterns of everyday talk and the types of writing which occur in different environments.

Such analysis leads to interpretation which depends on descriptions of contexts of talk and writing. Are there characteristics of written materials in work settings which differ from such features in home settings? Out of the stream of speech, how can we cut into chunks what is there? Are there genre conventions which tell us when one piece of text is one thing and not another? How do we know when a joke has ended? What role does anticipation play in the way we comprehend as we read or as we listen?

The search for understanding language is one in which teacher and students join as experts—all can use language, and yet all also join as novices in the exploration of ways to understand what it is. As students come to understand more and more through data collection, analysis, and comparison across types of settings for oral and written language, they will want to communicate their discoveries. Essays, reports, graphic representations, as well as other types of written messages can be the forms into which students place their interpretations of data. The audience for these writings can be those on the site in which the data were collected, for it is to those sites that the writer–researcher must return and seek verification of findings and interpretations. From brothers and sisters or parents at home, to ministers, or secretaries in college offices, those who are experts on their own language uses can be asked to read and discuss the reports on their language uses. Needless to say, students who go out into the world as ethnographers of communication must also be aware of the need to inform those who are being studied of the research; hence, to seek permission to carry out research, students must use written forms as well as oral explanations of what they are planning to do and what they have accomplished in their research. In essence, students at any level of the curriculum can become experts on their own language and that of the settings in which they can gain permission to observe, listen, record, and then analyze and interpret. These skills transfer to the study of literary texts and to roles as critics of one's own writing as well as that of others. Among those researchers who have repeatedly asked writers to engage in protocols in which they talk aloud as they write or read and explain what they are doing, there is acknowledgement that when students verbalize how they are using language as they write, this attention to language as such seems to be a treatment. It creates more interest in and awareness of one's writing and one's uses of language, which turns out to be a critical first step toward improved writing. Engaging students in language study before asking them to become essayists and literary critics in English classrooms enables students to come to know how to talk about language, and they find the enterprise entertaining, educational, and filled with positive transfer value to their own writing and speaking.

As students collect, analyze, and interpret their data, they generate rules about the structures and functions of language—oral and written. They do so to talk with each other and with those who helped create the data about the interpretations or findings. The tasks are not empty; they are filled with the rewards of detective work, and the types of writing the students do—from fieldnotes through brief summaries of small portions of data, to reports, essays, or the like—have the goal of communicating with the informants from whom they collected the data. These informants respond to such reports, because they, like most subjects of writing, enjoy seeing their words and thoughts on paper. Mechanics, waitresses, fathers, little sisters, or secretaries are not exceptions to the near-universal attraction of seeing one's seemingly trivial daily habits and routines valued enough by others to be their object of study and report. The transformation of the data into interpretive essays to be discussed with those who are the topics of the essays guarantees response and engagement with an expert and critical audience.

Just as the development of oral language depends on the context of the rich interaction between child and adults, so then does the development of written language depend on a rich responsive context. This context is especially critical for older students who have reached high school or college without opportunity to participate in any extended *interactive writing*—my title for this kind of writing. Young children acquiring language search for units of symbolic behavior, construct systems of elements and relations, and try to match their production to those of selected others in recurrent situational contexts. The new writer must follow similar steps to generate internal rules for writing to communicate. Responsive, interactive writing frequently occurring over a period of time provides the experience from which students may search out meaningful units and systems in writing. The opportunity to talk about the writing—with classmates, teachers, and with the subjects— forces writers to realize what they have not communicated through the written word—the assumptions they have made, the presuppositions they have not fully explained, the backgrounds of understanding which are not shared. As students begin to initiate interpretation for themselves and to have content they want to expand, they will use language not only for interactional and personal functions—Michael Halliday's terms (1975) for the functions to which young children put oral language—but for heuristic and imaginative purposes as well.

Moreover, in this kind of inquiry, imitation and rule generation play a part in the acquisition of written language. One goes beyond simply observing and recording the data in looking for the patterns by which language works—for example, the recurrent design of administrative forms versus the design of letters of inquiry from charitable agencies, or the relative length of sentences used in giving directions as compared with those delivered in a sermon. From creating fieldnotes (which must use primarily descriptive language), to writing summaries which demand transitions and connections among sentences within the piece, to framing interpretive essays, students have the opportunity to write in various genres. They not only explore patterns and rules by describing them at work, but they also generate the needed internal rules or knowledge about how to communicate in written form what they have learned about the uses of oral and written language in varying environments. In short, these students find the language arts or English classroom a place which does not give them grammar rules, but allows them to come to own rules which relate not only to grammar but also to the conventions of appropriateness for different genres and conventions of speaking and writing.

In their discussions of data and analysis with other students and with informants or outside researchers, students have to resolve real crises in communication—cases in which others simply do not understand or believe what the students are saying or writing. Resolution of these crises has to come in part from students learning in Virginia Woolf's terms, to see the "face beneath the page." The communicator–audience relation thus develops through a process of mutual adjustment, just as oral conversation or any other form of give-and-take discourse does. Listeners seek clarification, register misunderstanding and disagreement, and question their conversational partner's information. In writing, the same processes must occur within the head of the writer who must play both listener and speaker, writer and reader roles, as Louise Rosenblatt and contemporary literary critics tell us so frequently (Rosenblatt, 1976; Mailloux, 1982; Thompkins, 1985).

Myth #3. Lest we forget that my organizing theme to these remarks is myths about student writing, let us turn now to the third myth—thinking about one's writing is something entirely apart from talking about one's writing. One of the most frequent admonitions we give students who are learning to write is that they must think before they write. Writing should reflect the prior organization of one's thoughts, and we place great emphasis on thinking to organize thoughts, and then writing to represent *that* organization of ideas. We place very little emphasis on talking "out" one's ideas before or as one writes.

We have turned increasingly to conferencing in the revision process or for help in editing, and teachers of composition are running conferences with students to discuss pieces they have written. But such conferences are essentially dyadic; multiparty talk carries more potential for egalitarian rather than hierarchical distribution of power and knowledge. Talk as one prepares to write helps writers generate and test ideas; talk and reading aloud of drafts further tests the "reasonableness" of information conveyed. Though we must acknowledge the multiple approaches to writing which we find reported by writers in the *Paris Interviews* or the occasional interview of the Pulitzer Prize-winning journalist, we rarely acknowledge that the same types of variation may exist among our students. In teaching, we have generally prescribed the outline as the way to organize ideas before writing and to keep track of ideas as one writes. Yet, we laugh knowingly when years after we have taught students who have gone on to succeed in college, they return and tell us that they always had to write that needed outline *after* the essay, and not before. This familiar anecdote serves here just to remind us that there are many different ways in which writers organize their thoughts for writing, and outlining ahead of time may be one of the least frequently used means of doing so. Talking over one's ideas before and during writing and editing is the preferred strategy for professional writers.

One of the most common ways of organizing ideas is talking about what one is going to write before as well as during writing. I refer to these writers as the "in-process" creators. For them, either the act of talking and/or the physical act of writing stimulates creative thinking. "How can I know what I think until I've heard myself say it—or seen myself write it?" This is a common plea from children who have difficulty "getting it all right" on paper. Once again, strategies of the anthropologist in the field are helpful here. Find time to allow students to talk among themselves about a piece they will be writing; tape recording such sessions and allowing students to play tapes back to hear themselves think aloud is a very rewarding device for those students who are reluctant to think that this talk helps. Particularly for older students, years of imposed silence while writing can make it nearly impossible for them to adapt to the idea of talking out what they think before and during their writing. This experience seems to work best for those who consider themselves the poorest, the slowest, or the least creative writers. Once they have heard themselves argue on tape or try to persuade someone else of an idea and succeed, they gain confidence that they can transfer that idea to written form.

Another useful way of moving those students who have judged themselves entirely unsuccessful in writing is to ask them to transcribe a short portion of their talk from the tape and to work with the teacher or another student to turn the oral language into a written form (see Heath, 1982, for an account of high school students transcribing the audio portion of videotapes they had made and realizing the changes necessary to produce an acceptable written version of their videotapes).

Data of a different sort also suggest the benefits for writers and readers of talking about ideas gained from or about to be put into written form. A survey of several hundred literacy programs around the world indicates that for those programs for which data exist about the effects of the program after the initiators of the program left the region, all those programs from which learners retained literacy skills provided sustained opportunities for new literates to talk about what they had been reading and what and how they had been writing (Heath, *forthcoming*). It appears that a critical factor for the retention of both reading and writing habits is the opportunity to talk about knowledge gained and produced through literate behaviors. Textual communities (such as churches, health centers, agricultural self-help groups, etc.) allow such opportunities. The process of learning from written materials includes reflecting on the meaning of such knowledge for changed values and behaviors. For reading and writing to be sustained, interaction must take place around the ultimate goal of an agreed-upon meaning for the text. Thus the maintenance and extension of functions and types of literacy within a society depend upon opportunities for participation in redundant, multiple, and reinforcing occasions for oral construction of the shared background needed to interpret written materials.

Myth #4.   The final myth is one which teachers of writing have held for decades. This myth has been helped along by the interpretation of much of the research on the so-called oral–literate dichotomy. The myth maintains that oral language heavily influences written language, and that those who come from societies with "oral traditions" find it harder to learn to write than those who come from societies with "written traditions."

Scholars from the anthropologist Jack Goody (1977) to humanists such as Father Walter Ong (1982) have been interpreted as saying that particular ways of thinking go with those who write—especially those who write in the essayist tradition; those from oral societies are less likely to have the ways of thinking which allow them to decontextualize their materials and make their texts "autonomous" than are those from "literate" societies. Recent work by anthropologists who have done fieldwork in newly literate societies (Duranti & Ochs, 1986; Besnier, 1986) make clear the need to go beyond simple examinations of reading and writing to analyses of the integration of these activities in the social construction of different kinds of knowledge and the relative value of various types of information in the society. Scholars must answer the complex question: How are forms and uses of written and oral language interdependent with other features of the society? Moreover, the ways in which children learn the oral language of the society can affect their orientation to written language. If the society has ways of taking language apart and holding it up for examination for its own sake rather than keeping it exclusively embedded within the stream of communication, then members of that society seem to adjust more readily to learning to write in formal schooling than do members of societies who do not take language apart in such ways. For example, mainstream middle class school-oriented parents around the world have ways of stopping talk to focus on words as labels, to call attention to forms of language play, and to comment on particular genre conventions (e.g., reminding a child that telling a joke means getting the punchline in and just remembering the opening lines is not enough). These ways of approaching language are deeply embedded in language socialization practices of communities around the world (Schieffelin & Ochs, 1986).

A view that it is somehow "natural" to consider language *as such* underlies materials, methods, and motivations for teaching writing and reading around the world in formal schooling situations (Olson, 1984). For success in these situations, it appears that the ability to analyze language as a system of bits and pieces in patterns is fundamental to comprehension in reading and production in composition. This analysis requires the learning of a metalanguage used to dissect language as an artifact by segmenting, isolating, labeling, and describing bits of language apart from their communicative contexts. To become literate then is to be able not only to recognize patterns in print and to link these patterns in oral language, but also to talk about how one knows words, sentences, etc. Some sociocultural groups may carry within their habits of talking about language the precursors of the development of a metalanguage; other groups may have to acquire, along with literacy, new ways of viewing language and new occasions for interpreting what it is that written language signifies.

WHAT HAPPENS TO MYTHS EXPOSED?

Myths are never simple in their derivation or effects. Most myths are tightly intertwined with rationales for the existence of established institutions or behaviors; hence dismantling myths means altering established habits and organizations. Education is certainly an enterprise surrounded by myths, and most of its long-established practices, such as the veneration of essay writing, are much too organized to be easily dislodged. The thought-starters proposed here may provide an initial chisel with which to begin whittling away at some entrenched blocks of ideas.

To William Carlos Williams, such whittling had to begin with the smallest components of the education establishment. Without an understanding of the complexity of something seemingly so insignificant as the essay, academics had little chance of taking hold of larger components of academic learning. Of the essay, Williams said:

> Whatever passes through it—the essay—it is never that thing. It remains itself and continues so, pure motion. . . . So it is said "to essay" to stand firm, that is, during penetration by a fluid. . . . Its vitality is the same as that of fashions: changelessness. Without one there is not the other. Periods and places by their variety function as do the fashions, to establish man who essays. Geography and history deal wholly with fashion. But the rigidity of the essay is itself

human. . . . This is an essay: the true grace of fashion. The essay must stand while passion and interest pass through. This thing must move to be an engine; this in an essay means the parts are infinitely related to each other—not to 'unity' however. It is the crossing of forces that generates interest. The dead centers are incidental. But the sheer centrifugal detail of the essay, its erudition, the scope of its trial, its vanity or love, its force for clarity through change is not understood except as a force that is in its essence centripetal. The motion is from change to the variety of changelessness. (1970, pp. 322–323)

Williams argues that the genre of essay has no formulaic conventions as we have been prone to describe such; the essay is a form through which great varieties of content pass in the hands of journalists, historians, pop psychologists, physicians—other professional writers. In English classes, we have tried to create a set of conventions for the essay, but in reality, we have created a genre specific only to the classroom—the five-paragraph essay. In attempting to convey to students Williams' truth—that the essay must move to be an engine—its parts must be infinitely related to each other—we have provided a formula which we know is not that which Jonathan Swift or Matthew Arnold, or Edmund Wilson or John Ciardi could use to write essays. But we have replaced the vitality of the essay with an external skeletonized rigid frame.

The essence which Williams is trying to capture here is the self-generation of rules which drives the engine—the essay. It is the case not that essays under the pen of good writers are written according to a formula, but that they are written so that the structure is built within the essay. Put another way, the reader must know how to anticipate what is coming—anticipation must precede comprehension. We have to know what is coming at some level in order to understand what comes. Note that in the organization of this piece, I have kept your memories propped and your anticipation appetite whetted by telling you what was coming and by providing you with numbers as pegs by which to organize memory. Moreover, you know that the organizational theme for this essay (or formal talk—the two are very much the same at the organizational level, though not necessarily at the sentence level) is William Carlos Williams' notes on the essay. Thus each time I as author return to Williams, you as reader regain a sense of familiarity and confidence that your expectations—or your anticipations—have been met.

Williams goes on to say of the essay's structure: "Not only is it necessary to prove the crystal but the crystal must prove permanent by fracture." (1970: p. 323) The essay is like the crystal—its permanence in our memory cannot be fractured. Much of the recent work on remembering stories has shown that well-formed stories—that is those which conform to a story grammar—are better remembered than are those stories which do not conform to expected genre conventions. The same is true of essays in a different way—if the structure is built within the essay, and the reader is helped along so that he/she can anticipate what is coming. It is the clues or pegs for memory which enable the reader (or listener) to remember the essay's content. Thus the essay will not be fractured; it holds together because the essayist tells the reader the structure which will come and builds a temporary frame for the content which passes through the essay.

In essence both stories and essays (or expositions) are part of the same continuum of narrative—the basic way in which we describe past experience. The raw components of the essay are situation with possibilities which are either actualized or not actualized and which either succeed or fail in the sense of coming to closure. In stories, situation includes character (agent) doing something (action) which results through conflict in resolution; these events take place in space and time. In the essay, the situation has possibilities which must be stated; actualizing of these occurs within the text. Success or failure is determined by how well the text itself—form and content—actualizes (or says they cannot be actualized) the possibilities of the situation selected at the outset.

THIS ESSAY AS EXAMPLE

Human understanding is contractual; remember that Williams says that the essay is the most human literary form. Every writer (or formal speaker) makes a contract with readers (and listeners) at the outset of the essay. In this piece, I opened by setting up expectations and providing a framework for what was to come. To the extent that readers have been able to comprehend this essay's contents, they have done so because they have been able to anticipate the organization of this piece—by four myths and their counter thought-starters, and by the thematic structuring through Williams' writing on the essay. Several key topics have reappeared several times throughout the essay: oral and written language, their interrelationships, ethnography as linguistic exploration, rule generation as ownership and key to expertise, and defining oneself as language expert. Each reoccurrence of one of these has been reassuring for readers and has helped carry them along in the current of the essay's course.

The contractual nature of human understanding and the limits of the human memory make it such that written narrative must be so tightly structured through coherence and cohesion that word is tied to word. The essay, unlike the traditional story which is hierarchical, is encircling and enveloping. Stories have a master model of grammar which can be anticipated by a reader who has been socialized appropriately for understanding stories of certain forms. The essay has to build its own grammar or frame within each piece, in a new cooperative contract between reader and writer. Writers (and formal speech makers) must depend on internal form, must provide content and form so they are accessible, so readers can recover, reconstruct, and recompose the mental sequence of the writer responding to the conscious attended experiences which are narrated within the text. Process is recursive for good essays (and successful formal speeches), because writer turns text back again and again on itself, reassuring the reader that recovery is correct.

As essay writer, I have now fulfilled my contract with the reader by playing out the script I led you to anticipate in my opening, and I have exhausted Williams' points about the essay to the extent that I can without reproducing his full written text for your use as a text against which to play this text. My selection of his passages for discussion has been conditioned to some extent by the need for a visual image—the crystal—upon which the memory can hang certain abstract points. The essay and the crystal allow "things to pass through." The absence of conventional form ensures that each essay—like each crystal—"remains itself and continues so, pure motion."

As an ending note, I the author can engage you the reader in some sort of emotional commitment to the content of this essay. By laying out some questions which may have been in your mind as you read the piece, I can enter your frame of reference and sense of some future use you might make of the content of this essay. Why should scholars or educators who write and teach essays take up any of the ideas given here? Why should they entertain the idea that writing—and perhaps most especially writing essays— must be learned by the writer who through redundant, multiple experiences in responsive interactive writing generates rules for communicating through writing? What is it that opportunities for talk and taking language apart do to help ensure the retention of literate habits?

By enabling students to become inquirers or researchers of language which surrounds them, teachers and scholars together can strip away terms, fixed practices, expectations, routinized predictors of their own and their students' behaviors (see Myers, 1985). They can replace these with a spirit of imagination and intuitive knowledge—the stuff of which we as language-makers are made. Drawing out students' intuitive knowledge about language depends heavily on having them recognize the oral and written language they command. They come to this recognition as they collect, record, and analyze these data. All students can become experts, for they own the knowledge from which the group works together to determine what is in the data and what the data say about their system, its features, and their relevance to other kinds of data. For students in mixed-language or mixed-dialect classes, there is the extra bonus that the study of the various systems and repertoires of language uses enhances a sense of language as a vastly varied and versatile instrument.

Teachers engaged in this enterprise cannot be the overt directors; students must cast, script, direct, and evalute. They then become critics or analysts asking and answering what happened and why? The procedures described here do not mean that students will not come to know grammar or grammatical terms. They will instead find that as they cut apart and talk about language, they will need a metalanguage, and they can usually relate most readily—if they so choose—to terms they have already encountered (sentence, coordinate conjunction, temporal, etc.). But they come to internalize terms and rules for grammar as they shape its reality themselves and for their own purposes—to explain their data to their classmates and to their subjects. By so doing, they *own* the reality of language rules and conventions.

Teachers engaged with students in this researching force themselves to see knowledge in new ways. They become members of a classroom learning community—an oral and literate community learning together. They allow themselves to explore learning freely in order to have an empathy that enables them to improve their identification with students as learners. By so identifying, they can hope to better their explanations of habits they have heretofore viewed as "natural." Those habits, attitudes, ways of perceiving and expressing educators often regard as "natural" are learned; they are not instinctual and they do not come along with eye color, fingernails, and the suckling impulse. Habits of observing, valuing, and organizing fundamental to formal schooling come only through long years of reinforcement and repetition in and out of school—years of habitual action which many language minority students have not had. To the extent that teachers can recognize what it is they might explicate—or lead students to explicate—about the covert rules of oral and written language uses, they can allow students to become experts over their own knowledge. The task of understanding language is too great for one person to take charge of as transmitter. Teachers, scholars, and students must transmit and transmute for each other. A learning community is not only more efficient, but it is also much more thorough, effective, and encompassing than a teaching community.

Finally, for those teachers reading this essay, what might guide their decisions about whether or not they should bother to remember the four thought-starters offered here? Each teacher must answer this question on the basis of personal style, philosophy of teaching, degree of tolerance for unpredictability, and ability to obtain self-direction in the classroom. Some may teach in situations in which someone else dictates the curriculum, and some teachers may even be watched by superiors to ensure that a fixed format is followed. The goal here has been to raise the possibility that perhaps one class, two classes, or even one group within one class can work *with* teacher as learning partner. The spirit of exploration is sometimes easier for the young and for those who already feel disenfranchised than it is for those who feel "fixed" in a system. Any decision is, ultimately, however, a decision only when we can explore alternatives and feel the possibilities of those alternatives for ourselves.

In Williams' words, "ability in an essay is multiplicity, infinite fracture, the intercrossing of opposed forces establishing any number of opposed centres of stillness (1970, p. 323)." So is the learning of writing: it must be

filled with multiplicity, infinite opportunities to categorize, label, recate-
gorize, combine, and associate knowledge. It must engage the learner in the
intercrossing of opposed forces, leaving always the opportunity for the centripetal or inward turning forces which motivate learners, and the centrifugal or
sharing forces which lead us to want to spread, expand, and create knowledge—to realize the essential humanness of not only the essay as a literary
form, but the trying, the trial which pushes us toward clarity through change.

REFERENCES

Applebee, A.N. (1981). *Writing in the secondary school* (Research Report No. 21). Urbana,
    IL: National Council of Teachers of English.
Besnier, N. (1986). *Literacy in Fiji*. Ph.D. dissertation, University of Southern California,
    Department of Linguistics.
Duranti, A. & Ochs, E. (1986). Literacy instruction in a Samoan village. In B. Schieffelin & P.
    Gilmore (Eds.), *The acquisition of literacy: Ethnographic perspectives*. Norwood, NH:
    Ablex.
Ellen, R.F. (1984). *Ethnographic research: A guide to general conduct*. New York: Academic
    Press.
Freedman, S.W. (Ed.) (1985). *The acquisition of written language: Response and revision*.
    Norwood, NJ: Ablex.
Goody, J. (1977). *The domestication of the savage mind*. New York: Cambridge University
    Press.
Halliday, M. (1975). *Learning how to mean: Explorations in the development of language*.
    New York: Elsevier North-Holland.
Heath, S.B. (1982). Toward an ethnohistory of writing in American education. In M. Farr
    Whiteman (Ed.). *Writing: The nature, development and teaching of written communi-
    cation. Vol. 1, Variation in writing: Functional and linguistic-cultural differences*. Hills-
    dale, NJ: Erlbaum.
Heath, S.B. (1983). *Ways with words: Language, life, and work in communities and class-
    rooms*. Cambridge: Cambridge University Press.
Heath, S.B. (1985). Literacy or literate skills? Considerations for ESL/EFL learners. In P.
    Larson, E.L. Judd, & D.S. Messerschmitt (Eds.), *On TESOL '84*. Washington, DC:
    TESOL.
Heath, S.B. (forthcoming). Critical factors in literacy development. In K. Egan, S. DeCastell,
    & A. Luke (Eds.), *Literacy, society, and schooling*. Cambridge: Cambridge University
    Press.
Heath, S.B. & Branscombe, A. (1985). Intelligent writing in an audience community. In S.W.
    Freedman (Ed.), *The acquisition of written language: Revision and response*. Norwood,
    NJ: Ablex.
Mailloux, S. (1982). *Interpretive conventions*. Ithaca, NY: Cornell University Press.
Myers, M. (1985). *The teacher-researcher: How to study writing in the classroom*. Urbana, IL:
    National Council of Teachers of English.
Olson, D. (1984). "See! Jumping!" Some oral language antecedents of literacy. In H. Goel-
    man, A. Oberg, & F. Smith (Eds.), *Awakening to literacy*. Exeter, NH: Heinemann.
Ong, W. (1982). *Orality and literacy: The technologizing of the word*. London: Methuen.
Proust, M. (1934). *Remembrance of things past*. New York: Random House.
Rosenblatt, L. (1934). *Literature as exploration*. New York: Modern Language Association.
Saville-Troike, M. (1982). *Ethnography of communication*. Baltimore University Park.

Schieffelin, B. & Ochs, E. (1986). Language socialization. In *Annual Review of Anthropology* (Vol. 15). pp. 163–91.

Thompkins, J. (1985). *Sensatonal designs: The cultural work of American fiction 1790–1860.* New York: Oxford University Press.

Williams, W.C. (1970). *Imaginations.* New York: New Directions. [Selections from "Spring and All," first published 1923 and "An Essay on Virginia," first published 1921].

PART III
THE INFLUENCES OF SOCIETY
ON LANGUAGE SHIFTS

Chapter Six
Literacy and Language Change;
The Special Case of Speech Act Verbs

ELIZABETH CLOSS TRAUGOTT
Stanford University

The purpose of this chapter[1] is to explore the following question. Suppose that we have discovered that a certain class of words arose at a certain time in the history of a language; what evidence would we want from historical linguistics to help determine whether literacy had anything to do with the development of this set, and if so, what? Although the main thrust of the argument is methodological, it also touches on a number of theoretical issues, especially "explanation," and on the role of language in society.

ORAL AND LITERATE DISTINCTIONS
IN TYPES OF KNOWING

The class of words I have chosen to consider is the class of assertive speech act verbs like *recognize that, observe that, insist that, suggest that,* and so forth, all of which express the speaker's attitude toward the truth of the proposition. I have chosen these verbs because they have been the subject of much discussion recently, especially by David Olson and his students, in studies of acquisition of literacy. In a book currently in progress called *The World on Paper,* Olson is developing the argument that there is a distinct correlation between the development of "modern consciousness", and the development of speech act verbs like *observe, state,* and *claim,* and the spread of literacy. "Modern consciousness" is identified with the Enlightenment's search for autonomy through cognition, with Cartesian concepts of

[1] During 1983–1984 I spent much time in friendly debate with David Olson on literacy and especially mental verbs and speech act verbs. I am grateful to him for inspirational discussions, for allowing me to play devil's advocate on questions of literacy, and most especially for inviting me to share with members of the McLuhan Center an earlier version (Traugott, 1985) of the present paper, which arose out of those discussions.

Thanks are also due to Judith Hochberg for extensive help in collecting the data, to Suzanne Kemmer for comments on an earlier draft of this paper, to Penelope Eckert and James Fox for discussion of some of the issues, and to Edith Bavin for the reference to Warlpiri. I gratefully acknowledge support from the Center for Advanced Study in the Behavioral Sciences, from NSF grant BNS 76-22943, and from the Guggenheim Foundation.

knowing, with the increased attention during this period to distinctions between meaning and saying, and with a rapid growth in vocabularies for
propositional attitudes. All of these, Olson argues, were made possible by
increased literacy.

In a paper by Olson and Astington, called *Children's Acquisition of Metalinguistic and Metacognitive Verbs,* it is pointed out that:

> the differentiation of what is said and what is meant is of particular impor-
> tance to writing and the interpretation of text, the traditional problem of her-
> meneutics. (Olson & Astington, 1986, p. 194)

The authors go on to say that there is supporting evidence for a correlation
between the elaboration of speech act and mental state concepts and the
development of literacy:

> Hundert *(in preparation)* points out that in the 17th century there developed
> "increasing lexical distinctions in many European languages between the verbs
> employed for knowing, for acquaintance, and for the possession of moral vir-
> tue or prudence" and that this development "struck Vico as a significant
> transformation in human consciousness". (p. 194)

Further, the authors provide a table of mental state verbs and assertive
speech act verbs to demonstrate that although there were four basic mental
state verbs in Old English, the ancestors of *know, mean, think,* and *understand,* there were only two speech act verbs, *say,* and *tell;* they also show
that additional mental state verbs like *believe, discover, doubt,* date from
Middle English, while most corresponding assertive speech act verbs date
from the sixteenth and seventeenth centuries, e.g. *assert, admit (that), con-
cede,* etc. (p. 195, Table 3). They conclude with the observation that the sixteenth and seventeenth centuries were a period in which the Royal Society
and other bodies sought to "improve English as a medium of prose":

> Presumably, when written English had to serve the needs of science and gov-
> ernment, it became important to make the differences marked by those terms.
> (p. 194)

There is no question that vocabularies are developed to fulfill the needs
of certain situations. We see ourselves doing that every day as academics,
constraining meanings of words already in use for our own purposes, or in-
venting new words. At certain periods certain types of neologisms and mean-
ing-extensions are favored, given general cultural interest—our fad right
now is the extension of computer language, as mimicked in these words from
a comic about a familiar scene at a cocktail party: "I know we've interfaced
before, but I can't access your name." It is part of linguistic competence to
use vocabulary from one domain in a different one, and the proliferation of
speech act verbs at certain periods of English presumably reflects this. The
question I want to raise is what significance these kinds of facts can be given

when we take a broader view of the history of literacy and of thought and culture in general. The answers to this question are enormously complex, and will not be solved for some time. But I would like to suggest some issues to be considered as one goes about trying to answer it.

Before getting into the data, I should state a few assumptions. In my view, literacy is not the same as the ability to write or the presence of a writing system. Writing is an enabling factor, perhaps a prerequisite (see, however, Pattison, 1982) but not the same thing. Writing is a technology. Literacy involves a special use of writing: it is a register associated with linear, noninteractive strategies, and may be expressed orally as well as in writing (cf. Chafe, 1980; Tannen, 1982); it is typified by "objectification" of the subject matter, by talk about texts, and by self-conscious attention to distinctions between what a text assets and its interpretation, in other words, by certain kinds of attitudes toward language (cf. Stock, 1983).

Secondly, I am certain that literacy, and even writing, have some effect, even a considerable one, on a language. A position such as that expressed by Bloomfield in *Linguistic Aspects of Science* (1939, p. 7) that "Languages are quite the same whether their speakers practice writing or not" seems totally mistaken. Nevertheless, the fact that writing and especially literacy can have a significant effect on language structure does not, in my view, necessarily mean that they enable a *radically* different kind of consciousness from nonliteracy, specifically a consciousness that enables one to talk in metalinguistic terms about the difference, for example, between *mean* and *say* [as proposed by Olson (personal communication)].

ABSTRACT REASONING IN TRADITIONAL LANGUAGES

I am skeptical about the theory of a radical difference, or "cognitive divide", between the literate and nonliterate consciousness for a number of reasons, most of which have to do with a tendency to project our own notions of literacy and of language structure onto other times, other languages, and other cultures. For example, in the absence of detailed studies of literacy in different cultures, there is a danger of projecting our contemporary psychological views of literacy and therefore of concluding that it is everywhere a psychological/cognitive phenomenon, whereas in many cases it appears to be primarily a cultural one (cf. Frake, 1983; Heath, *in press*). Another problem is the claim that I have heard repeatedly that nonliterate languages do not have ways of expressing certain abstract logical ideas. But if one is looking for semantic equivalents, and not equivalent parts of speech, one often finds that native American, Australian aboriginal, and other "traditional" languages have various ways of expressing causal and conditional, including counterfactual, relations (hence fairly abstract reasoning), and of making distinctions between what is known by hearsay, by experience, and by inference. A few examples must suffice here, from Warlpiri, an aboriginal Australian language (Laughren, 1982):

(1) nganta "they say, reportedly (and I doubt it)"
     murra "they say, reportedly (and I think it's likely)"
     kari "I know from personal experience"
     karinganta "I know the proposition to be true and am its author"
     kulanganta "I know the proposition is false but I/someone formerly believed it
         to be true"
     ngarra "I assert in denial of what you just said"
     marda "possibly"

Such propositional particles serve epistemic and evidential functions that have only recently been recognized as very important factors in the structure of languages. They certainly seem to suggest that a considerable amount of abstractness and indeed objectification of language is possible in nonliterate languages.

Furthermore, similar distinctions are made in "traditional languages" to those that appear in French, German, Old English (but not Modern English) between knowing in the sense of being acquainted with and knowing that. One may compare:

(2) Fr.   *connaitre* vs. *savoir,*
     Gm.   *kennen* vs. *wissen,*
     OE   *cunnan* vs. *witan, gecnawan,*
     Warlpiri *milya pinyi* "know, recognize" vs. *pina mani* "know, have knowledge of" (data courtesy of Edith Bavin).

Such distinctions between types of knowing would appear to require quite sophisticated epistemologies.

It may seem surprising that a historical linguist should be so concerned to find evidence from modern nonliterate languages—historical linguistics is after all typically based on written texts, and data from nonliterate languages may seem to be excluded. It is true that almost all data for historical linguistics were in the nineteenth century written, but in this century this has been far from true (cf. especially the call to use the present to explain the past in Weinreich, Labov, and Herzog, 1968; and Labov, 1974). People reconstruct Proto-American languages, many of which had no writing until recently. There are, of course, limits to reconstruction. All the evidence suggests that the root *men* of "mind" existed in Proto-Indo-European, some five thousand years B.C., presumably therefore in preliterate times; but this does not tell us what exactly was meant by "mind". Yet, since there is a fundamental principle—reconstruct only what is known to be possible in a living language —it is legitimate to speculate that the meaning of "mind" was not totally different from that available in a modern nonliterate community. Whether the preliterate mind is different or not from the literate is therefore of crucial interest for reconstruction—various paths of endeavor obviously cross-fertilize each other fruitfully.

Once we allow ourselves to check our claims about reconstruction against modern nonliterate languages, some interesting things emerge. For example, Ong (1982, p. 80) has suggested that the fact that the word *idea* is based on Greek "see" and English *wit* on Lat. *videre* reflects a shift from the oral world, in which "hearing" is understanding, to a literate one where "seeing" is understanding—in other words he implies that the sight/understanding metaphor requires a literate society in which words and especially propositions can be literally seen. But *see* and *know* are covered by the same word not only in Greek and English but also in some Polynesian languages, in Australian languages, and in Kobon, a language of Papua New Guinea (Viberg, 1983). These languages have not been written down until recently, and in some cases only by linguists. So the presence of literacy may encourage the use of visual metaphors for understanding but it does not appear to cause it —which is hardly surprising since vision is such an important factor in most everyday decision-making processes. Clearly, we have to be sensitive to the various possibilities allowed by the world's languages before we can draw conclusions about literacy as a necessary motivating factor in language change.

THE HISTORY OF ENGLISH SPEECH ACT VERBS

So much for general assumptions and cautions. I turn now to the specific question of how to interpret the history of English speech act verbs. Since we have written records in English from the seventh century on, virtually nothing in the history of English can be said to be preliterate. Toon (1983) has shown how literacy in English did not just develop slowly in happenstance fashion. Rather, it was a central element in the establishment of political hegemony over neighboring kingdoms in three successive periods. The story of the last of these periods, the West Saxon, is fairly well known. In the late 9th century King Alfred established his own hegemony, and instituted an educational program that called for all sons of freemen to learn to read English, and for the elite to learn Latin as well. In addition, he called for the translation of major classical works into English, among them the *Consolation of Philosophy* by Boethius, the most widely read philosophical treatise on free will and predestination in the Middle Ages. A hundred years later with the flourishing of the Benedictine reform, we find Winchester in the South of England as the center of literacy, and among its greatest scions, Aelfric, the homilist and grammarian, who wrote the first grammar of Latin in a European vernacular (Zupitza, 1966).

Despite so much writing, grammar-writing, translation, as well as original composition in the vernacular, the Old English period is typically thought of as one in which prose style was not yet well developed—there are some features often associated with orality, such as inadequate distinctions among referents, corelative constructions such as ponne...ponne "when...then", forpon...forpon "because...therefore", and so forth. On the other hand, it has other features that contradict this. One example is the presence in Old English of the conditional connective *gif*. Old English, along with its descendents, Middle and Modern English, is one of the relatively few languages which has a conditional marker signalling just this very complex and abstract meaning, rather than a marker that is essentially ambiguous with a temporal (cf. German *wenn*) or some other connective. Whatever we may finally want to say about Old English, it appears to have been adequate to expressing at least the kinds of propositions that were written by a Roman philosopher.

Between Old English and Early Modern English is the Middle English period. The early part of this period is associated by Brian Stock with a new interest in literacy, specifically a new experience concerning the relationship between interpreter and text, ultimately leading to a "change in mentality" (1983, p. 34). It was first a period of French dominance and the development of many new genres including romances, later the period of Chaucer. From earliest Old English times till the sixteenth century the chief language of the church and law was Latin, with French a strong second during the Middle English period. In 1362, the Statute of Pleading was passed, in which it was stated that all pleas "shall be pleaded, shewed, defended, answered, debated, and judged in the English tongue, and...be entered and enrolled in Latin" (Mellinkoff, 1963, pp. 111–112). Nevertheless, the language of the law remained French throughout the fifteenth century, and continued to be used up to the seventeenth century. Indeed, the Statute of Pleading was actually written in French; the quotation above comes from an eighteenth century translation. Furthermore, the first book on English law not written in Latin was written in French (and printed in 1481) (cf. Pollock & Maitland, 1905; Mellinkoff, 1963).

Against this background, let us start with Olson and Astington's observation—that a large number of speech act verbs came into being in the Early Modern English period, that is, after 1500 (or some 20 years earlier if one wishes to date the period from the time that Caxton opened his printing press). I will discuss only the performative speech act verbs (that is, those that like *say* and *insist,* but unlike *tell* and *explain,* can under the right circumstances have *illocutionary* force), because most of Olson and Astington's examples are of performative verbs. However, it appears that the kinds of issues I will discuss with respect to performative verbs can be generalized to nonperformative speech act verbs.

Fraser (1975) has provided us with a convenient list of some 275 modern English performative verbs. A quick glance shows that about 75% of these derive from French or Latin. One has to go to the Oxford English dictionary and Middle English Dictionary, however, to find out how old they are.

We will shortly look at a selection of the assertive/representative speech act verbs listed by Fraser along with some information about the period at which the speech act meaning was current.

But first: How do we know when we have found a speech act verb meaning—virtually all words with speech act meanings come in with non-speech act meanings first. For example, *insist* comes in in its old spatial use "stand on", and then is used for talking in a long drawn out way; it is only when it comes to mean *insist that somebody do something* that we have what can count as a speech act meaning: a name for an act that can be achieved in saying *I insist that. . .* Similarly, to *state* originally (c. 1590) means to place or station, to be given a certain rank (or "status"), hence to state a case (lay it before a judge), and finally (c. 1800) to declare that something is the case.

All speech act theorists point out that a speech act verb does not have *illocutionary* force except in the first person singular present. However, I presume that for purposes of talking about lexicalization of propositional attitudes and so forth, we do not need to insist on first person present tense examples, that is, instances of performativity, but rather on examples that simply report on events that must have been verbal actions (e.g., *he insisted that. . . , it was stated that. . .*).

There is a trickier problem—as is well known, most verbs of assertion have *that*-complements and also plain (NP) complements, e.g. *report that* the commission failed to solve the problem, beside *report* the commission's failure to solve the problem, *observe that* the sun was in its eclipse, beside *observe* the sun's eclipse. Sometimes the *that*-clause and the NP are fairly similar in meaning, as in the *report* case, sometimes they are somewhat different, as in the *observe* case. Historically, for reasons that probably have more to do with the development of English syntax than anything else, the *that*-complements tend to develop later than the NP complements. What must we say about this? I propose that when the NP is a deverbal noun then what we have is a potential speech act verb (pSAV). The cases are clearest when the deverbal NP occurs along with its subject (*report the commission's failure*) or object (*submit an account of the war*). We need therefore to contrast:

(3) submit a book (the NP is not deverbal): submit ≠ SAV
     submit an account of something (the NP is deverbal) = pSAV
     submit that the account is false = SAV

These three distinctions are labelled as follows in the tables I will be discussing:

(4) W: verb form (i.e. word) exists, but not in speech act meaning
     pSAV: verb form exists, with potential SAV functions (the NP is deverbal)
     SAV: verb form exists, with a verbal complement (*that*-clause; *to* infinitive, as in *promise to go;* or *-ing* construction, as in *I deny saying that*)

We turn now to a sample of the 63 speech act verbs with assertive meaning listed by Fraser. Table 1 gives periods of origin for assertive SAVs from the beginning and end of his list.[2] It is striking that of the verbs listed in Table 1, 4 appear in Old English (OE), 10 in Middle English (ME) (with 5 potential speech act verbs), 15 in Early Modern English (ENE) (with 1 potential speech act verbs), and 5 in Modern English (NE). In other words, many of the speech act verbs originated in the Middle English period. So if the proliferation of assertive speech act verbs has something to do with modern consciousness, that consciousness seems to predate Descartes by a long time. Particularly interesting is the relative paucity of new assertive speech act verbs after 1700.[3] Since literacy has by and large increased since 1700, literacy can certainly not be regarded as a necessary cause for the development of this type of verb.[4]

What of the speech act verbs that developed in the Early Modern English period? Before assigning them any particular significance beyond expansion of labelling, one would like to see whether only assertives were expanded and thus specially privileged in this period, as Olson (in preparation) suggests. In Table 2 I give some examples of other speech act verbs, including (a) expressives, (b) directives, and (c) commissives. It turns out that the story is very similar to the one for assertives. Note this time there are 4 speech act verbs in Old English, 12 in Middle English (with 3 potential speech act verbs), 16 in Early Modern English (with 1 potential speech act verb), and 4 in Modern English—much the same profile as for the assertives. Again, Middle English appears to have been an only slightly less active period than Early Modern English, which seems to have been the most active period for the development of the speech act verbs. In any event, Early Modern English is not strikingly different from Middle English with respect to the proportion of assertive and nonassertive speech act verbs, so assertive verbs do not appear to be in any way privileged by the sixteenth and seventeenth centuries.

What can we make of the massive rise of speech act verbs in the Middle English period? I believe it has much to do with the law courts, with the need to explain feudal practices and specify powers and duties in contexts of territorial litigation (the Hundred Years' War attempting to regain parts of France) and civil war (the Wars of the Roses). This was a period of new

---

[2] A few verbs listed by Fraser have been omitted here and in later discussion of other types of speech act verbs. Omitted verbs are either very rarely used in the category to which Fraser assigns them, e.g. *accuse,* or do not usually have sentential complements, e.g. *apprise.*

[3] *Agree* occurs as an SAV in Middle English, but as a permissive, not an assertive.

[4] Derrick de Kerckhove suggests (personal communication) that the relative paucity of new SAVs in the Modern English period (after 1700) might be the result of printing and the establishment of rhetorical norms. Another possibility is that, since Fraser's list does not include phrasal expressions like *I put it before you that,* most recent innovations have simply not been listed.

Table 1.   Assertive speech act verbs

	OE (600–1130)	ME (1130–1480)	ENE (1480–1700)	NE (1700–pres)
acknowledge			SAV	
add	SAV			
admit		pSAV	SAV	
advocate			SAV	
affirm		SAV		
agree (that)			SAV	
allege		SAV		
announce			SAV	
apprise			SAV	
argue		pSAV	SAV	
assent		SAV		
assert			SAV	
attest			SAV	
aver		SAV		
claim		SAV		
comment		pSAV	SAV	
concede			SAV	
conclude		SAV		
refuse		SAV		
remark				SAV
remind			SAV	
repeat		pSAV	SAV	
reply		SAV		
report		SAV		
respond			W	SAV
retort				SAV
say	SAV			
state			W	SAV
submit		W	pSAV	SAV
suggest			SAV	
swear	SAV			
tell	SAV			
verify		pSAV	SAV	
warn	W	SAV		

developments in commerce, with attendant needs for clarifying claims, asserting rights, reporting, assuring, and promising; it was also the time of the rise of universities, and of considerable interest in rhetoric and of new ideas about chronicling and historiography. (For some examples of early official English, including King Henry V's letters and petitions to King, Parliament, and Chancery in the 15th century, see Fisher, Richardson, and Fisher, 1984.)

Schlieben-Lange's (1983) account of the development of historiography in the Middle French period is very relevant to the present argument. She is concerned with speech act verbs of chronicling (*narrate, say, tell*), and

Table 2.   Non-assertive speech act verbs.

	OE	ME	ENE	NE
(a) *Expressives*				
admonish		SAV		
apologize			SAV	
applaud			SAV	
approve		W	SAV	
blame		W	SAV	
object		W	SAV	
question			SAV	
recognize		W	SAV	
regret		SAV		
sympathize		pSAV	SAV	
thank	SAV			
toast				SAV
wish	W	SAV		
(b) *Directives*				
appeal		SAV		
ask	SAV			
beg	W	pSAV	SAV	
bid	SAV			
call upon		W	SAV	
command		SAV		
pray		SAV		
prohibit		pSAV	SAV	
request			SAV	
require		SAV		
solicit			SAV	
(c) *Commissives*				
assure		SAV		
bind oneself	W		SAV	
commit oneself		W	SAV	
dedicate oneself			SAV	
guarantee				SAV
offer		SAV		
pledge		pSAV	SAV	
promise		SAV		
undertake		SAV		
swear	SAV			
volunteer				SAV
vow		SAV		

evaluating (*blame, praise, question*), and with related non-speech act verbs like *extract, put in order, compile*. She argues that these new vocabularies for historiography arise out of new concepts of what writing is for. Similarly, I would argue that the new Middle English vocabularies arose in response both to the need to say things in English that had not been said before because there was no context for saying them, and in response to new academies and new bureaucracies. In other words, they were encouraged by literacy. But still, what evidence is there that they were caused by it? If we go back to our data in (3) and (4), we see that there are only a very small number of native words. What does this mean? Were there very few speech act verbs in Old English? Or were there Old English words for similar concepts that got ousted? If we expect the Old English period to be only on the way to literacy, and if we expect terms like those we have discussed to be the result of new institutions and ways of thinking made possible by literacy, because they are more explicit in distinguishing propositional and other attitudes, then we might expect there to be a rather small set of speech act verbs in the Old English period. Furthermore, if we correlate verbs of assertion with modern consciousness, or with literacy in general, we might expect to find particularly few assertives in Old English [a position implied by the Olson and Astington paper (in preparaton)].

The data are hard to get a hold of, since there are no adequate dictionaries as yet—Bosworth-Toller did not think to distinguish between verbs with NP and *that*-complements (we anxiously await the computerized Old English dictionary from Toronto). Still, I found it possible to identify about 60 speech act verbs, including the following examples of assertives:[5]

(5)	andettan	"admit, confess that"
	cwedan	"say"
	fulfealdan	"explain"
	(ge) cypan	"proclaim, announce that, testify that"
	geswutelian	"declare, make manifest"
	mapelian	"say in public, testify that"
	oncnawan	"admit, confess that"
	onsacan	"deny that"
	sedan	"attest, affirm as true" (cf. sooth)
	secgan	"say"
	sprecan	"say"
	tellan	"narrate"
	spellian	"announce"
	wanian	"lament, deplore that"
	wissian	"declare, make known"

Many, but by no means all, occur in translations from Latin—as I have said, the Alfredian translation of Boethius does not seem to suffer at all from lack of ways to translate very elaborate abstract ideas about mental states and propositional attitudes; since it is a dialogue between Boethius and Philosophy, it contains speech act verbs (even in the first person present), as well as a large number of mental verbs.

---

[5] Ashley Amos points out (personal communication) that sixty SAVs in Old English may not appear to be a great number when compared with the numbers of modern SAVs; however, in terms of percentage of the total Old English vocabulary it is actually quite high.

These data do not show that the existence of considerable lexicons of speech act verbs is unrelated to literacy—on the contrary, my argument would be that Old English prose is much more literate than many seem to envisage. But what these data do show is that the existence of a relatively large lexicon for assertive speech act verbs cannot be directly correlated with either the modern consciousness developed in the sixteenth and seventeenth centuries (despite the claims of the eighteenth century Italian philosopher, Vico, and later others including Hundert, and Olson and Astington), or with the rise of the new mentality in the medieval period that Stock identifies.[6]

We must, of course, ask why the Old English terms were replaced. I submit that that is because the language of education and of the courts, and the contexts where literacy was practiced, was primarily Latin (and French). English vocabulary, even if it meant the same thing semantically, did not carry the same social meaning—don't we ourselves prefer latinate metalanguage to simple English when we lecture? Furthermore, in many cases English vocabulary did not actually fit very well in the Middle English period, because the social institutions had changed. This point has indeed already been made in Green (1982) in connection with the history of some commissives in English. In discussing the replacement of Old English and Middle English verbs of promising like *behatan* by *promise* in the 15th century, he notes that notions of royal prerogative had changed, new types of promise were required by the development of commerce, and even notions of time were changing. All of these could have led to the rejection of the older term for the new.

Now, strange though this may seem, promising seems to be a very interesting topic to look at where matters of literacy are concerned, possibly more interesting than verbs of cognition. In her paper on Ilongot speech act verbs, Rosaldo (1982) points out that there are rough equivalents to assertives and directives in Ilongot, although in Ilongot asserting truth is less important in explaining something than establishing relationships with others. (Of course, this is also truer of English than Searle's (1979) approach to assertive speech act verbs might suggest. If I explain and state something in a classroom situation, I do so not just because I think what I am saying is true—in fact I might know it wasn't really true at some level of detail—but because I also wish to establish, reconfirm, indeed reconstitute the student–teacher relationship: in other words, assertives are at some level also directive [cf. Bach & Harnish 1979].) The striking thing is that there are apparently no Ilongot equivalents to commissives like *promise,* nor are there expressives like *I'm sorry.* There are oaths, but these have to do more with

---

[6] This point is given further support by evidence from the Old High German *Evangelienbuch* by Otfrid (completed 862 a.d. in Alsace). In his study of native and non-native (Latin and loan-translation) vocabulary in Otfrid, Siebert (1971) lists over fifty speech act verbs, several of them assertives, e.g. *gi-unnan* 'admit that', *rediôn* 'explain', *werdôn* 'vouchsafe'.

supernatural laws than with personal commitments. Again, investigation of a Warlpiri dictionary revealed a lot about propositional particles, but nothing about promising. Benveniste's (1973) book about Indo-European institutions suggests the same thing for early Indo-European society: the chapter on vowing and swearing is not about swearing that the speaker commits himself to something, so much as a chapter on interactive negotiations between man and gods. The gods were supposed to respond favorably, therefore to vow was to consecrate oneself in anticipation of support from the gods.

Old English seems to be well equipped with words for promising that are not too far afield from ours. But Schlieben-Lange's study brings up an interesting point. She rightly says that it is not enough in working out the discourse practices of a time, whether oral or literate, simply to look for forms. Instead, one should consider the whole spectrum of speech act verbs—which types of speech act verbs are well represented at any one period (and then, if possible, one should try to find out why). Her table of Old French speech act verb types (Schlieben-Lange 1983, p. 143) appears as Table 3, translated (+ = many different verbs, − = few different verbs). What is striking, of course, is that Schlieben-Lange finds few directives (like ordering) and few commissives (like promising). The speech act verbs connected with truth are, however, fairly well represented.

It is at least possible, then, that there may be more of the modern consciousness in speakers committing themselves to do something without immediate interactive benefit and in face of an indeterminate future than there is in asserting that something is the case, or in being concerned about the truth of the proposition.

To sum up my argument so far: I have said that vocabularies that make fine distinctions among various kinds of propositional attitudes, judgements, and commitments may well be enabled by literacy, but they are not caused by it (otherwise, how would an aboriginal language like Warlpiri have so

Table 3. Speech act verbs in Old French.

Representatives Type: assert	+	Type: agree deny explain
Directives Type: order	−	
Commissives Type: promise	−	
Expressives Type: congratulate	+	Type: publicly praise. blame
Declarations Type: nominate	+	Type: challenge, various legal activities

many epistemics, and why would speech act verbs be so important in ritual?). Presumably, these distinctions are in part made possible by the extended memory that literacy allows, and to some extent even required by the disassociation from immediate context that literacy fosters. But it is far from clear that they actually represent new mentalities. Indeed, it is questionable whether speech act verbs are an especially appropriate set to relate directly to literacy since speech act verbs, even when they do not have or cannot have performative function, nevertheless by definition involve speaker–hearer (or writer–reader) contract, and have very specific interpersonal functions as part of their meaning. In this respect they do not fit the supposed objectifying function of language.

As I pointed out earlier, virtually all speech act verb meanings derive from other meanings. How do such changes come about, and what does that suggest about the relation to literacy? This is not the place for an investigation of the etymologies of speech act verbs. But a few brief comments are in order. Let us take the case of speech act verbs like *find, guess, agree, assume, blame,* and *observe,* all of which derive from mental verbs. (These mental verbs themselves often derive from other, more concrete, meanings, as does *find.*) There are clearly at least two paths of change which apply not only when mental verbs give rise to speech act verbs but also to other sources of speech act verbs. One path of change has to do with first person contexts. If I say *I find this subject boring* I am expressing my own opinion, and the social, contractual consequences are presumably negligible beyond those that accompany any statement. But if I say *I find this man guilty,* the proposition is one of the kind that is likely to be interpreted as more than a statement; if I have the right authority, the consequences of my saying this may indeed be severe—it is surely not by chance that many of the speech act terms mentioned in this papar are first cited with speech act meanings in legal and other bureaucratic contexts. It is the kind of change that is perfectly natural, once the appropriate situations arise.

A far stronger condition for the shift from mental or other non-speech act sources is the passive construction. If I hear the statement *He was found guilty* I am going to infer that whoever found him guilty must have said (or written) something, in other words the mental state was manifested in some verbal way. *State* is only one among many that first appear in potential speech act verb or speech act verb form in the passive, according to the OED, cf.:

(6a)   Clarendon 1647. Whereupon it was thought fit that the whole affair...should be stated and enlarged upon in a conference between the two Houses (W with clear implicature that the activity is verbal) (OED *state* 8.a.)

(6b)   Farmer's Mag. 1802. It has already been stated that 3,000,000 of acres are required to be in wheat (OED *state* 8.b.)

The changes in first person and in passive contexts both result from what Geis and Zwicky (1971) call the principle of invited reference. For a while in the history of a word, language users may draw certain conclusions about what is meant. These conclusions go well beyond the literal sense of the sentence to what is variously called utterance meaning or pragmatic meaning. At a later stage this meaning may be directly linked with the word as part of its inherent semantics and no longer be merely an inference. This is what seems to have happened in many cases in the development of speech act verbs. So, when *insist* meant to persevere, and especially to persevere in talking, the inference was surely invited that a person would not persevere unless they believed in the truth of what they were saying: when belief in the truth of what was said came to be automatically linked with the verb, it became a speech act verb.

Since the changes discussed here seem so natural, it would seem they are in fact only very generally related to literacy—they are undoubtedly more likely to occur in a society that is conscious of language, is oriented to making fine distinctions, and where the truth of the proposition is important. They reflect a literacy that is supported and maintained everywhere by *speaking*—in the law courts, in lectures, in debate, and now in the media. It would after all not be much use just to think *Cogito ergo sum*—it might even not be too much use to read it; it is the dialogue, the interaction of readers with the text and with each other that makes Descartes so influential. This suggests the much larger issues that it is important to investigate the extent to which literacy must be upheld by speech events.[7]

SUMMARY

The history of assertive speech act verbs in English suggests that the ones we currently use were developed in both the Middle English and the Early Modern English periods, presumably in response to various institutions, such as schools of rhetoric, feudal politics, the law courts, legal pleading, and expanding commerce. The histories of individual words such as *state* or *observe* may reveal specific attitudinal developments in very specific areas of knowledge, but the history of the class does not provide evidence that there was any massive, privileged change in the lexicon of assertive speech act verbs that can be correlated with radical changes in consciousness. It appears that the class of assertive speech act verbs may in fact not be particularly associated with literacy as such, but rather with specific practices, some oral, some literate, in different societies. If anything, it is awareness of the necessity for reconstituting the speaker–hearer relationships of interactive language such as tend to get lost in the objectivizing force of literacy,

---

[7] This is a topic on which Shirley Brice Heath is currently working.

that is reflected in the growth of speech act verbs in English—and presumably in other languages as well. Finally, I have tried to show that conclusions about significant links between culture and language cannot be made without careful assessment of evidence from whole, not partial, domains of vocabulary.

REFERENCES

Bach, K. & Harnish, R.M. (1979). *Linguistic communication and speech acts.* Cambridge, MA: MIT Press.

Benveniste, E. (1971). Subjectivity in language. *Problems in general linguistics* (M.E. Meek, trans.). Coral Gables, FL: University of Miami Press.

Benveniste, E. (1973). *Indo-European language and society* (E. Palmer, trans.). Coral Gables, FL: University of Miami Press.

Bloomfield, L. (1939). Linguistic aspects of science. *International encyclopedia of unified science.* Chicago, IL: University of Chicago Press.

Chafe, W. (Ed.). (1980). *The pear stories: Cognitive, cultural, and linguistic aspects of narrative production.* Norwood, NJ: Ablex.

Fisher, J.H., Richardson, M., & Fisher, J.C. (1984). *An anthology of Chancery English.* Knoxville: University of Tennessee Press.

Frake, C. (1983). Did literacy cause the great cognitive divide? (Review article on Sylvia Scribner and Michael Cole, The psychology of literacy). *American Ethnologist, 10,* 368–71.

Fraser, B. (1975). Hedged performatives. In P. Cole & J.L. Morgan (Eds.), *Syntax and semantics III: Speech acts.* New York: Academic Press.

Geis, M.L. & Zwicky, A. (1971). On invited inferences. Linguistic Inquiry 2, 561–66.

Green, E. (1982). *Felicity conditions and the history of some commissives in Middle English.* Paper presented at the annual meeting of the Modern Language Association.

Heath, B. (In press). Critical factors in literacy development. In S. de Castell, K. Egan, & A. Luke (Eds.), *Literacy, society and schooling.* Cambridge, MA: Cambridge University Press.

Hundert, E.J. (in preparation). Enlightenment and the decay of common sense. In F. van Holthoon & D. Olson (Eds.), *Common sense.*

Labov, W. (1974). On the use of the present to explain the past. In L. Heilmann (Ed.), *Proceedings of the Eleventh International Congress of Linguists.* Bologna: il Mulino.

Laughren, M. (1982). A preliminary description of propositional particles in Walpiri. In S. Swartz (Ed.), *Papers in Walpari grammar: In memory of Lothar Jagst.* Work Papers of Summer Institute of Linguistics, Australian Aborigenes Branch, Series A. Vol. 6. Darwin: SIL-AAB.

Lyons, J. (1982). Deixis and subjectivity: *Loquor, ergo sum?* In Robert J. Jarvella & Wolfgang Klein (Eds.), *Speech, place, and action: Studies in deixis and related topics.* New York: Wiley.

Mellinkoff, D. (1963). *The language of the law.* Boston: Little, Brown.

Olson, D. (In preparation). *The world on paper.*

Olson, D. & Astington, J. (1986). Children's acquisition of metalinguistic and metacognitive verbs. In W. Demopoulos & A. Marras (Eds.), *Language learning and concept acquisition.* Norwood, NJ: Ablex.

Ong, W. (1982). *Orality and literacy: the technologizing of the word.* New York: Methuen.

Pattison, R. (1982). *On literacy: The politics of the word from Homer to rock.* New York: Oxford University Press.

Pollock, F. & Maitland, F.W. (1905). *The history of English law before the time of Edward I* (2nd ed.). Cambridge, MA: Cambridge University Press.

Rosaldo, M.Z. (1982). The things we do with words: Ilongot speech acts and speech act theory in philosophy. *Languages in Society, 11,* 203-37.

Schlieben-Lange, B. (1983). *Traditionen des Sprechens: Elemente einer pragmatischen Sprachgeschichtsschreibung.* Stuttgart: Kohlhammer.

Searle, J.R. (1979). *Expression and meaning.* Cambridge, MA: Cambridge University Press.

Siebert, E. (1971). *Zum Verhaltnis von Erbgut und Lehngut im Wortschatz Otfrids von Weissenberg.* Munich: Wilhem Fink Verlag.

Stock, B. (1983). *The implications of literacy: Written language and models of interpretation in the eleventh and twelfth centuries.* Princeton, NJ: Princeton University Press.

Tannen, D. (1982). Oral and literate strategies in spoken and written narratives. *Language, 58,* 1-21.

Toon, T.E. (1983). *The politics of Early Old English sound change.* New York: Academic Press.

Traugott, E.C. (1982). From propositional to textual and expressive meanings: Some semantic-pragmatic aspects of grammaticalization. In W.P. Lehmann & O. Malkiel (Eds.), *Perspectives on historical linguistics.* Amsterdam: John Benjamins.

Traugott, E.C. (1985). *Literacy and language change: The special case of speech act verbs.* The McLuhan Program in Culture and Technology, University of Toronto. Working Paper 11.

Traugott, E.C., & Dasher, R. (1985, September). *On the historical relation between mental and speech act verbs in English.* Paper presented at ICHL VII, Pavia.

Vendler, Z. (1972). *Res cogitans: An essay in rational psychology.* Ithaca, NY: Cornell University Press.

Viberg, A. (1983). The verbs of perception: A typological study. In B. Butterworth, B. Comrie, & O. Dahl (Eds.), *Explanation for language universals, Linguistics, 21,* 125-62.

Weinreich, U., Labov, W., & Herzog, M. (1968). Empirical foundations for a theory of language change. In W.P. Lehmann & Y. Malkiel (Eds.), *Directions for historical linguistics.* Austin: University of Texas Press.

Zupitza, J. (Ed.) (1966). *Aelfrics Grammatik und Glossar.* Berlin: Max Niehans Verlag.

Chapter Seven
The Community As Educator*

WILLIAM LABOV
University of Pennsylvania

Much of the research that I have done on language change and variation has been motivated by the thought that the results may help to understand the failure of the school system to teach reading and writing to inner city youth. Almost all of this work has been done outside the schools, in the wider community where people use language without paying too much attention to it. Much language learning, as we know, takes place in this wider community, and not within the schools. One way of understanding the learning that takes place, or doesn't take place, in schools, is to find out as much as we can about the nondirected learning outside the schools, where the community is the educator.

The following discussion is an attempt to assess the general principles that govern the transfer of linguistic forms and abilities from one person to another, from one group to another, as these principles have emerged from studies in the speech community. When we think about literacy, we are primarily concerned with the transfer by conscious training, in learning to read and write. But by examining the unplanned transfer, or non-transfer of other linguistic skills in the community at large, we may be able to learn something about the failure to transfer literacy within the schools.

A central theme here will be the distinction between two conceptions of language. One is the set of socially significant symbols: the words and sounds that are perceived and recognized by most members of society as identifying a particular language variety: I will refer to this as "language" in quotes. The other is the liinguistic system, as the linguist describes it, and I will refer to it as the linguistic system. These two types of language show radically different patterns of transmission and learning.

---

* The bracket notation [ ] is used for the sound of the language, without relation to meaning. The slash notation / / encloses the linguistic categories known as "phonemes": the units of sounds that make one word different from another, and the notion that must be entered into the mental dictionary of the language learner. The parenthesis notation ( ) indicates sociolinguistic variables, which carry social and stylistic information in addition to their dictionary uses.

THE SOURCES OF LANGUAGE LEARNING

In the course of the discussion we will have to take into account several sites of language learning. The one site that we will not consider is the individual psyche, molded by the innate capacity and particular make-up of the language learner. We begin with language as a social fact—the system of communication used in everyday life and controlled by the social compact to assign certain meanings to certain forms and their arrangements. Accordingly, our first site for language learning is the transmission of language forms within the family. In this social configuration there is sexual asymmetry: the primary source is the female caregiver, with some auxiliary input from male adults, brothers and sisters.

The next site for language transmission is the peer group. The first serious influence of non-family peers occurs at various ages, anywhere from two to five, depending on the play and nurture patterns of the community. In the United States and Western Europe, the full force of peer group influence begins around eight or nine, when the child is first recognized as a member of the pre-adolescent group.

The influence of the pre-adolescent group overlaps that of the school, the institutionalized source of language learning. It also overlaps the influence of the mass media, which is widely believed to be a major transmitter of linguistic influence in modern society. Finally, we must consider the multiple sites of language transmission in the wider society as the adult becomes fully socialized: the job, the neighborhood, the church, and a host of formal and informal organizations.

ACQUISITION OF THE LINGUISTIC SYSTEM

Before systematic means of studying the speech community were developed, linguists tended to believe that a language was nothing but a conglomerate of individual systems or idiolects. Now we are coming to see that the social contract that lies behind Saussure's conception of *langue* is a linguistic reality. The set of forms and meanings that is transmitted to the language learner rests on a fundamentally homogeneous structure, which like other social facts is binding on every individual.

An illustration of this homogeneous base can be observed in the Philadelphia vowel system. The city is a model laboratory of sound change in progress, with two thirds of the vowel phonemes involved. But these changes take place within a well defined system of word classes that is unique to Philadelphia and uniform within it. The short *a* words give the clearest example: *man, pass, that,* etc.. From New York to Baltimore, words spelled with short *a* are divided into a "tense" and a "lax" set, which varies from town to town. The tense vowel is usually similar to the mid-

Table 1.   Philadelphia Division of Short *A* Words Into Tense and Lax Forms

Tense						Lax			
[1]	[2]	[3]	[4]	[5]	[6]	[7]	[8]	[9]	[10]
man	laugh	bath	pass	mad	bang	cash	bat	cab	sad
stand	calf	path	last	bad	hang	smash	cap	bag	dad
dance	after	lath	ask	glad	sank	bash	sack	badge	sad
etc.	etc.	etc.	etc.	etc.	etc.	etc.	etc.	etc.	etc.

front ingliding vowel of *yeah*; the lax vowel is the short front central [æ]. The Philadelphia system can be illustrated as shown in Table 1.

Each of the columns represents a phonetically defined subclass that has many members, except column [5], which has three members: the three common affective adjectives *mad, bad, glad*. The fourth such adjective, *sad*, with all other words ending in /d/, is found with lax vowels in column [10]. No other speech community has such a system, but it governs the speech of Philadelphia with an iron hand. Table 2 shows the distribution of tense and lax words in subclasses of [5] and [10] in the spontaneous speech of 100 Philadelphians. The uniformity of this pattern extends across the social spectrum, including the Philadelphia upper class: in spontaneous speech, all but one of the upper class speakers adhered to this core pattern without exception.[1] We still do not know how such citywide patterns are arrived at, but it is clear that Philadelphians have learned this pattern, and learned it in a uniform way.

There is other evidence that language learning goes on steadily throughout life. Sankoff and Lessard (1975) showed in their regression analysis of the Montreal Corpus that all speakers steadily increase their vocabulary with age. In English, a pattern of adult acquisition appears in the simplification of final consonant clusters ending in /t/ or /d/. Every child studied so far shows at an early age the variable constraints on this process: clusters formed by past tense suffixes (as in *walked* or *missed*) are simplified less often than monomorphemic clusters (as in *act* or *fist*). But the adult treatment of ambiguous clusters as in *lost* or *kept* is a different matter. Here there are several possible analyses: one may consider the whole words *keep* and *kept* to be irregular forms of present and past; or the vowel alternation of /iy/ and /e/ as the distinctive feature signalling present versus past; or view the /t/ suffix as the chief signal of the past, parallel to the /t/ in *missed* /mist/. Boyd and Guy showed in 1979 a significant age-grading in the probability of

---

[1] The one exception in the series of upper class speakers studied by Anthony Kroch was a person who corrected all tense vowels to lax. It should be noted that the uniformity of this pattern appears only in spontaneous speech: word lists and other formal means of elicitation produce a confused picture, with errors in both directions (Labov, in press).

Table 2.   Tense and Lax Vowels in Short A Words
Ending in /D/ for 100 Philadelphians

	Tense	Lax
mad	73	0
bad	143	0
glad	18	1
sad	0	14

consonant cluster simplification of this ambiguous /t/. Pre-adolescent children behave as if there was no final /t/ at all: adolescents and young adults treat the final /t/ as if it was a part of the stem, as in *fist,* and the regression coefficient for age shows that older speakers tend to identify the final /t/ with the past tense /t/. From this pattern we can infer that speakers continue to analyze the linguistic patterns of their language as they grow older, developing a more abstract grammar over time.

The two patterns just discussed—short *a* distribution and *t,d* deletion—are part of the linguistic system. We have no record as yet of any overt comment or recognition of these variable on the part of the speakers who are not linguistically trained.[2] There is no social differentiation of short *a* distribution, and very little for *t,d* deletion. The community transmits this information in one way or another, but does not discuss it, develops no social awareness, and finds it almost impossible to focus on.[3] This is characteristic of most grammatical regularities, which have no sociolinguistic correlations.

THE ACQUISITION OF SOCIALLY SIGNIFICANT SYMBOLS

Sociolinguistic Markers

Almost all of the social affect devoted to language is concentrated on the surface: the words and the sounds rather than the pattern. In the case of the tensed short *a* it is the particular quality of the sound used which is the sociolinguistic variable. As the phoneme /æh/, it can be realized in a wide variety of phonetic forms, from a slightly raised low vowel to a high inglid-

---

[2] I have found one or two outside observers who could replicate the Philadelphia pattern, but only partially. One New Yorker had moved to Philadelphia at the age of 12, and gone through high school there. At 40 he could remember how Philadelphians pronounced each of the words that differed from his native pattern; but he had no idea about any word that was the same.

[3] This difficulty in calling features of the linguistic system to the attention of members of the speech community affects efforts to communicate the results of linguistic research. It may have something to do with the difficulty in creating interest in the teaching and learning of grammar.

ing vowel, similar to the vowel of *idea*. There is tight social stratification of this variable: the lower the social class of the speaker, the higher the vowel.[4]

Many sociolinguistic variables show regular stylistic stratification as well as social stratification. The variable (r) is a typical example. It represents the realization of final and preconsonantal /r/ in words like *car, card, beer, beard,* etc., either as a consonantal [r], or a vocalic inglide or long monophthong. The New York City variation has been the most closely studied (Labov, 1966; Labov, Cohen, Robins, & Lewis, 1968): among both blacks and whites, we find that the higher the social class, the more consonantal [r] is used: the lower the social class the less. At the same time, for almost every speaker we find that the more formal the style, the more attention is directed to language, the more use of consonantal [r], and the less vocalization. To a greater or lesser extent, the same phenomenon is found in all of the "*r*-less" dialects of the Eastern Seaboard: in Boston, Richmond, Charleston and Savannah. In many cases, this variation is not a part of the vernacular pattern, but only appears in careful speech and the reading of word lists. It is not a matter of conscious imitation as a rule: members of the community acquire this superposed variable by unconscious imitation of others. One might think that the pattern is the result of school teaching or the conscious imitation of radio announcers. This may be true for some part of the variation, but there are several reasons to believe that the main transmission route is in the wider community.

First, we can note that most older New Yorkers show the same variable use of (r) that younger ones do. Yet if they attended school before 1945, they would have been exposed to an entirely different ideology and practice concerning this variable. In the 1930's New York City schools endorsed a prestige pronunciation based on the Southern British "*r*-less" pattern where the vocalization of (r) was considered the only correct form. It is only after World War II that this "international English" was demoted to the status of a local or foreign dialect and an *r*-pronouncing variety of American English took its place.

Second, we can find much evidence from the study of ongoing changes in practice that the mass media do not affect speech habits of most people directly, though an isolated minority may submit to such influence. Rather, it seems that the prestige patterns captured in the broadcast standard of the mass media reflect changes that have already taken place in the wider community, including redefinitions of "careful," "correct," or "non-local language."

---

[4] In fact, the correlation is so regular that we were able to use it as a test of normalization: the proper algorithm for reducing all Philadelphia vowels to the same reference grid, removing variation due to differences in vocal tract length, but preserving social differences that are real characteristics of the data. The algorithm selected was the one that preserved most sharply the social stratification of (æh).

Stereotypes and Folk Labels

The term *stereotype* is used here to refer to a part of "language" that is talked about by members of the community. It may or may not be a part of the linguistic system: there are stereotypes that are so far divorced from anything that people do or say that they have a life of their own. Stereotypes are sometimes conveyed in the form of folk labels such as "Brooklynese," or fixed phrases that register the categorical use of some nonstandard feature in conventional spelling: "toity-toid street" or "dese, dems and doses." As far as linguistic research can determine, there is no such thing as "Brooklynese" or any other regional subdialects of New York City, which is a single linguistic unit with systematic stratification by social class and race. White working class speakers in Brooklyn have the same speech pattern as white working class speakers in Jersey City or the Bronx.

Furthermore, the vowel [oi] has never been used in words like *third* by any New Yorkers except a small group of Irish-American speakers; the older vernacular vowel has a midcentral nucleus. No native speakers of English use more than an occasional voiced /d/ in words like *these*; the variable alternates between a lenis flap, an affricate, and the voiced interdental fricative. These linguistic descriptions of fact are irrelevant to the social construct of "Brooklynese," which is the only type of "language" that is overtly recognized by society, and the only type that is ever discussed in public.

Some stereotypes have a closer relation to the linguistic structure. The idea that some people "drop their *g*'s" in alternations like *working ~ workin'* is founded on reality, and there is consistent social and stylistic stratification of the variable (ing) in such words. In a wide variety of speech communities, we find that (ing) is a sociolinguistic marker: the use of the *-in'* variant is inversely related to social class and formality of style, and is favored more by men than women.

The phonetic realization of the tensed short *a* has this character. It is a marker of social class and style, but also a *stereotype* of Philadelphia speech. It is the feature of Philadelphia "language" that is most often mentioned (and condemned) by Philadelphians as the "harsh, nasal *a*," in particular words like *Camden* and *bad*. Though spontaneous speech is not highly corrected in Philadelphia, there is a considerable amount of correction of the vernacular pattern in word lists.[5]

---

[5] The correction of a short *a* by Philadelphians is relatively mild compared to New Yorkers, and largely confined to middle class speakers. (One upper class speaker consistently corrected tense /æh/ to lax /æ/ in spontaneous speech.) In New York, all social classes show the correction of tensed /æh/, even in spontaneous speech, and there is even more self-conscious discussion and condemnation. In the Northern Cities like Chicago, tensed short *a* is part of an ongoing change in progress, and shows some social correlation, but very little social consciousness. The selection of a particular element of the sound system as a social variable, part of the recognized "language" of the area, is the result of historical and dialect-specific developments.

The small number of stereotypes available to members of the community provide the concrete materials for discussions of the community's "language." They almost always refer to surface features of the linguistic system.[6] The ideas conveyed are vague, overparticular, misleading and very often dead wrong, if they are taken as referring to the linguistic system that people actually use. Statements of phoneticians, dialectologists or linguists about the linguistic system can only be interpreted by the general public in terms of the ordinary conception of "language," which is based on such stereotypes. There has been a great deal of public discussion recently of our finding that the "Black English Vernacular (BEV)" is diverging from other local dialects in northern cities, and I have been able to observe the transfer of information to reporters, columnists, and the general public on radio and television talk shows. The reporting has been quite accurate on the general issues. But the facts of the linguistic system, such as the status of subject–verb agreement and third singular /s/, do not transfer. Instead, the issues are discussed in relation to the folk labels "ghetto language," "blood talk," or "black language." The only concrete language features connected with these labels appear to be certain marked words and phrases like "blood" or "getting down," some intonation contours, and one grammatical element, habitual *be* in such fixed phrases as "What it be like?"

The transfer of information about language to teachers and educators is equally difficult, in spite of the fact that they have more knowledge of the linguistic system than the general public. The information developed by linguists about nonstandard dialects usually appears in a stereotyped and inaccurate form in textbooks and curricula, so that it may be difficult for teachers to connect the language of children in the classroom with the "black language" they are said to speak. One critic of "Black English" said at a conference of educators on the Ann Arbor "King" case that he had asked a dozen participants to tell him what "Black English" was and he never got the same answer twice. I have no reason to think that he was wrong.[7]

Stereotypes are not only the centers of public discussion of "language," but also the central themes of many school curricula designed to correct students' speaking and writing.

THE RELATIVE INFLUENCE OF FAMILY AND PEERS

For most researchers on the acquisition of language, the caregivers within the family are the sole transmitting agents considered.[8] But if we take one

---

[6] One exception is the stereotype of "double negatives", which refers to the nonstandard linguistic rule of negative concord. This is a structural feature, which makes reference to the incorporation of negative particles into following indetermines *any, ever,* and *either.*

[7] This was Benjamin Alexander, president of Chicago College, in a film made by the BBC Open University crew at the Wayne State Conference organized in February 1980 by Geneva Smitherman.

[8] One consequence of this fact is that the early publications of the research group on acquisition headed by Roger Brown and Ursula Bellugi did not report that one of the three

step wider, we must ask about the influence of the child's earliest peer groups: what are their influence compared to that of the family?

This is a serious problem for dialectologists, since they want to select informants who are fully representative of a community. It has been the practice to look for speakers whose parents are native speakers—that is, the third generation of immigrants or later. Allen (1973) had to include a number of second generation informants in his dialect atlas of the North Central states, where the Scandinavian immigration was large and recent. He therefore compared the data he obtained from second and third generation informants and found no difference between them for the great majority of regional dialect words. There were however a few words that were becoming obsolete in the general community that were better represented among the third generation informants. This indicates that the wider community is an effective source of transmission for the vocabulary as a whole, but that the family can play an essential role in the preservation of forms that are no longer common currency.

In New York City, it was also impossible to confine the study to third generation speakers. Labov (1976) restudied second and third generation New Yorkers for their use of the sociolinguistic variable (eh) and (oh). It was possible to match second and third generations for two subgroups: younger lower-middle class Jews and middle-aged working class Italians. Their use of these variable was almost identical. Here the influence of the peer group was predominant. But in the case of new immigrants, the cards are stacked against the influence of the family, since the non-native English of first generation speakers is not a socially accepted model. Payne's study of the acquisition of the Philadelphia dialect (1980) was designed to observe the opposite situation, where the non-native dialect had more prestige than the local dialect. In the newly formed suburb of King-of-Prussia, about 50% of the population was drawn from outside of Philadelphia, to work in electronic, computer and chemical industries. The newcomers had higher professional qualifications than the local Philadelphia people, as a whole. In Payne's sample of 34 out-of-state families, the dialects of Eastern Massachusetts, New York City, and the near Midwest were well represented.

Payne's study of the Philadelphia regional vocabulary confirmed what Allen had found: there was no difference between second and third generation speakers, and little difference between the children and their immigrant parents. The characteristic sound features of the Philadelphia dialect were acquired rapidly by the out-of-state children within a few years of their entrance into the community: the fronting of /ow/ in go but not in goal, the

---

children studied, Adam, was black. Adam's family was middle class, and undoubtedly exposed him to standard forms, so it appeared to the researchers as an irrelevant fact. Adam's development of negative concord in his fourth year in forms like "Nobody don't know that" was described as an internal development, not the result of any transfer from the environment, though this is in fact a dominant form in the BEV. We would need a much wider view of Adam's social network to understand what is happening here.

fronting of /uw/ in *too* but not in *tool,* the raising of /aw/ in *down* and *out,* and the centralization of /ay/ in *sight* but not in *side.* On the other hand, parents showed only a few traces of these sound changes, and their original system was maintained intact. This confirmed systematically the general observation that children of parents who move into new areas do not "sound like" their parents as a rule, but like their peers.

This sound pattern included the tensed and raised sound for the phoneme /æh/ in *mad, bad,* and *glad.* However, it did not include a short *a* distribution discussed above. Only one of the 34 out-of-state children acquired the core pattern of tense and lax forms of the short *a* that was shown above to be the uniform characteristic of the Philadelphia dialect.

We can conclude that the peer group can transmit rules of the sound system, primarily additive rules of the output, with simple phonetic conditioning, and under this influence, speakers can remold their local accents to conform with the peer group patterns that are socially significant. But no amount of peer group influence can alter consistently the original dictionary entries that determine the categories of the phonological system: these are acquired in their most consistent form from the original caregivers when language is first learned.

Consequences for School Literacy

The research findings on the differential acquisition of linguistic forms raise serious questions for the teaching of reading and writing in standard English form within the schools. Let us accept the idea that this teaching must be done on the basis of the linguistic system that the child brings to school in the early grades. If there are systematic differences between the target and the starting point, how can the target system be taught?

As far as I know, every effort to teach new phonological systems to children speaking other dialects has run into serious difficulties. In France, there are many children in northern schools who speak dialects of the Midi, where there is a consistent five vowel system. Teachers have the task of teaching the standard French seven vowel system, with the distinction between open and closed /e/ and /o/. The former is particularly important because it is needed to distinguish the imperfect ending with open /e/ in *était* as against the closed /e/ of the participle in *été.* In China, pupils throughout the country are faced with the problem of mastering the distinction between a dental and a retroflex series of consonants that is not found in their own dialects but is institutionalized in standard Mandarin or *pu tong hwa* (Lehmann, 1975). In the United States, black children in northern cities are faced with a standard spelling and speaking system that includes the distinction between /i/ and /e/ before nasal consonants /m/ and /n/, distinguishing *pin* from *pen, since* from *sense.* In all three cases, there has been very little success in teaching children who have acquired one set of underlying forms a new set. Instead, we find that even those who have worked their way through the educational process and acquired advanced degrees maintain the phonological system of their youth with very little modification. The conclusion that we might come to is that educators should abandon the effort to teach a standard language based on phonological distinctions that are not general to the population as a whole, and accept the fact that these, like other historical residues, are registered in spelling but not in the pronunciation of most educated people.[9]

The same policy could not be applied to the problem of unpredictable grammatical forms like the irregular past forms of English: the selection of *come* or *came, saw* or *seen, ate* or *eaten* for the simple past or part participle.[10] Here the problem that the schools and the language learner faces is immense, and there is no immediate possibility of shortening the labor of relearning each form one at a time.

Is it possible for young adults to relearn such complex distributions? Is there any evidence that this has happened in the course of undirected learning in the wider community? On reflection, it would seem that the answer must be positive. If the only speakers who mastered the Philadelphia short *a* pattern were children of Philadelphia parents, we could not have the uniform pattern of Table 1. The present-day Philadelphia population includes many descendants of out-of-state parents who may not have mastered these patterns in their youth. But they did not pass on their irregularities to their children. If third and fourth generation speakers have a uniform pattern, they must have acquired it from parents who gradually acquired themselves an unconscious knowledge of the city wide distribution. There must be some pattern of slow but effective learning in later life that makes it possible for second generation Philadelphians to gradually acquire the specifics of the community pattern and transmit it to the third and later generations. Otherwise, we could not explain how the dialects of New York City, London, Paris, Berlin and Philadelphia are built on such a uniform structural base. It is not impossible that such an undirected learning pattern can be put to work within the school system to accelerate the immense task of learning the standard use of unpredictable forms.

THE EFFECT OF PEER GROUP NETWORKS ON SOCIOLINGUISTIC VARIABLES

Teachers do not have a direct view of the operation of peer group networks, since their effects are diluted and dispersed within the classroom. In their attempts to socialize students into classroom patterns and ideology, teachers

---

[9] In China, the spelling distinction is made only in the roman alphabet of *pin yin,* but not in characters, which serve admirably their normal purpose of a common representation for all dialects of the language.

[10] Wolfram and Christian, 1975, attempt to find regularity in the distribution of these forms in Appalachian English, but the degree of order is quite limited.

may suspect that they are up against powerful and resistant forces of this type, from the fourth grade onward (see Labov, 1982; Ogbu, this volume). In the inner city classrooms we find an odd mixture of children with many different orientations to the peer groups that dominate life in the wider community. There are "lames" or isolates; peripheral, marginal and secondary members of the dominant peer groups; and core members. The socially significant symbols that the teacher receives in the classroom—the "language" of the students—may not differ appreciably from one subgroup to the other. But an examination of the linguistic system used by the various subgroups often shows a direct relation between peer group membership and the realization of sociolinguistic variable. Figure 1 shows the probabilities of contraction and deletion for five subdivisions of the Jets, a South Harlem adolescent club studied by Labov et al. in 1968 (Labov, 1972, p. 279). The core members, with primary status, are united by reciprocal sociometric choices in sociometric namings of hang-out preferences; the secondary members, with secondary status, are defined by their nonreciprocal relation to core members. The groups marked "I" live in the block where the Jets originated; the groups marked "II" live in the block to the west, and joined the Jets later. Marginal members are partially detached from the group because they are older, live at a distance, or have other interests. The probability of contraction and deletion of the copula form *is* registers the variable likelihood of full forms, "He is doing it," contracted forms "He's doing it," and zero forms "He doing it." The contraction rule is the same as the contraction rule of the general population, and its proba-

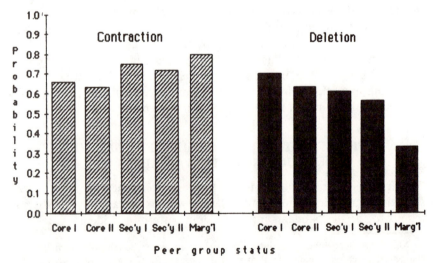

FIGURE 1.   Relation of Contraction and Deletion Rules to Peer Group Membership for South Harlem Adolescents.

bility is directly related to distance from the peer group core. The deletion rule is specific to the BEV, and is inversely related to distance from the core.

The pattern of Figure 1 can be extended further. The lames or isolated individuals, who have no relationship to the peer groups, usually show linguistic features that are even more distant from the peer group pattern, and the whites of New York are categorically different. There are marked educational correlates of these patterns. Peer group members show much lower reading scores than isolated individuals as a whole, and in fact showed an absolute ceiling of Grade 4.9 in the New York City school reading scores (Labov & Robins, 1969). A correlation was found between the ability to interpret the *ed* past tense suffix and the peer group norm of consonant cluster simplification (Labov, 1970). The evidence points to the fact that the adolescent peer group in the inner cities institutionalizes resistance to the norms, the ideology, and the practices of the school system. This resistance appears to be the result of a political and cultural conflict between the vernacular speakers and the school authorities (Labov, 1982). The linguistic behavior of peer group members is a reflection and a symbol of this conflict.

The linguistic reflection of antagonism between adolescent peer groups and school norms can be found in many sources far beyond the inner cities. Eisikovits (1981) found evidence of covert norms that strongly opposed the standard English patterns among Australian high school students. She showed that girls shifted towards the standard norms of the adult female interviewer for a larger number of grammatical variables whenever they responded directly to the interviewer. But boys did precisely the reverse for the majority of these variables: when they responded directly to the interviewer they moved further away from her norms than when the last speaker was a member of the group. Eckert's ethnographic studies of a Michigan high school (1986) locate the opposition between ''Jocks'' and ''Burnouts'' in alignment or nonalignment to adult norms and institutions. Linguistic reflections of this opposition are found in the differential participation of youth in the ongoing sound shifts of the Northern cities.

The educational consequences of this institutionalized peer group opposition to the schools are clear. In the previous section, it appeared that many of the tasks of language learning that lead to literacy involve the relearning of large numbers of individual forms, as well as acquiring new vocabulary and new skills. Powerful motivations are required to achieve that end, and those peer group structures that are opposed to the school are motivated in the opposite direction. The reorientation of peer group pressures towards the work required to achieve high levels of literacy must be one of the primary goals of an educational policy that would reduce unequal opportunities in our society.

ADULT LANGUAGE LEARNING

Everything that has been said so far about the uniformity of the structural base of the Philadelphia dialect must be restated. That uniform base is used only by the white population. The 38% of the Philadelphia population that is black does not share the underlying system of categories found in the white population, and does not participate in the ongoing changes in progress. From 1981 to 1984, the Linguistics Laboratory at the University of Pennsylvania conducted research on the relations between black and white dialects in Philadelphia, and in particular on the transmission of linguistic features between the two groups (Labov & Harris, 1983).

One of the most prominent features of the black vernacular is the absence of subject–verb agreement as a general rule, which is reflected in other American English dialects in the consistent use of the /s/ suffix on the third singular present of the regular verb and a number of irregular verbs like *do*. The [BEV] shows a low frequency of /s/ in the third singular subjects, a consistent use of *have, do,* and *was,* and a widespread tendency for the /s/ to appear in other persons and numbers. There is no phonetic conditioning of this variation among core speakers of the vernacular. Torrey's studies of second graders in Harlem (1983) showed that they had no capacity to interpret this inflection as a mark of the singular, and did not learn to do this easily. The general conclusion of all studies is that the third singular /s/ inflection has no systematic place in the BEV grammar.

The BEV speakers studied in Philadelphia showed an even lower frequency of third singular /s/ than in previous studies, partly because we had succeeded more than before in overcoming the effects of observation and the tendency to move away from the vernacular in the presence of a microphone. The core members of the social networks studied used almost 90% forms without /s/, and the majority of the /s/ forms used were concentrated in narrative contexts in a use from the subject–verb agreement of other dialects.[11]

However, this absence of subject–verb agreement is not characteristic of the population as a whole. Figure 2 shows the level of third singular /s/ for 34 members of the social networks studied in North Philadelphia. The darkest circles indicate a very high level of absence: they are characteristic of the core group of BEV speakers in the center, the Puerto Ricans who associate with blacks, the senior citizens, and the subjects born in the South. All of these are black speakers who have associated primarily with blacks, and very little with whites. Members of the same social network with different

---

[11] This concentration of /s/ in narrative contexts is a new phenomenon of younger speakers, not observed before, and is one of the main bases for our conclusion that BEV is moving further away from other dialects. For most young black Philadelphians, verbal /s/ is beginning to function as a marker of past narrative (Myhill & Harris, 1983).

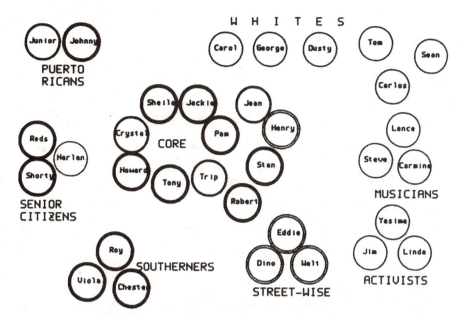

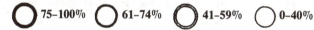

FIGURE 2. Social Types in the No. Philadelphia Black Community in Relation to
Absence of Third Singular Verb Marking.

social histories are grouped at the right. A set of street-wise blacks who may
be considered "hustlers and con-men" show moderate use of the third singular /s/: these are men who have engaged in various confidence games,
hustling and other illegal occupations that have required extensive dealing
with whites. Next are a group of three activists who are engaged in militant
black politics and labor activities: they show a very low level of third singular /s/ absence. Three musicians show the same pattern.

It should be emphasized that this grammatical feature does not alter the
impression for most listeners that the speakers are blacks using "black
dialect". In subjective reaction tests, the presence of third singular /s/ does
not alter the speakers' identifications as blacks, while controlled alteration
of certain vowels towards the white Philadelphia pattern had a radical effect. The change in the linguistic system is not perceived by members of the
community: it is not a socially significant symbol.

All of the speakers studied have had extensive exposure to standard
English through the mass media and the schools. But it appears that this
type of contact has had no significant effect upon them. It is only when
members of the black community engage white speakers in face-to-face
dealings that affect their life chances that they begin to acquire features of

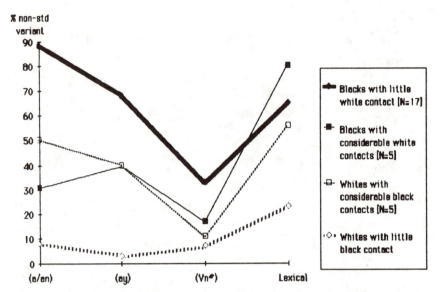

FIGURE 3. Use of BEV-Marked Variants of Phonological and Lexical Variables by Philadelphia Blacks and Whites.

the other dialects. The rule of subject–verb agreement is acquired unconsciously from the dominant culture and appears in vernacular speech.

Again we observe a sharp differentiation in the behavior of several different kinds of linguistic material. Figure 3 shows several phonological and lexical variables for this population, divided into four groups according to an index of contact developed on the basis of a systematic questionnaire and confirmed by participant observation (Ash & Myhill, 1983): blacks who have little contact with whites, the core speakers of BEV; blacks who have considerable contact with whites; whites who have considerable contact with blacks; and whites who have little contact with blacks, the majority. The three phonological variables studied here are the alternation of *a* and *an* before vowels, as in *a apple* versus *an apple;* the monophthongization of /ay/ in words like *high* and *shine;* and the nasalization of the vowel in words ending in nasal consonants, with the loss of the final nasal, as in *ma'* versus *man.* The fourth variable registers knowledge and use of a number of words specific to BEV: names of card games like *tonk* and *pitty pat;* terms for clothing, like *stacys* and *old man comforts;* for cars, like *hog* and *deuce and a quarter;* for friends, like *dude.* For all these variables, we see more or less of a continuum: the more contact with whites that blacks have, the less they use them; the more contact with blacks that whites have, the more they use them.

A very different situation emerges when we examine grammatical variables in Figure 4. Here the same speakers are plotted for their use of

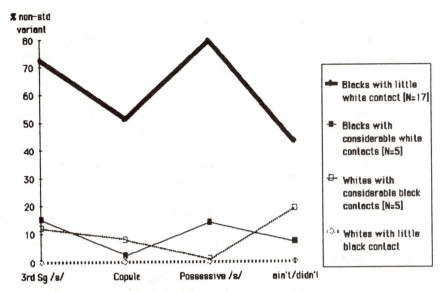

FIGURE 4.   Use of BEV-Marked Grammatical Variables for Philadelphia Speakers by Race and Degree of Contact.

third singular /s/; the copula; the possessive /s/ in attributive position as in *my sister's house* versus *my sister house;* and the use of *ain't* for the simple negative past, as in *He ain't do that yesterday.* Instead of a continuum, there is a dichotomy. The blacks who have little contact with whites use a very high level of these BEV features, and all others are at a very low level, practically zero.

It appears that there is active language learning in later life, which can assume a systematic character, almost as systematic as first-language learning. The wider community acts as educator under very particular conditions: when speakers of a lower-status dialect deal with and negotiate with speakers of the dominant dialect, they acquire unconsciously the very kinds of linguistic rules that the schools failed to teach.

IMPLICATIONS FOR EDUCATIONAL POLICY

This view of the community as educator has shown a variety of forms of language learning in the wider community, which must be matched against the absence of language learning in American schools—in the inner cities and in many rural areas. Even in the most prosperous sectors of the educational establishment, in the metropolitan suburbs, we find a parallel failure in the teaching of foreign languages. In this final section, I would like to develop some suggestions on how these research findings might bear on the central problems of American education.

The fundamental problem of American education is racism—beliefs and practices that are motivated by and reinforce the view that one race is superior to others. Its most obvious expression is residential, economic and educational segregation. The most obvious implication of our research is that integration within cities and across city lines is required to reduce the isolation of black and Hispanic youth. It is not necessary that the integration of white and black groups leads to a friendly and equal participation of black and whites in all activities. The simple mixing of black and white populations in the schools will lead in the opposite direction of the results shown in Figures 2–4. It is not necessary for a person to like someone else to be influenced by and learn from the other person's speech pattern. It has been shown that the learning of grammar in the wider community is entirely unconscious, and there is no reason to think that the same learning cannot take place in the schools.

The early exposure of black youth to speakers of other dialects is the essential ingredient here. The gradual divergence of black and white dialects is only possible because such exposure is missing. The issue is not simply that blacks should be exposed to whites, but simply to children who speak other dialects closer to the standard English of the classroom. The increasing residential segregation of the inner cities is not only a segregation of black and white, but a segregation of poor, economically deprived blacks from middle class blacks. It is a new development in the United States that large numbers of black youth go to school only with children from the same dialect background and same economic background as themselves.

One consequence of early exposure is that children will have a better opportunity to reorganize their underlying forms. Though I have not emphasized the point in the earlier sections, all studies show that the younger the children are when they arrive in a dialect area, the more rapid their acquistion of the new forms. It is not only the forms of irregular verbs that are involved here: many phonological patterns become binding on black youth, so that it is very difficult for them to hear certain contrasts: between /f/ and /s/, between final /-nd/ and /-d/, between /-sts/ and /-s/.

Exposure to other dialects will allow some of the fundamental skills of language learning to operate. But it is also evident that a great deal of social engineering is required to permit this learning to take place. We must do in the classroom what the community does, but in a concentrated and coherent way.

One goal for this type of engineering is to reduce the distance between the socially significant symbol and the linguistic system. Students, like other speakers of the language, react to certain symbols with a strong social evaluation that determines the effort that they can devote to language learning. For many students who are aligned towards street culture and against classroom culture, certain of the sounds and words identified with classroom

English are identified with a set of values that have already been rejected. They are associated with a set of polarities: white versus black, middle class versus working class, female versus male. They are associated with high culture versus popular culture in music, poetry, film and drama. They are associated with the school values of patterns of surveillance, submission to authority and informing on fellow students versus the street values of respect for privacy, resistance to oppression and loyalty to friends and equals. They are associated with fussiness, weakness and delicacy as against simplicity, strength and decisiveness. The effect of these socially significant symbols is to contaminate the straightforward goals of learning to read and write with an extraneous set of moral alignments that have nothing to do with the main task at hand.

It seems to me that any program of language arts that would integrate our society must break through these traditional associations. The language of the classroom must be seen as a common property of all social classes and ethnic groups; free from identification with male or female style; neutral to the opposition of high culture and popular culture; independent of the other socialization processes of the school system; and restored to the vigor of everyday life. One step in this direction is to strip away the socially significant symbols that carry such a heavy social loading. These include overprecise articulation and the strong release of final consonants; the preservation of outmoded or fictitious rules of grammar that produce *It is I, Whom do you see?* and *We shall;* the passion for sentence combining and the substitution of words for thought. In their place we need to develop the capacity for observation and attention to detail. We need to re-establish the connection between speech and writing so that all speakers of the language can draw upon their native skills to achieve literacy.

If we could put some or all of these suggestions into effect, one result would be to reduce the distance between the school and the wider community. The title of this chapter would then lose all significance, since the school would be the community as educator.

REFERENCES

Allen, H. (1973). The use of Atlas informants of foreign parentage. *Festschrift Kurath.*

Ash, S. & Myhill, J. (1983). *Linguistic markers of ethnic identity.* Paper presented at NWAVE XII, Montreal.

Boyd, S. & Guy, G. (1979). *The acquisition of a morphological category.* Paper presented at the Linguistic Society of America annual meeting, Los Angeles.

Eckert, P. (1986). *The roles of high school social structure in phonological change.* Paper presented at the meeting of the Chicago Linguistic Society.

Eisikovits, E. (1981). *Cultural attitudes and language variation..* Paper presented at the 6th Annual Congress of Applied Linguistics, Canberra, Australia.

Labov, W. (1966). *The social stratification of English in New York City.* Washington, DC: Center for Applied Linguistics.

Labov, W. (1970). The reading of the -ed suffix. In H. Levin & J. Williams (Eds.), *Basic studies in reading,* (pp. 222–245). New York: Basic Books.

Labov, W. (1972a). *Sociolinguistic patterns.* Philadelphia: University of Pennsylvania Press.

Labov, W. (1972b). *Language in the inner city.* Philadelphia: University of Pennsylvania Press.

Labov, W. (1976). The relative influence of family and peers on the learning of language. In R. Simone et al. (Eds.), *Aspetti Socioling. Dell' Italia Contemponea.* Rome: Bulzoni.

Labov, W. (1982). Competing value systems in the inner-city schools. In P. Gilmore & A. Glatthorn (Eds.), *Children in and out of school* (pp. 148–171). Washington, DC: Center for Applied Linguistics.

Labov, W. (in press). The exact description of the speech community. In D. Schiffrin & R. Fasold (Eds.), Proceedings of NWAVE XI, Washington, DC.

Labov, W. & W. Harris (in press). De Facto Segregation of Black and White Vernaculars. In D. Sankoft (Ed.), Proceedings of NWAVE XII The Hagve: J. Benjamius.

Labov, W. & Robins, C. (1969). A note on the relation of reading failure to peer group status in urban ghettos. *Teachers College Record, 70,* 395–405.

Labov, W., Cohen, P., Robins, C. & Lewis, J. (1968). *A study of the non-standard English of Negro and Puerto Rican speakers in New York City.* Philadelphia: U.S. Regional Survey.

Lehmann, W.P. (Ed.). (1975). *Language and linguistics in the People's Republic of China.* Austin: University of Texas Press.

Myhill, J. & Harris, W. (1983). *The use of the verbal -s inflection in BEV.* Paper presented at NWAVE XII, Montreal.

Payne, A. (1980). Factors controlling the acquisition of the Philadelphia dialect by out-of-state children. In W. Labov (Ed.), *Locating language in time and space,* (pp. 143–177). New York: Academic Press.

Sankoff, D. & Lessard, R. (1975). Vocabulary richness. A sociolinguistic analysis. *Science, 190,* 689–690.

Torrey, J. (1983). Black children's knowledge of standard English. *American Educational Research Journal, 20,* 627–643.

Wolfram, W. & Christian, D. (1975). *Sociolinguistic variables in Appalachian dialects.* Final report to the National Institute of Education, Grant No. NIE-G-74-0026.

PART IV
CULTURAL AND HISTORICAL EFFECTS ON LITERACY

Chapter Eight
Opportunity Structure, Cultural Boundaries, and Literacy

JOHN U. OGBU
University of California, Berkeley

It is commonly believed that in an urban industrial society like the United States adults are judged competent if they are functionally literate. It is also commonly known that many members of the lower class and some minority groups do not achieve satisfactory levels of functional literacy. My research has been mainly among those minority groups who, on the average, do not achieve satisfactory levels of functional literacy.

A disproportionate number of these minority group members do not successfully learn to read, to write, and to compute. At least, they are unable to demonstrate the ability to read, write, or compute in social and work situations requiring them to do so. Many find it difficult, for example, to fill out job application forms and income tax forms, and to read and understand instructional manuals and utilize the information. At school their children do poorly on teacher-made tests and on standardized tests.

In the United States minority groups who lag in functional literacy include American Indians, black Americans, Mexican Americans, Native Hawaiians, and Puerto Ricans. The problem is, however, not confined to the United States. The Burakumin in Japan, Maori in New Zealand, and West Indians in Britain, to name a few, experience similar difficulties with literacy.

Why do these minorities lag in acquisition of literacy? Why do they experience difficulties learning to read? Many explanations have been advanced by scholars in various disciplines. Even within one discipline like anthropology there are competing explanations. Furthermore, the explanations have changed from time to time even among proponents of one particular point of view. An example of this periodic shift in explanation is found among those who claim that the problem is due to language and communication factors. Thus, in the 1960s the proponents of language and communication factors claimed that black children experienced difficulties learning to read because they lagged in language development or had inadequate language (Feagans & Farran, 1981; Williams, 1970). Later the low reading achievement was attributed to language or dialect differences, to inadequate language socialization, and then to a mismatch in communication (see Simons, 1979, for a review). In the late 1970s it was said that black children and similar minorities come from "oral cultures" or "residual oral cultures" and that conflicts between these cultures and the "literate culture" of the schools and mainstream America caused their reading problems (Ogbu, 1983a).

I am not going to challenge the assertion that black American culture is an oral culture. But I do want to begin by pointing out that children from the so-called oral cultures of small-scale societies and children of "residual oral cultures" of more complex societies do not manifest the kind of school learning problems found among black American children. Examples of the former are Ibo children in Nigeria (personal knowledge—a member of the "tribe"), Kpelle children in Liberia (Gay and Cole, 1967), and Melpa children in New Guinea (Lancey, 1983). Children from residual oral cultures include Chinese peasant immigrants to the United States in the 19th and early 20th centuries, Japan's outcaste immigrants (Ito, 1967) and Punjabi Indian immigrants (Gibson, 1983).

I have argued that the explanations based on language and communication differences are not satisfactory for a number of reasons. One reason is that they lack an adequate comparative base. They are based on research among only those minority groups that are not particularly successful in acquiring literacy; they do not consider the case of other minority groups who are relatively successful in acquiring literacy even though they, too, possess different languages and communication styles (Ogbu, 1981; 1982).

Another reason why the explanations are not satisfactory is that they do not take into account certain societal forces which can enhance or discourage the acquisition of literacy in the society, or a segment of it. Yet, studies of literacy development, such as that in 15th and 16th century England by Cressey (1980), show that acquisition of literacy is enhanced when it is socially and economically functional and rewarded. A third reason for considering conventional explanations unsatisfactory is that they lack an historical perspective. Finally, I believe the explanations err by assuming that acquisition of literacy is primarily a matter of individual or family attributes and efforts. Perhaps because the explanations lack an historical perspective, they fail to consider the collective origins and collective basis of literacy behaviors of individual members of minority groups, or of members of any other population.

Other explanations of minority children's difficulties in learning to read and to compute have been advanced on the basis of difference in cognitive styles (Ramirez & Castenada, 1974; Shade, 1982), interaction styles (Erickson & Mohatt, 1982), teaching and learning styles (Boykin, 1980; Philips, 1983), and so on. Again, I will not challenge the claim that black Americans and similar minorities possess different cognitive styles, different communication styles, different interaction styles, different teaching and learning styles, or that their styles of language socialization and the general upbringing of children are different from that of the mainstream. But I do want to point out that members of small-scale societies and immigrants to the United States do not manifest the same kind of school learning problems that are found among black Americans and similar minorities even though the former, too, possess different cognitive styles, different teaching and learning styles, and different styles of language socialization and general upbringing (Heyneman, 1979; Freed & Freed, 1981).

I propose that the real issue in the acquisition of literacy among the minorities, as in their academic striving generally, is not whether children possess a different language or dialect, a different cognitive style, a different communication style, a different participant structure or interaction style, or a different pattern of language socialization and upbringing. Rather, the real issue is twofold, namely, first, whether or not the children come from a segment of society where people have traditionally experienced unequal opportunity to use their literacy skills in a socially and economically meaningful and rewarding manner; and, second, whether or not the relationship between the minorities and the dominant-group members who control the education system has encouraged the minorities to perceive and define acquisition of literacy as an instrument of deculturation without true assimilation.

As an alternative explanation I am suggesting that the problems experienced by the minorities in acquiring literacy and in academic performance generally are a function of their adaptation to the limited opportunity historically open to them for jobs and other positions in adult life requiring literacy, and where literacy pays off. The problems are further reinforced by the expressive responses—identity and cultural frame of reference—that the minorities have developed to cope with their subordinate relationship with the dominant group. Although the adaptation is manifested by individual minority group members, it is a collective response to a situation the minorities faced *as a group*. Furthermore, although the adaptation arose historically in response to the treatment of the minorities by dominant-group members, it persists: (a) because the barriers in opportunity structure and other forms of differential treatment of the minorities continue and are perceived to continue in one form or another; (b) because of the way the schools continue to treat the minorities; and (c) because of the types of responses the minorities have developed to cope with their situation.

The problems of literacy among the minorities are a part of the broader problem of low academic performance. The minorities who have difficulties learning to read also experience difficulties learning to compute and to perform in other areas of the school curriculum (Ogbu, 1978). Therefore, in the following pages I will treat literacy and academic or school performance interchangeably.

SOME PREREQUISITES FOR UNDERSTANDING
MINORITY ADAPTATION

Academic performance and literacy problems of the minorities are due to complex forces not only within the classroom and school, but also within the historical, economic, and sociocultural domains in the society at large. There are a number of prerequisites for comprehending how these forces create and perpetuate the problems. One prerequisite is to recognize that there are different kinds of minority groups and that they vary in the kinds of problems they experience in school. A second prerequisite is to recognize that school performance depends in part on the role of school success or school credentials in people's folk theory of getting ahead. A third prerequisite is to recognize that there are different kinds of cultural/language differences and that not all of these differences are implicated in the disproportionate and persistent difficulties with school learning. Let me expand on each of the prerequisites.

Different Kinds of Minorities

One key to understanding the difficulties some minority groups encounter with literacy is to distinguish between different kinds of minorities, since some groups are more successful than others. Toward this end I have classified minority groups into three types. One type, *autonomous minorities,* consists of people who are minorities primarily in a numerical sense. They may possess a distinctive ethnic, religious, linguistic, or cultural identity. However, although they are not entirely free from prejudice and discrimination, they are not socially, economically, and politically subordinated. Autonomous minorities do not experience disproportionate and persistent problems in learning to read and to compute partly because they usually have a cultural frame of reference which demonstrates and encourages school success. This type of minority is typically represented in the United States by Jews and Mormons.

Another type of minority group is the immigrant. *Immigrant minorities* are people who have *moved more or less voluntarily* to the United States because they believe that this would lead to more economic well-being, better overall opportunities, or greater political freedom. These expectations continue to influence the way the immigrants perceive and respond to schooling in the host society. Partly for this reason, although the immigrants often experience initial difficulties due to language and cultural differences, they do not experience lingering or disproportionate school failure. The Chinese in Stockton, California, the Punjabi Indians in Yuba City, California, are representative examples (Gibson, 1983; Ogbu, 1974).

I do not classify refugees and migrant or "guest" workers as immigrant minorities. Although they may share certain features with immigrants, the contexts in which refugees and migrant workers operate are different in some important respects. For example, migrant or "guest" workers tend to face legal barriers which may limit their access to equal education and to equal employment opportunity in their host society (Organization for Economic Co-operation and Development, 1983; Rist, 1979; Castle & Kosack, 1973). Refugees, like immigrants, face problems of resettlement, language and cultural discontinuities, employment, and so on. Like the immigrants, they may anticipate a better future in their host society. However, they may live with uncertainty about the permanence of their status, such as whether they will return to their country of origin which they did not leave voluntarily. They also may live with considerable guilt and anguish about family separation, deaths, or other hardships of friends and kinsmen whom they could not help or left behind (Suarez-Orozco, 1986; Bryce-LaPorte, 1980).

Finally, the third type of minorities, *castelike* or *subordinate minorities,* is made up of *people who were originally brought into the United States society involuntarily* through slavery, conquest, or colonization. Thereafter, they were relegated to menial positions and denied true assimilation into the mainstream. American Indians, black Americans, Mexican Americans, and native Hawaiians are examples. The Burakumin in Japan and the Maori in New Zealand are non-United States examples. It is the castelike minorities that usually experience most difficulties in acquiring literacy, and in general academic achievement. The reasons for their disproportionate and persistently lower school performance will be explored later in this chapter.

Status Mobility System and Literacy: Re-establishing The Missing Link

From society's point of view, schools are structured to prepare citizens to support existing economic systems as workers/producers and consumers, as well as to believe in the system. Schools are also structured to train citizens to support other institutions in society. Schools try to accomplish their tasks, especially the task of recruiting people into the labor force (a) by teaching young people the beliefs, values, and attitudes that support the economic system; (b) by teaching them some practical skills like reading and computing that make the system work; (c) by enhancing the development of some personal attributes compatible with the habits required at the workplace; (d) by credentialing people to enter the workforce. However, the success of the schools in educating children of a given population depends, in part at least, on the people's folk theory of getting ahead and on the part played by school success or school credentials. An example of such a folk theory is that of White middle class Americans which asserts that one gets a good job that pays well by getting a good education. Consequently, schooling in America (controlled by the middle class) has usually been based on the common sense goal to prepare young people in marketable skills and to offer credentials for labor force entry, remuneration, and advancement on the job. American people have usually perceived and responded to schooling from this point of view.

Status mobility system is a concept which allows us to capture the connection between people's folk theory of getting ahead and their school perceptions and strivings. A status mobility system is basically the socially approved mode of getting ahead in a society or a population (LeVine, 1967). Every society or population has its own folk theory of getting ahead, however getting ahead is defined. Each folk theory tends to generate its own ideal behaviors and ideal successful persons or role models—the kinds of persons widely perceived by members of the population as people who are successful or people who can get ahead because of their personal attributes and behaviors. The personal attributes of the role models tend to influence the values of childrearing agents and the attitudes and behaviors of the children themselves as they get older and begin to understand their status mobility system. Thus, if being literate is a quality that enables members of a population to get ahead, say, in terms of good jobs that pay well, then those who have good jobs with good pay will usually be literate people and possess the qualities that enhance literacy skills. The acquisition of literacy and effective strategies for transmitting literacy will be high in the ideology and behaviors of parents and others responsible for the upbringing of the children.

When there are externally imposed barriers that prevent people from getting ahead according to the prevailing folk theory, people will initially try to eliminate, lower, or circumvent those barriers. If the barriers persist they will tend to create an alternative folk theory that promotes other ways of getting ahead. Minorities in the United States have often faced such barriers that prevent them from using education or literacy to get good jobs with good pay, according to American folk theory. Some of the minorities continue to pursue education in spite of the barriers, partly because they have other uses for their school success in or outside the United States. This appears to have been the case of earlier Chinese immigrants who could return to China where their American education was highly valued and rewarded (Sung, 1967; Ogbu, 1983b). In the case of black Americans and other castelike minorities they have had no "homeland" to return to where they can be rewarded for their "American education"; nor do they have alternative activities in the United States requiring and rewarding academic success to a sufficient degree. As a consequence, these castelike minorities appear to have developed a somewhat different folk theory of getting ahead that does not necessarily emphasize the strategy of academic pursuit.

Different Types of Cultural/Language Differences

My comparative study of cultural and language difficulties encountered by minority children in school suggests that there may be three types of cultural/

language differences (Ogbu, 1982). One is *universal cultural difference,* in the sense that for all children, the transition from home to school involves adjusting to new behavioral requirements, social relations, style of language use or communication, and style of thinking (Cook-Gumperz & Gumperz, 1979; Scribner & Cole, 1973).

Another type is *primary cultural/language difference.* These are differences that existed before two population groups came in contact, such as *before* immigrant minorities came to the United States. The Punjabi Indians in Yuba City, California, for example, spoke Punjabi, practiced Sikh, Hindu, or Moslem religion, had arranged marriages and wore turbans before they came to America where they continue these beliefs and practices to some extent. Due to these cultural/language differences these immigrants experienced initial adjustment difficulties in school and society (Gibson, 1983). However, because their cultural/language differences did not arise from a need to protect their identity and maintain a sense of security under white American domination and subordination (i.e., because the differences did not arise in opposition to the identity, culture, and language of white Americans), the immigrants' differences are not so emotionally charged as to constitute a barrier to learning the things they perceive will help them achieve the objectives of their emigration. Thus, for example, the immigrants do not perceive or interpret learning the standard English language and the academic aspects of the school curriculum as threatening to their language, culture, and identity. Rather, they appear to interpret school rules of behavior and standard practices for academic achievement as appropriate means to acquire the literacy, knowledge, and skills they need in order to obtain the school credentials required for future employment and self-advancement in America. Immigrant minority students thus tend to adopt what Gibson (1983) calls a strategy of "accommodation without assimilation." That is, while they may not give up their cultural beliefs and practices, the immigrants are willing and strive to "play the classroom game by the rules" and try to overcome "all kinds of difficulties in school because they believe so strongly that there will be a payoff later" (Gibson, 1983). With this kind of attitude, the immigrants are able to cross cultural boundaries and do well in school.

In contrast, the third type of cultural/language difference, *secondary cultural difference,* arises *after* two groups have come in contact, especially where one group dominates the other. For example, secondary cultural differences between blacks and whites arose after blacks were involuntarily brought into American society as slaves, relegated to menial status and denied the chances of true assimilation, even after they were emancipated from slavery. Under this circumstance, blacks, like other castelike minorities, developed new or "secondary" cultural ways of coping, perceiving, and feeling. Indeed, they developed a new cultural frame of reference, or ideal way of behaving, in opposition to the cultural frame of reference of their "white oppressors." Furthermore, the secondary frame of reference emerged to protect their collective or social identity and to maintain boundaries between them and the dominant whites. Another contrast with primary cultural differences is that secondary cultural differences are often differences in style rather than in content. Research among castelike minorities in the United States has usually emphasized differences in communication style (Gumperz, 1981; Kochman, 1982), and in teaching and learning styles (Boykin, 1980; Philips, 1976, 1983). Furthermore, although the primary cultural differences of the immigrants have their own "styles" in cognition, communication, teaching and learning, the "styles" of the secondary cultural differences of castelike minorities are distinguished by the element of opposition or opposition process. That is, these "styles" are a part of an oppositional cultural frame of reference discussed earlier. Rather than due to differences in content of "style", because of their oppositional cultural frame of reference, castelike minorities do not perceive and respond to learning standard English and academic aspects of the school curriculum as do immigrants or people from small-scale societies. Instead, castelike minorities tend to equate such learning with linear acculturation which is threatening to their culture/language, identity, and sense of security. I will return to the influences of cultural differences on literacy acquisition of castelike minorities later.

In summary, there are different kinds of minorities of which one type, castelike minorities, experience disproportionate and persistent difficulties in education. Although all minorities may have their distinctive cultures and languages, some are more able than others to cross cultural and language boundaries in pursuit of education partly because of differences in the quality of their relationship to the dominant group who control schooling. Of the three types of cultural differences that I have identified, secondary cultural differences found among castelike minorities tend to be most associated with persistent learning difficulties. Finally, although education or literacy enhances the chances of social and economic advancement in adult life, barriers against educated members of the minority groups tend to cause minorities to develop alternative folk theories of getting ahead and alternative strategies to achieve success that do not necessarily emphasize or require literacy or school success. I will now use the case of black Americans to illustrate how these complex factors influence acquisition of literacy among castelike minorities.

THE CASE OF BLACK AMERICANS

As I pointed out earlier, the literacy and school learning difficulties experienced by black Americans in general are due: (a) to societal barriers that have historically prevented black people from having access to good schooling, making appropriate use of their education, and receiving societal rewards commensurate with their education; (b) to the way that American schools have treated blacks; and (c) to the types of responses that blacks themselves have made to their societal and school treatments. In this section I take up each of these sources of literacy problems in turn.

Societal Contribution

American society has historically contributed in two ways to the problems of literacy and school learning among blacks. One is the denial of access to a good education to generations of blacks. For example, during slavery there were laws forbidding teaching blacks to read and write. After slavery there were both formal and informal mechanisms used to exclude blacks from a good education. Because of this exclusion, and because of inferior education, blacks did not have the chance either to acquire the level of literacy or to build a tradition of literacy that would strengthen their competitive skills for desirable positions (Ogbu, 1978; see also Bond, 1966; Bullock, 1970).

The other mechanism by which American society has discouraged literacy among blacks is the use of a *job ceiling*. That is, by means of formal statutes and informal practices, white people who control the economy denied blacks access to good jobs with good pay (or to equal pay when they have the same jobs as whites) as well as access to other desirable positions in adult life, thus preventing blacks from benefiting from their education to the same extent as whites. The use of the job ceiling against blacks and similar subordinate groups is illustrated at the national level by the action of AT&T that continued until the 1970s. This case was investigated by the Equal Employment Opportunities Commission which in 1974 reported that the giant company "saved" about $362 million a year by not paying women, blacks, and Hispanic workers what they would have earned had they been white males (DeWare, 1978). The difficulties faced by blacks in using and benefiting from their education and literacy at the local level can be illustrated with the situation in Stockton, California, in the late 1960s and early 1970s (when I did my fieldwork there). Although the situation was changing because of new federal and state laws against employment discrimination and because of affirmative action, I recorded several events that showed that local blacks faced employment barriers in the past and that some of those barriers still remained (Ogbu, 1977, 1986). For example, between 1967 and 1973 blacks had to picket, boycott, and threaten several local business establishments before they were hired or received job promotions.

The job ceiling against blacks and similar minorities benefits employers and corporations economically, as can be seen in the case of AT&T. It also benefits white workers, especially white male workers: It gives even the less qualified whites access to better jobs, wages, and promotion opportunities which they might otherwise not have achieved if blacks and other minorities were permitted to compete for these jobs on the basis of training and ability. But the point I would like to stress here is that this unequal opportunity for rewards of literacy and education has probably worked to discourage blacks and similar minorities from developing the kinds of attitudes and behaviors that promote literacy and school success.

Schools' Contribution

Schools contribute to the problems of literacy among blacks and similar minorities because their actions often reflect society's view and treatment of the minorities. One gains a sense of how the public schools have contributed to the educational problems of blacks by reading historical accounts of black education in a particular American city, and from interviews with school officials and with blacks themselves in that city. Using information from such sources in my research in Stockton, California, I came to the conclusion that the education of blacks and similar minorities in Stockton was both segregated and inferior before the 1960s. In the 1960s Stockton schools seemed definitely to be making serious efforts to improve minority education. However, even in the late 1960s minority education was still segregated and inferior to some extent. Evidence for this comes from the replies made by the Superintendent of Schools to petitions presented to the Board of Education by representatives of the black and Mexican communities. The community groups sought changes in school curriculum, counseling, tracking, textbooks, teacher attitudes, and the like. In his replies, the superintendent seemed to admit that the differences and inadequacies mentioned in the petition indeed existed.

I will use the grading system in the elementary school I studied as an example of a specific mechanism by which Stockton schools, *without deliberately intending to do so,* discouraged literacy among blacks and Mexican American children who in the first grade in the 1964–65 school year received the letter grade of C for their academic work. In the 1968–69 school year these children were in the sixth grade and all but one of the 17 had continued to receive the letter grade of C every year. The one exception received a C+ to B− one year. This means that throughout their elementary school career and under several teachers, about 94% of these students maintained the same level of school performance. Yet, written comments by teachers suggest that some children were definitely doing better than C work and others doing worse.

There were several possible adverse consequences of this grading practice (or reward system) for the acquisition of literacy. One is that if the a minority children were not rewarded on the basis of their real performance, ability, or "progress", the grading system did not help them learn to associate doing well in school with making a greater effort in schoolwork. Another is that it did not seem to help the children develop proper work habits, good performance strategies, or pride in their academic achievement. Instead, the children "learned" to be content with an average grade of C, which got lower and lower as they progressed beyond elementary school (Ogbu, 1974, 1977).

I suggest that the reward system experienced by the children in school is a reflection of the reward system they would later experience as adults in the larger community. In that adult world, blacks and similar minorities were not, until recently, hired, paid, or promoted on the basis of education and ability. The schools were more or less preparing the children for a predictable future.

Black Contribution

The extent that minority children, as a group and as individuals, succeed or fail in school depends not only on how society and schools treat them but also on how they themselves perceive and respond to schooling. As noted earlier, different types of minorities perceive, interpret, and respond to the same societal and school treatments differently. In this section I will consider the perceptions, interpretations, and responses of black Americans as representative of one type of minority group which contribute to the problems of literacy and academic work.

1. Responses To Instrumental Barriers. One of the responses blacks have made to barriers against them in American economic, political, and social life is to evolve distinctive folk theories of getting ahead. Thus, although blacks like whites say that they desire education as a means to improve their social, political, and economic status, their operative folk theories of "making it" in America have apparently been different and have led them to develop strategies that are actually in competition with schooling. But it is not easy to discover what the operative folk theories are, because when blacks are asked direct questions about how they get ahead they tend to give the same answers that white Americans give, saying that they need good education to get ahead. Blacks in Stockton illustrated this when they responded to my research questions, saying that to get ahead a black Stocktonian "needs good education just like anyone else." Yet, as my research interviews with students, parents and other adults proceeded, they would indicate that they did not really have as much chance of getting ahead on the basis of education and ability as white Stocktonians. They also expressed this feeling of lack of equal opportunity in discussion of the problems faced by blacks when trying to get jobs, to get loans, to start businesses or to buy homes in predominantly white neighborhoods. And there is some objective evidence to support their claims of unequal opportunity, such as the finding by the County Planning Department in its comparative analysis of the relationship between median years of schooling completed and median family income for blacks and the general populations (mainly whites) in selected city census tracts. This study found that although in most of the census tracts analyzed, blacks have higher median years of schooling completed, they generally have lower median family income (San Joaquin County, 1973) than whites. Based on my ethnographic observation of their efforts to change the rules of school credentialing and of employment, as well as on my observation of the alternative survival strategies they used to increase the pool of jobs and other resources available to them during my research, I also concluded that Stockton blacks do not have equal opportunity to use and benefit from their literacy and education.

Not only do blacks not really believe that the rules for getting ahead that work for white Americans necessarily work for them in those domains controlled by whites, they also try to change those rules rather than conform to them. Attempts to change the rules for advancement in school and society can be seen in the attacks on criteria for school credentialing and for employment, as mentioned above. During my research in Stockton, blacks criticized these criteria on several occasions when there were public discussions of "tests" given in school and for employment purposes (Ogbu, 1977). Students, parents, and other blacks also criticized the tests during research interviews. On the whole, blacks appear to feel that the tests given in school and for employment purposes, whether given by whites or by their black representatives, are designed to keep them down, not to help them "make it".

In addition to trying to change the rules or criteria, blacks have developed several "survival strategies" to eliminate, lower, or circumvent the barriers they face in trying to get desirable jobs and to advance in other ways. One well known strategy is "collective struggle" or "civil rights activities." But collective struggle includes more than the activities which white Americans legitimate as civil rights. It includes rioting and other forms of collective action that promise to increase opportunities or the pool of resources available to blacks. Patron–client relationship or "Uncle Toming" is a survival strategy that was appparently common in the past. Other survival strategies are opting for sports, entertainment, hustling, and pimping.

While these instrumental responses affect the school performance of blacks, the situation is paradoxical. Blacks have historically demanded more and better education, and blacks continue to demand more and better education, as was the case in Stockton throughout my research there. And as I have already indicated, blacks assert that education is the means to improve their social and economic status. It was reported in Stockton that prior to my research in 1968 the people of the neighborhood I studied carried a coffin at one of their annual parades and on the coffin was written "A DROPOUT IS DEAD," to emphasize their belief in the importance of education. This, although their expectations about the benefits of education have historically not been met in terms of good employment opportunities.

One likely consequence of the failure to meet their expectations is that instead of individual blacks persevering for a good education, blacks tend to endorse collective action as offering the best chances for advancement. I suspect that this pooling of efforts may weaken realistic perceptions and sidetrack the pursuit of schooling as a strategy for self-advancement. Furthermore, collective struggle for employment, for better jobs, better education and better housing, such as occurred during my study in Stockton, may affect the extent to which *blacks as a minority community* sanction (as distinct from wishing) school success as a cultural goal, accept the schools' criteria for success, and sanction and implement the instrumental attitudes and behaviors that enhance academic success. Other survival strategies, such as patron–client relationship, hustling, sports, and so on become serious competitors with schooling as a strategy for making it. Another likely consequence is that these survival strategies may require and stimulate attitudes, skills, and behaviors that are not necessarily compatible with those required for academic success.

Going from community to the family level, it appears (from my research interviews in Stockton and from ethnographic observations) that parents very much want their children to get good education. At the same time, however, they do not seem to implement effectively appropriate instrumental attitudes and behaviors, including teaching their children the use of time and work habits that will help them do well in school. In addition, they seem to be teaching their children, *without knowing it,* contradictory or ambivalent attitudes about schooling. On the one hand, parents tell their children to get a good education and encourage them verbally to do well in school; those who can, help with homework. But on the other hand, *the actual texture* of these parents' lives in terms of low level jobs, underemployment, and unemployment also comes through strongly, reproducing a second kind of message powerful enough to undercut their exhortation. The result is that the children increasingly become disillusioned about their ability to succeed in adult life through the mainstream strategy of education, and become doubtful about the real value of schooling for themselves.

Turning to the students, judging from my observations both at school and at home and judging from what the children and their parents said at research interviews, it seems that they do not invest enough time and effort or persevere sufficiently in their schoolwork. I found in those interviews that the students, like their parents, say that they want education and that the school credential is important for anyone who wants to get mainstream jobs. But at the same time they do not match their wishes and aspirations with effort. That is, they do not put enough time, effort, and perseverance into their schoolwork. This is not because black students do not know what to do in order to do well in school, because they explained during research interviews that one of the reasons Chinese, Japanese, and some white students do well in school is that they expend more time and effort than do blacks in doing their schoolwork. Moreover, this lack of serious academic attitude and effort appears to increase as black students get older and apparently more aware that as members of a minority group they have limited future opportunities for getting good jobs as a result of their education. They also begin to learn about, and turn to, other ways of advancing, influenced by their observations of how older people in their community or neighborhood make it, and by the prevailing folk theories of success in their community. Accordingly, they increasingly divert their time and efforts away from schoolwork into nonacademic activities. In so doing, they further contribute to their low academic adaptation and problems of literacy.

One may gain some idea about the mindset of black youngsters in the inner city from Dearich Hunter's article "My Turn," in *Newsweek,* August 18, 1980. Hunter is a 15-year-old high school student from Wilmington, Delaware, who has also lived in Brooklyn. In the article, he describes several categories of inner-city Black teenagers. The "rocks" are the majority who have given up all hope of making it in the mainstream economy by means of school credentials. Consequently, they have stopped trying to do well in school. They do not bother to look for work, because not even their parents can find work. The "hard rocks," Hunter says, are "caught in the deadly, dead-end environment and can't see a way out, a life that becomes the fast life or incredibly boring—and death becomes the death that you see and get used to every day." The "ducks" are the few who still believe that they can make it by succeeding in school. The "ducks," unfortunately, often become the target of ridicule and rip-off by the "hard rocks." And a "hard rock" who tries to change, to become one of the "ducks," usually falls into the category of "junkies." For, often, those attempting to change find themselves abandoned and despised, eventually becoming drug addicts. Thus, we can see the job ceiling not only discourages blacks from developing a strong tradition of pursuit of literacy as a cultural norm, it also creates disillusionment that discourages black youths from maximizing their school efforts.

When survival strategies like collective struggle succeed in increasing the pool of jobs and other resources for the black community, they may encourage black youths to work hard in school. But such success can also lead the youths to blame "the system" and rationalize their lack of serious schoolwork efforts. Clientship or Uncle Toming is dysfunctional for the youths because it does not create good role models for school success through hard work. Clientship teaches black children manipulative knowledge, skills, and attitudes used by inner-city adults in dealing with white people and white institutions. In my research in Stockton, I found that many blacks, both adults and children, believed that most blacks who are successful had played the "Uncle Tom" game to achieve and maintain their positions (Ogbu, 1977).

Familiarity with other survival strategies, like hustling and pimping, has also some adverse effects on children's schoolwork. For one thing, in the norms that support these strategies, the work ethic is reversed by the insistence that one should make it without working, especially without "doing the white man's thing." Also, social interactions like those between teacher and students and among students in the classroom are seen as opportunities for exploitation, i.e., opportunities to gain prestige by putting the other person or persons down. This may lead to class disruptions and suspensions. Finally, the skills involved in hustling and similar activities, as noted before, may conflict with those required for completing schoolwork successfully.

2. Expressive Responses: Identity and Cultural Boundaries. The barriers and responses to the barriers described above are important reasons for the literacy problems encountered by black children and similar minorities. But they do not answer three related questions: (a) Why are some individual black children successful, although they also face a job ceiling and inferior education, although they too share the same status mobility system or folk theories of making it with other blacks? (Fordham, 1982); (b) Why do some minority groups who also face a job ceiling and other opportunity barriers, and who experience inferior education, do better in school and in literacy acquisition than blacks and other castelike minorities? (Ogbu, 1978); (c) Why are some minority groups doing well in school and in literacy acquisition, although they possess cultures or languages different from the culture and language of American public schools and of white Americans who control and teach in these schools (Ogbu & Matute-Bianchi, 1986)?

To answer these questions it is essential to recognize two factors which make the realtionship between blacks and whites in America qualitatively different from the relationship between immigrant minorities and white Americans. One is that the collective or social identity which blacks have evolved in the course of their history in America appears to be not simply different from, but rather in opposition to, the social identity of white Americans (Green, 1981). The other factor is that in some but not all domains, the cultural frame of reference of black Americans is in opposition to the cultural frame of reference of white Americans (Ogbu, 1982, 1984). The oppositional or ambivalent identity and the oppositional cultural frame of reference are *properties of blacks as a population or group* and, as already indicated, arose out of their collective experience in America. The social identity and cultural frame of reference are transmitted and acquired as other aspects of black identity and culture in the course of black children's upbringing. They do not influence the attitudes and behaviors of all black children and adults to the same degree.

I am indebted to Edward Spicer and his students and followers as well as to my colleague, George DeVos, for pointing out the nature of the opposition process in relationships between dominant groups and minority groups in traditional and modern urban industrial societies (Castile & Kushner, 1981; DeVos, 1967; Spicer, 1966, 1971). Through comparative and historical analysis, these scholars show that in both pre-industrial and modern urban industrial societies some populations become "persistent" or "enduring peoples" through mechanisms of opposition which maintain boundaries between the minorities and their adversaries. Furthermore, their studies suggest that the boundary-maintaining mechanisms can be studied ethnographically. And when the opposition process is carefully analyzed it is usually found that it has led to formation of a collective oppositional identity as well as to an oppositional cultural frame of reference. *In general, the opposition process creates a situation in which intercultural learning or crossing cultural/language boundaries becomes problematic.* I conclude from reviewing these studies that such a situation would adversely affect minority acquisition of literacy, especially when literacy or education is perceived by the minorities to be a part of the culture of their adversary or "oppressors." I have also concluded after studying the history of the relationship between blacks and whites in America that the same kind of situation has existed between blacks and whites (i.e., the relationship between blacks and whites has been characterized by both oppositional social identity and oppositional cultural frame of reference).

Oppositional Identity.   How and why did black oppositional identity arise? Blacks, like other involuntary or castelike minorities, developed their sense of collective identity or sense of peoplehood in opposition to white American social identity because of the way white Americans have treated them economically, politically, psychologically, and socially, including exclusion from true assimilation; it also emerged because blacks perceived and experienced the treatment by whites as collective and enduring oppression. Like other castelike minorities, blacks eventually came to realize and to believe that regardless of their place of origin (in Africa) or place of residence (in America), regardless of their individual ability and training, individual economic status or physical appearance, they could not expect to be treated exactly like white Americans, their "fellow citizens"; nor could they easily or freely escape from their more or less birth-ascribed membership in a subordinate and disparaged group (Green, 1981).

There are many incidents in black American history which illustrate the kind of collective treatment that led them to develop their collective oppositional or ambivalent identity. One example was the treatment of blacks after Nat Turner's "insurrection" in Southampton, Virginia, in 1831. Following that event, the geographical mobility of all black people was highly restricted throughout the country, as was their contact amongst themselves, regardless of their personal involvement in the matter (Fordham, 1984; Haley, 1976; Styron, 1966). In Washington, D.C., whites even excluded black children from attending Sunday school with white children, although black children in that city were not involved in the insurrection in Southampton,

Virginia; the black children in Washington, D.C., were excluded simply because they were black. All black people were thus judged responsible for Nat Turner's behavior and somehow punished for it (Fordham, 1984).

Another illustrative incident occurred long after blacks were emancipated from slavery, in January 1923, to be precise. This incident was reported by the CBS television magazine, "60 Minutes," on August 5, 1984. It began with an allegation that a black man had raped a white woman in Rosewood, Florida, a town of some 200 people. The accused black man was not brought to court trial. Instead, some 1,500 white men from the surrounding communities went to Rosewood the night of the alleged rape, and "in retaliation," on the following day killed about 40 black men, women, and children. Here again, all black people were made responsible for the alleged offense of one black person.

It was through countless incidents of this nature, throughout their history, that black Americans developed their sense of peoplehood (or their social identity system) which they perceive not merely as different from white Americans' social identity but in many respects in opposition to it (i.e, as in opposition to the social identity of their white oppressors). Events which reinforce this oppositional identity have continued, although their specific forms have changed (Spicer, 1971).

The oppositional identity was also generated and reinforced by black people's knowledge that the door of true assimilation into the mainstream is not as open to them as it is to white ethnic immigrants; that they do not have a homeland to return to like some non-white immigrant minorities; and that their "oppression" and inferior status are not due to something inherently wrong with them. They know also that individual blacks who try to "pass" often encounter or suffer discouraging social and psychological costs. For these reasons blacks, like other castelike minorities, responded with what DeVos (1967) calls "an ethnic consolidation," i.e., a collective sense of peoplehood (see also Castile & Kushner, 1981; Green, 1981; Spicer, 1966, 1971).

Oppositional Cultural Frame of Reference.   Along with the formation of an oppositional identity, blacks also developed an oppositional cultural frame of reference which includes devices for protecting their identity and for maintaining boundaries between them and white Americans. The oppositional cultural frame of reference includes "cultural inversion" (Holt, 1972) which in the present context has two meanings. In one sense, the broader sense, it means the various ways that black Americans express their opposition to white Americans. In a narrower sense, cultural inversion refers to specific forms of behavior, specific events, symbols, and meanings which blacks regard as not appropriate for themselves because they are characteristic of white Americans. At the same time, blacks emphasize other forms of behavior—other events, symbols, and meanings—as more appropriate for themselves because these are not a part of the white American way of life or culture. That is, what blacks consider appropriate or even legitimate for themselves in terms of attitudes, beliefs, preferences, behaviors or practices are sometimes defined in opposition to the attitudes, beliefs, perferences, behaviors or practices of white Americans.

The point I want to emphasize is that cultural inversion in the broad or narrow sense results, from the point of view of black people, in a coexistence of two opposing cultural frames of reference guiding behaviors. One cultural frame of reference is appropriate for whites; the other is appropriate for blacks. As in the case of similar minorites, black people's cultural frame of reference is emotionally charged because it is intimately bound up with their sense of social identity and security. Therefore, individual blacks who try to behave like whites (i.e., those who try to "cross cultural boundaries," in forbidden domains), face opposition from other blacks. Their behaviors tend to be interpreted not only as "acting white" but also as a betrayal of black people, as "trying to join the enemy." The individual blacks trying to cross cultural boundaries or pass may also experience internal stress or what DeVos (1967), calls "affective dissonance," partly because their sense of social identity may lead them to feel that they are, indeed, abandoning or betraying their people; and partly because such individuals are often uncertain that they would be accepted by white people even if they succeed in learning to "act white."

The opposition process, in terms of identity and cultural frame of reference, distinguishes the responses to schooling and literacy of blacks and similar minorities from the responses of immigrant minorities, and from the responses of people from the oral cultures of small-scale societies. It is also the opposition process which appears to account for the fact that the elimination of instrumental barriers like job ceiling does not necessarily lead to immediate disappearance of the difficulties encountered by castelike minorities with respect to literacy and academic performance. The problems created by the oppositional identity and cultural frame of reference may persist after the barriers in economic and other domains have been removed *because* reformers and policymakers are not usually aware of them and do not, as a rule, address them in policies and programs designed to help the minorities. Nor do the minorities demanding changes recognize them; in fact, minority spokespersons are likely to resist an analysis pointing to the identity and cultural frame factors.

How, exactly, do the oppositional identity and cultural frame of reference enter into the process of education and the acquisition of literacy? They enter into the process of schooling through the perceptions and definitions of school learning by blacks and similar minorities as learning white American culture and as "acting white." That is, school learning is viewed consciously or unconsciously as the learning of white people's culture that eventually leads to identification with white people, both actions further interpreted as abandoning black cultural frame of reference and loss of black identity. In other words, adopting attitudes and behaviors that lead to successful acquisition of literacy or academic work is defined consciously or unconsciously as a one-way or linear acculturation. Thus, although blacks and similar minorities say, like white Americans and immigrant minorities, that they want education or literacy, they simultaneously assume and fear that by adopting attitudes and behaviors typical of whites who are successful in school they would be giving up a part of their own identity, culture, and language. In summary, castelike minorities appear to think that following rules and standard practices of the schools that eventually lead to academic success is "acting white" and rejecting minority identity and culture. Some blacks, of course, elect to "act white" and thereby do well in school but the social and psychological costs are often high.

Up to this point I have mainly discussed the historical and collective aspects of the twin issues of identity and cultural frame. Now I want to talk about how they become a part of the history, knowledge and identity of individual black students and how they influence the individual students' acquisition of literacy and schooling. To begin with, black children of all social classes and all regions learn from their parents and other socialization agents, in varying degrees, black people's interpretations of their experiences in America, and black people's collective sense of peoplehood or social identity vis-a-vis white American social identity. The children also learn black people's cultural frame of reference. Black children's sense of social identity increases as they get older, especially as they approach adolescence. Furthermore, the children increasingly acquire knowledge of and competence to participate in the distinctive black cultural frame of reference, as well as an understanding of appropriate emotional or affective response states.

It is possible that the influence of oppositional identity and cultural frame of reference begins at an earlier age, but thus far research evidence has been found among children approaching adolescence and among adolescents. Studies by Erickson and Mohatt (1982) among Odawa Indian students and by Philips (1983) among Warm Springs Reservation Indian students suggest that older elementary school students are already influenced by the twin phenomena. These children come to class "resisting" school rules and standard practices of the classroom. That is, they enter the classroom with a sort of cultural convention which dictates that they should not adopt the classroom rules of behavior and standard practices expected of children in the public schools and presented by the white teacher in charge.

Studies among black adolescents reveal that they tend to define academic tasks or behaviors and academic success as "white", "not black" (i.e., as not appropriate for blacks). On the other hand, they define certain extracurricular activities traditionally open to minorities, and where black students excel, as appropriate for blacks. Strong peer pressures are applied to black students who try to excel in academic work or who become involved in "white" extracurricular activities. Such students are called "Uncle Toms" (Petroni, 1970), "crazy," and "brainiacs" (Fordham, 1985).

Petroni's study (1970) provides a good example of the difficulty created by this situation for bright black students. Initially black students in the high school told this researcher that they were excluded from certain courses and extracurricular activities by "white racism." But later Petroni found that black students stayed away from these courses and activities in part because of pressures from fellow black students; furthermore, blacks who participated in the so-called "white activities" like student government, madrigals, senior play, and the like, were called "Uncle Toms" and rejected by other black students. The following interview excerpt shows the dilemma of one black male student who had all A's in his courses:

> Well, I participate in speech. I'm the only Negro in the whole group. I find it kind of interesting that I'm the only Negro. I'm always contrasted in pictures of the group. The Negroes accuse me of thinking I'm white. In the bathroom one day, some Negroes wrote in big letters, "B.B. is an Uncle Tom." It's this kind of pressures from other Negro kids which bothers me most.

On the other hand, black students who excel in nonacademic activities, or "black things," like sports, were highly praised. Petroni suggests that the fear of being called "Uncle Toms" or being accused of "acting white" may prevent black students from working hard to do well in school.

The dilemma of a black student, then, is that he or she has to choose between "acting black" or "acting white" (i.e., adopting appropriate attitudes and behaviors that other black students consider appropriate for blacks but are not necessarily conducive to school success). Thus, unlike immigrant minority students, black students and similar minorities are not able or are not willing to distinguish between attitudes and behaviors that result in academic success and school credentials for future employment and attitudes and behaviors that may result in linear acculturation or replacement of their cultural identity with that of white Americans.

The phenomenon of opposition process may also partially explain differences in academic performance among castelike minority students themselves. Fordham (personal communication) has suggested, on the basis of her study of high school students in Washington, D.C., that black students vary in their degree of encapsulation or involvement in the opposition process. Students who are very much encapsulated tend to experience greater difficulty crossing cultural boundaries and are usually poor students. Those who are marginal to the process find it easier to cross cultural and language boundaries and are, therefore, more successful academically. However, such students may pay a high price in terms of isolation and peer criticism. In between are students who utilize a number of strategies to camouflage their academic striving and success. The camouflage (e.g., clowning) may result in less schoolwork effort, and thereby in lowering the students' grades. Some good students acquire protectors in the person of "bullies" and "hoodlums" whom they assist with their schoolwork and homework in exchange for protection. In any case, good students must be careful not to brag about their school success or otherwise bring too much attention to themselves (Fordham, 1985).

Conflict and Distrust.   The last response of blacks which I will discuss is the development of deep distrust toward white Americans and the institutions they control, such as the schools. Throughout their history there have been many episodes which have left blacks with the feeling that white people and the institutions they control cannot be trusted. Public schools, particularly in the inner city, are generally not trusted to provide black children with the "right education." This distrust arises partly from perceptions of past and current treatment of blacks by the schools as discriminatory. This discriminatory treatment has been documented in several studies throughout the United States (Bond, 1966, 1969; Kluger, 1977; Ogbu, 1978; Weinberg, 1977).

For over a century, blacks have "fought" against total exclusion from the public schools and have been "fighting" against inferior education in segregated and integrated schools. In the totally segregated Southern school systems, blacks identified strongly and cooperated with "black schools." But the positive influence of this identification and cooperation was undermined by their simultaneous rejection of the same schools as inferior to white schools and by their continued struggle for school desegregation. In other words, blacks were diverted from striving for achievement in black schools to the "collective struggle" for equal resources in desegregated schools.

But in desegregated schools throughout the United States, blacks still express dissatisfaction and distrust because they perceive inferior education as being perpetuated through many subtle devices like "biased testing," misclassification, tracking, biased textbooks, biased and inadequate counseling, and so on, and because blacks doubt that the public schools understand their children or their educational needs. This is particularly true in the case of black male students. Black Americans tend to attribute the low school performance of black males to the schools' inability to "relate to black males in ways that will help them learn" (Scherer & Slawski, 1978).

Elsewhere (Ogbu, 1985a, 1985b) I have illustrated this phenomenon of distrust and have suggested how it might interfere with black children's learning. During my fieldwork in Stockton, California, I recorded several instances of conflict between blacks and the schools. The conflicts occurred at Board of Education meetings, public hearings on school desegregation, meetings with particular school officials, and at particular school sites where blacks demanded "better education" or "equal education." In my interviews, the blacks generally expressed dissatisfaction with their children's education, from preschool through high school. They seemed to believe that white children were given superior education while black children received inferior education. In one interview a parent claimed that white children learn to read well in the early grades because they are taught their alphabet, their numbers and to read and write their names at preschool. In contrast, according to this parent, preschool programs for black children focus on teaching them how to get along with one another. This parent was not only expressing her personal views, she was voicing the common belief in her community about the discrepancies in the education of black and white children. She was also discussing the discrepancies in the presence of her children, as many other parents do. So, the children grow up believing that there are discrepancies in the education of local blacks and whites. And they learn to distrust the schools and white people who control them.

Furthermore, because white people are not trusted, and because the knowledge that schools teach is regarded as white people's knowledge (Weis, 1985) blacks tend to be skeptical about the information they learn. My ethnographic research in Stockton provides several examples of occasions where this skepticism was expressed. One occasion involved an incident at a public meeting after a riot in a predominantly minority high school in 1969. The hero of the occasion was a black youth who had been in and out of jail several times. Holding a high school history textbook called *The Land Of The Free,* and strolling from one end of the platform to the other, he repeatedly asked the teachers if, while teaching their classes, they ever stopped for a moment to ask whether the title of this textbook has the same meaning for blacks, Indians, and Mexican Americans that it has for whites. And each time he asked the question he was cheered by black students and parents as well as by other minorities present.

The following excerpt from an interview with a student and his parent is another good illustration of the skepticism toward school knowledge.

Mother:	Them books. Them books. Them lily white books. (Laughter). Them lilly white books. Change them books. Do you know, let me tell you, John. Do you know what? You can go, say, the last year, two years you can go, to town, to J.C. Penney's, and so on and you can see black statues in the windows. Show me a book that you can pick up (in school) and say it is about black people.
Anthropologist:	Well, you can come to George Washington School and I will show you many of them.
Mother:	Yea, but that's just—were they there last year?

Anthropologist:	I don't know but at least we are getting them now. We are getting them now in school.
Mother:	But you asked me what you can do to change?
Anthropologist:	Yea.
Mother:	But do every classroom have black books? You can read that Cortez conquered—whatever Cortez conquered. You can read about that but you can never read nowhere where black man conquered nothing. You know that's a lie. You know, you know they even told me Tarzan was black and do you know that I was grown with 7 kids before I ever learned that Tarzan was black? He was raised and born in Africa.
Anthropologist:	Really?
Mother:	And when you look on television what do you see? Black Tarzan swinging on the tree?
Son:	I had a good point a while ago—
Mother:	But this is true. You don't see black something. But you see, they have, they got it (i.e., the books) now. But last year they didn't have them.
Son:	This is what it is.
Mother:	You got your point?
Son:	No. This is not the point. *Now, the white man, like I say, will not teach you something where he will hurt himself. He is not going to do this. And he is not going to fully teach you. I mean—they might bring out a book that will tell you something about black history but then he's going to kind of mix it up and make it sound as though the white man was good. Like they always said, it was a white man that was there when a black man invented something, see? First, they said the white man invented something but it was the black man that was with him. But now they sort of change it saying the black man invented it but it was the white man that helped him. See? It changed, so that the white man always helped him. See? The white man always won.*
Mother:	*Like the black man never do nothing for himself.*
Son:	*That's it.*
Anthropologist:	You know, as you go higher in your education you will find that there are some books written by black people and that they didn't change things the way you have been pointing out.
Mother:	But wait, John, let me ask you something: Is it better for him (points to her son) to learn when he goes to college or learn before ever, before he flips off the ground? Why hang yourself before you know that if you kick long enough you're going to hang yourself? Why don't they reverse it? If they reverse it and let them (i.e., black children) know while they are in grammar school about the black people? Why does he have to go to college to learn about his own culture?
Son:	Why should I go to college to learn about my own culture? Yea!
Mother:	He's bitter about the time he gets to college. He's a militant by the time he gets to college.

Son:	Why did they keep, like I say, they kept you down for so long?
Mother:	That is why we don't have many more blacks and Mexican Americans going to college. Because by the time they make it to college they're so fed up and so, they've been kicked so long that by this time they say, "forget it." They don't have patient to fight, some of them. They don't have much face to fight harder.
Anthropologist:	The Mexican Americans?
Mother:	The blacks.—I am more concerned about the blacks. This is what I am saying about blacks. The Mexican Americans have got somewhere. They read about themselves, not everyday. But every now and then they read about what Mexicans did. They're going to read he fought some Indians somewhere, you know. He'd going to read every now and then. But the black, he never did read something. Just like they say (that) Columbus discovered America. He didn't. The black man did. He had nothing to do with it.
Son:	Hey! Wait a minute. (He mentioned some other discovery which he claimed wasn't made by the white man, but it was mostly unclear.)
Mother:	No. They just accidently stumbled upon it.
Son:	America was already here, it was already occupied by the Indians. How are they going to discover it?
Anthropologist:	Well, it is the same way they claimed to have discovered Africa. We were there all the time, you know.
Son:	How are they going to discover something?
Mother:	You see what I am saying is that they said that they discovered it while nobody discovered it but them before the Indians got here. But still they say the white man did it. Columbus did it but all the books that I have, I was grown before I found out that it wasn't; it was a black man and he looked through that thing and they accidentally went into the place they called America while they were going somewhere else.
Son:	*Have you ever noticed this, that when a black man wants something he asked a white man and the white man says no, he (the black man) can't have it at the time. But then when the white man say, "This is what the black people need," he give it to him. But then, when a black person asks for something that he wants they don't want to give it to him. Have you noticed that?*

To complicate matters, the conflicts between the schools and blacks often force the schools to approach black education defensively—through control, paternalism, or "contest"—strategies which divert attention from the real task of educating the children. Another consequence of the type of relationship between blacks and the schools, characterized as it is by conflicts, distrust and skepticism, is that blacks and whites tend to interpret school requirements differently. Thus, white middle class parents and their children may see completion of a given school task or conformity to school standard practices as necessary, desirable, and compatible with their educational goals. Inner-city black parents and their children may interpret the same requirements as deception or as an unnecessary imposition that does not meet their "real educational needs." I would suggest that under these circumstances it is difficult for black children, especially as they get older, to accept and follow school rules and to persevere at their academic tasks.

SUMMARY AND IMPLICATIONS

I have argued in this chapter that the difficulties encountered by black children and similar minorities in learning literacy and in academic striving are not merely due to the fact that they come from oral cultures or residual oral cultures. Nor are the difficulties merely due to the fact that the children come from cultures with differences in cognitive, communicative, or interactional style.

A comparative study of the academic attitudes and behaviors of different types of minority students and of children from small-scale societies attending Western-type schools suggests that black Americans belong to a particular type of minorities, castelike minorities, whose difficulties in school are distinctive in many respects. For this reason it has been necessary to go beyond identification of cultural, language, and other conflicts, and the search for "solutions" for those conflicts in the education of these minority children. The next important task has been to try to understand the reasons for the distinctive problems of the castelike minorities, especially their disproportionate and persistent low school performance, including low success in learning to read. This is what this chapter has been about: to explain why learning and teaching difficulties and the cultural and language differences that create them appear to persist among castelike minorities. One explanation that is emerging from the comparative research presented in the present chapter certainly implicates the treatment of the minorities by both society at large and the schools; but it also implicates the kind of responses that the minorities themselves have developed.

What are the policy and practical implications of the analysis presented in this chapter? The analysis suggests several things that can be done to enhance the acquisition of literacy and school success among castelike minorities. First, the job ceiling and related barriers should be eliminated and opportunity for gainful employment improved for minority adults and youths. These changes should improve the perceptions and response of minority youths to schooling. Second, both the gross and subtle mechanisms that now differentiate the schooling of minorities from the schooling of whites should be eliminated where they exist. Third, the "adaptive" responses that the minorities have developed which now appear to adversely influence their schooling should be recognized and taken into account in policies and programs designed to improve their school performance. Similarly, distrust and skepticism which also appear to adversely influence the minorities' responses to schooling should be recognized and taken into account in policies and programs designed to improve their education.

The unique problems created by the process of opposition or ambivalence in identity and cultural frame of reference need to be addressed both from within the schools and from within the minority community. School personnel need to understand how castelike minority children's sense of social identity and and cultural frame of reference influence their school attitudes and behaviors. If school personnel understand this, then they will be in a better position to design effective programs and find ways to help children avoid equating academic success with linear acculturation or "assimilation." The children will then be able to adopt appropriate academic attitudes and behaviors that will help them succeed.

The minority community can play an important part in helping the children make the distinction between attitudes and behaviors that lead to academic success and attitudes and behaviors that lead to loss of ethnic identity or to linear acculturation. Furthermore, just as society can help reorient minority youths into more academic striving by eliminating the job ceiling and providing more and better employment opportunities, so also the minority community can help divert the time and effort of minority children into a more academic world. One example of how the minority community can do this is to provide the youths with sufficient concrete evidence that the minority community appreciates and honors academic success as much as it honors success in sports and athletics.

REFERENCES

Bond, H.M. (1969). *The education of the Negro in the American social order.* New York: Octagon.

Bond, H.M. (1969). *Negro education in Alabama: A study in cotton and steel.* New York: Atheneum.

Boykin, A.W. (1980, November). *Reading achievement and the social/cultural frame of reference of Afro American children.* Paper presented at NIE Roundtable Discussion on Issues in Urban Reading, Washington, D.C.

Bryce-LaPorte, R.E. (Ed.). (1980). *Sourcebook on the new immigration: Implications for the United States and the international community.* New Brunswick, NH: Transaction Book.

Bullock, H.A. (1970). *A history of Negro education in the South: From 1619 to the present.* New York: Praeger.

Castile, G.P. & Kushner, G. (Eds.). (1981). *Persistent peoples: Cultural enclaves in perspective.* Tuscon: University of Arizona Press.

Castle, S. & Kosack, G. (1973). *Immigrant workers and class structure in Western Europe.* New York: Oxford University Press.

CBS Television Network. (1984). Transcript of "The Rosewood Massacre." *60 Minutes, xvi* (47):16–22

Cook-Gumperz, J. & Gumperz, J.J. (1979). From oral to written culture: The transition to literacy. In M.F. Whiteman (Ed.): *Variation in writing*. Hillsdale, NJ: Erlbaum.

Cressey, D. (1980). *Literacy and the social order: Reading and writing in Tudor and Stuart England*. Cambridge, MA: Cambridge University Press.

DeVos, G.A. (1967). Essential elements of caste: Psychological determinants in structural theory. In G.A. DeVos & H. Wagatsuma: *Japan's invisible race: Caste in culture and personality* (pp. 332-384). Berkeley: University of California Press.

DeWare, H. (1978, July 4). Affirmative action plan at AT&T is permitted. *Washington Post*, pp. A1, A7.

Erickson, F. & Mohatt, J. (1982). Cultural organization of participant structure in two classrooms of Indian students. In G.D. Spindler (Ed.) *Doing the ethonography of schooling: Educational anthropoligy in action* (pp. 132-175). New York: Holt.

Feagans, L. & Farran, D.C. (Eds.). (1981). *The language of children reared in poverty: Implications for evaluation and intervention*. New York: Academic Press.

Fordham, S. (1984). *Cultural inversion and black children's school performance*. Unpublished manuscript, University of the District of Columbia, Washington, DC.

Fordham, S. (1985). *Black students' school success: Coping with the "burden of 'acting white.'"* Unpublished manuscript, University of the District of Columbia, Washington, DC.

Fordham, S. (1984). *Afro-Caribbean and Native Black American School Performance in Washington, DC: Learning To Be Or Not To Be A Native*. Unpublished Manuscript, University of the District of Columbia, Washington, DC.

Freed, R.S. & Freed, S.A. (1981). *Enculturation and education in Shanti Nagar*. New York: American Museum of Natural History Press.

Gay, J. & Cole, M. (1967). *the new mathematics and old culture*. New York: Holt.

Gibson, M.A. (1983). *Home-school-community linkages: A study of educational equity for Punjabi youths*. (Final Report). Washington, DC: National Institute of Education.

Green, V. (1981). Blacks in the United States: The creation of an enduring people? In G.P. Castile & G. Kushner (Eds.). *Persistent peoples: Cultural enclaves in perspective* (pp. 69-77). Tuscon: University of Arizona Press.

Gumperz, J.J. (1981). Conversational inferences and classroom learning. In J. Green & C. Wallat (Eds.), *Ethonographic approaches to face-to-face interaction*. Norwood, NJ: Ablex.

Haley, A. (1976). *Roots: The saga of an American family*. Garden City, NY: Doubleday.

Heyneman, S.P. (1979). Why impoverished children do well in Ugandan schools. *Comparative Education Review*, 15 (2), 175-185.

Holt, G.S. (1972). Stylin' otta the black pulput. In T. Kochman, (Ed.), *Rappin' and stylin' out: Communication in urban black America*. (pp. 189-204) Chicago: University of Illinois Press.

Hunter, D. (1980, August 18). Ducks vs. hard rocks. *Newsweek*, pp. 14-15.

Ito, H. (1967). Japan's outcasts in the United States. In G.A. de Vos & H. Wagatsuma (Eds.), *Japan's invisible race: Caste in culture and personality* (pp. 200-221) Berkeley: University of California Press.

Kluger, R. (1977). *Simple justice*. New York: Vintage.

Kochman, R. (1982). *Black and white styles in conflict*. Chicago: University of Chicago Press.

Lancey, D.F. (1983). *Cross-cultural studies in cognition and mathematics*. New York: Academic Press.

LeVine, R.A. (1967). *Dreams and deeds: Achievement motivation in Nigeria*. Chicago: University of Chicago Press.

Organization for Economic Co-operation and Development (1983): The Education of Minority Groups: An Enquiry into problems and practices. Paris: Centre for Educational Research and Innovation.

Ogbu, J.U. (1974). *The next generation: An ethnography of education in an urban neighborhood.* New York: Academic Press.

Ogbu, J.U. (1977). Racial stratification and education: The case of Stockton, California. *ICRD Bulletin, 12,* (3), 1–26.

Ogbu, J. (1978). *Minority education and caste: The American system in cross-cultural perspective.* New York: Academic Press.

Ogbu, J.U. (1981). Societal forces as a context of ghetto children's school failure. In L. Feagans & D.C. Farran (Eds.), *The language of children reared in poverty: Implications for evaluation and intervention.* (pp. 117–138) New York: Academic Press.

Ogbu, J.U. (1982). Cultural discontinuities and schooling. *Anthropology and Education Quarterly. 13* (4), 290–307.

Ogbu, J.U. (1983a). Literacy and schooling in subordinate cultures: The case of black Americans. In D.P. Resinick (Ed.), *Literacy in historical perspective* (pp. 129–153) Washington, DC: Library of Congress.

Ogbu, J.U. (1983b). Minority status and schooling in plural societies. *Comparative Education Review, 27* (2), 168–190.

Ogbu, J.U. (1984). *Understanding community forces affecting minority students; academic effort.* Unpublished manuscript, The Achievement Council of California, Oakland.

Ogbu, J.U. (1985a). Cultural-ecological influences on minority school learning. *Language Arts, 62* (8), 860–869.

Ogbu, J.U. (1985b). *Educational preparation of minority youths for labor force, Stockton, California: A report to California Policy Seminar.* Unpublished manuscript.

Ogbu, J.U. (1986). Stockton, California, revisited: Joining the labor force. In K. & J. Reisman (Eds.), *Becoming a worker* (pp. 29–65). Norwood, NJ: Ablex.

Ogbu, J.U. & Matute-Bianchi, M.E. (1986). Understanding sociocultural factors in education: Knowledge, identity, and adjustment. In D. Holt, (Ed.): *Beyond language: Social and language factors in schooling and language minorities.* Los Angeles: Evaluation, Dissemination and Assessment Center, California State University, Los Angeles.

Philips. S.U. (1976). Commentary: Access to Power and Maintenance of Ethnic Identity as Goals of Multi-Cultural Education. In M.A. Gibson (Ed.), *Anthropological Perspectives on Multicultural Education. Anthropology and Education Quarterly,* Special Issue, *7(4)*30–32.

Philips, S.U. (1983). *The invisible culture: communication in classroom and community on the Warm Springs Indian Reservation.* New York: Longman.

Petroni, F.A. (1970). Uncle toms: White stereotypes in the black movement. *Human Organization, 29* (4), 260–266.

Ramirez, M. & Castenada, A. (1974). *Cultural democracy, bicognitive development and education.* New York: Academic Press.

Rist, R. (1979). On the education of guest-worker children in Germany: Public policies and equal educational opportunity. *Comparative Education Review, 23,* (3), 355–369.

San Joaquin County. (1973). *Median family income, 1970: By race and census tract.* Stockton, CA: Department of County Planning.

Scherer, J. & Slawski, E.J. (1978). *Hard walls—soft walls: The social ecology of an urban desegregated high school* (Final Report of Field Research in Urban Desegregated Schools). Washington, DC: National Institute of Education.

Scribner, S. & Cole, M. (1973). Cognitive consequences of formal and informal education. *Science, 182,* 553–559.

Shade, B.J. (1982). *Afro-American patterns of cognition.* Unpublished manuscript, Wisconsin Center for Educational Research, University of Wisconsin at Madison.

Simons, H. (1979). Black dialect, reading interference, and classroom interaction. In L.B. Resnick & P.A. Weaver (Eds.), *Theory and practice of early reading* (Vol. 3), pp. 111–129). Hillsdale, NJ: Erlbaum.

Spicer, E.H. (1966). The process of cultural enclavement in middle America. *36th Congress of International de Americanistas, Serville, 3,* 267–279.

Spicer, E.H. (1971). Persistent cultural systems: A comparative study of identity systems that can adapt to contrasting environments. *Science, 174,* 795–900.

Stockton Unified School District (SUSD). (1969). *Board of Education minutes.* Unpublished manuscript, Office of the Superintendant, Stockton, CA.

Styron, W. (1966). *The confessions of Nat Turner.* New York: Random House.

Suarez-Orozco, M.M. (1986). *In pursuit of a dream: New HIspanic immigrants in American schools.* Unpublished doctoral dissertation, Department of Anthropology, University of California, Berkeley.

Sung, G.L. (1967). *Mountain of gold: The story of the Chinese in America.* New York: Macmillan.

Sung, G.L. (1971). *The story of the Chinese in America.* New York; Collier.

Weinberg, M. (1977). *A chance to learn: A history of race and education in the United States.* New York: Cambridge University Press.

Weis, L. (1985). *Between two worlds: Black students in an urban community college.* Boston: Routledge and Kegan Paul.

Williams, F. (Ed.), (1970). *Language and poverty: Perspectives on theme.* Chicago: Markham.

Chapter Nine
A Socio-Historical Approach to Literacy Development: A Comparative Case Study from the Pacific

THOM HUEBNER
Stanford University

Third World countries, as well as countries with highly developed technologies and linguistically heterogeneous populations, are increasingly focusing on literacy issues, with campaigns to increase reading and writing abilities of children. However, the course of literacy development differs from one locality to another, as does its effects. When, as is most often the case during these last years of the twentieth century, the motivation for the acquisition of literacy is access to more highly developed technologies, the introduction or promotion of reading and writing skills is often complicated by the presence of two languages, the vernacular and the language of wider communication, through which the more developed technology is accessible. This forces difficult decisions about whether, when and how best to introduce literacy in each code. At stake are the optimal access to technology on the one hand, and the maintenance of linguistic and cultural traditions on the other.

Since responsibility for the teaching of literacy is most often assumed by schools of one kind or another (Gardner, 1983), language policy and planning decisions overlap to a considerable degree with educational policy and planning decisions. It is the assumption of sociolinguists concerned with the relationship of linguistic phenomena such as societal bilingualism, literacy, language loss and language spread to political, economic, social and cultural factors comprising the context for these phenomena that historical, comparative case studies can reveal patterns to these relationships which will inform contemporary language planning and policy making. At the same time, case studies are a prerequisite to the formulation of typologies and a litmus test of proposed universals which will form the basis for a sociolinguistic theory of literacy.

This chapter employs a comparative case study approach, examining the socio-historical contexts in two societies as they undergo the transition from traditional preliterate learning, through traditional religious learning involving vernacular reading and writing, to secular technological learning through a language of wider communication (Gardner, 1983). The two cases, Hawaii and Samoa, viewed together make an interesting comparison, since many facets of the socio-historical contexts are parallel. The short term outcomes of the introduction of literacy in the two situations are also comparable. The long term effects of the introduction of literacy, however, are quite different in the two situations and can be seen as resulting from differences identified in the socio-historical context.

Vernacular literacy was introduced in Hawaii and Samoa, at the time two preliterate Polynesian cultures, within a decade of each other in the early part of the 19th century by Protestant missionaries. In both cases, the introduction of vernacular literacy was initially very successful, with universal literacy reported in both island groups by the middle of the century. During the latter half of the nineteenth century, however, both Hawaiian literacy skill and the use of Hawaiian as a spoken language were lost to an immigrant language prior to the colonization of that society. In Samoa, on the other hand, the spoken and written use of indigenous language remained widespread through the period of Western colonization, well into the twentieth century.

Examination of the differences in demographics such as the relative sizes of the indigenous and immigrant populations, degree of economic development, and the types of political structures in place at the time of introduction of traditional religious schooling and native language literacy, provide insight into the effects of the socio-historical context on issues of language maintenance and language shift. The comparison calls into question some factors which have been identified as prerequisites for the introduction of vernacular literacy. It suggests that the types of knowledge valued in preliterate society and types of literacy introduced may influence the degree of success of the introduction of that skill. It also suggests what while strong, locally controlled educational institutions supporting vernacular literacy may be a necessary condition for its maintenance, the strength of and control over those institutions is often a function of changing social, political and economic conditions.

LITERACY FROM A SOCIO-HISTORICAL PERSPECTIVE

From a historical perspective, a distinction has often been made between pre- or nonliterate and literate societies. The work of Scribner and Cole (1981) demonstrates that there are several kinds of literacy and that each entails a set of specific cognitive skills. Ethnographic work on the development of literacy in a variety of cultures (Scollon & Scollon, 1981; Heath, 1983) suggests that just as there are many kinds of literacy, there are also many kinds of preliteracy, each drawing on different sets of skills. Gardner, in his theory of multiple intelligences (1983), maintains that members of various preliterate as well as literate societies excel in aspects of linguistic competence which are essential for the roles they perform in that society and to which they are socialized through various educational processes. One might conclude that in moving from a preliterate to a literate state, societies will experience varying degrees of success depending on the degree of congruence between skills emphasized, taught and valued in the preliterate society and those needed for the kinds of literacy introduced.

In examining the transition from preliterate to literate society, one must distinguish, at the broadest level, between initial literacy in the mother tongue and initial literacy in another language. Among those conditions necessary for the successful introduction of vernacular literacy, Spolsky, Engelbrecht, Guillermino, and Ortz (1983) list the perceived utility of literacy by traditionally influential members of the community and the establishment of native functions for literacy. It is the functions of literacy which determine the skills employed and developed through literacy in the mother tongue.

The development of literacy in a language other than the mother tongue may occur subsequent to or along with, as well as without any prior or simultaneous, vernacular literacy development. The introduction of literacy in an additional language other than the mother tongue often accompanies a shift in education from one type to another (Gardner, 1983). For example, the acquisition of literacy necessary to read and write sacred texts in Koranic schools in Iran or Christian schools in medieval Europe entailed languages other than the vernacular. Likewise, the medium of secular technological instruction is often a language other than the mother tongue. This additional language (Fishman, Cooper & Rosenbaum, 1977) is learned in order to expand the communication networks of individuals within a society to include the worlds of science and technology.

These changes in patterns of language use may result in language shift, or "the gradual displacement of one language by another in the lives of the community members" (Dorian, 1982, p. 44), either partially or completely. Complete societal language shift results in an additional language becoming the mother tongue of community members. A partial language shift may be manifested in the displacement of one language by another for specific functions. Partial language shift sometimes is accompanied by lanaguage skill attrition, the loss of proficiency in one or more of the language skills: writing, reading, speaking, or understanding (Oxford, 1982: p. 120). Before a language can spread as the mother tongue of members of the society, it must spread as an additional language within the society (Fishman et al., 1977, p. 78). Language shift can occur rapidly, sometimes within a generation (Hinojosa, 1980).

THE PRELITERATE CONTEXT FOR THE INTRODUCTION OF VERNACULAR LITERACY

When the missionaries arrived in Polynesia, they found cultures organized around villages, which were sustained through farming, supplemented by hunting and fishing.

Traditional Polynesian educatin involved the enculturation of the young into the roles of society and the cultural values, knowledge and skills entailed in those roles. One historian observes that many of the local inhabitants had been

> trained in schools or under the directions of selected teachers. The young man who was to be a chief or leader studied astronomy, law, geography, and particularly history and language. Besides his regular studies, he must be trained as a warrior and a speaker and taught to read the meaning of the habits of the fish, the blossoming of trees, the flight of birds, and the movement and shape of clouds. In some Polynesian islands each young man learned some trade, such as house builder, wood carver, fisherman, sailor or farmer...(Kuykendall, 1926, pp. 41–42).

Within this system the function of teaching differed from established Western concepts in that teaching was tied to particular relationships between teachers and those being taught. Older siblings took on much of the responsibility of socializing younger siblings. The master craftsman, hunter, fisherman, etc. taught his skill to those who sought it. In short, teaching was "a function rather than a determinant of status in the group" (Sanchez, 1956, p. 125).

Verbal creativity was highly valued in traditional Polynesia, as evidenced in the everyday use of puns, proverbs, and similes as well as in the highly stylized formal speeches of ceremonial occasions. In Samoa, the value placed on oratorical skill can be seen in the *a'a ti*, one of the first tests of a newly selected chief or *matai*. In this speech delivered before his village council or *fono,* the new matai was "expected to show his wisdom and his grasp of oratorical protocol and expertise in turning a phrase or alluding to a mythological or legendary event" (Holmes, 1974, p. 21). An unacceptable performance was grounds for refusing to recognize his right to sit on the council. The best examples of oratory as fine art, however, were demonstrated by talking chiefs, who were aligned to matais, for whom they functioned as councilors and whom they represented, both within the village and beyond, as ambassadors and spokespersons. The duties of a talking chief included accompanying his matai on visits to other villages and welcoming visiting parties to his own (Turner, 1861; Mead, 1928). They were also responsible for the delivery of the *lauga,* a genre of ceremonial speech which opened every meeting of the fono and was used on other occasions as well. It usually contained the official list of names and titles of the village chiefs as well as mythological and metaphorical references to past historical events and to the current social and political structure of the village (Duranti, 1981). The talking chiefs were also the poets of Samoan society, creating verse characterized by rhyming couplets, a predictable meter, and allusions to myths and legends.

In Hawaii, too, eloquent use of oral language held an esteemed position among the indigenous population. Early missionary journals report on the Hawaiians' fondness for poetry and the preservation of memorable historic events and traditions through songs committed to memory by persons attached to the kings or chiefs, or strolling musicians who travel through the islands and recite them on occasions of public festivity. Formal oratory was also evidenced at public occasions. One missionary writes:

> I never was more deeply affected than by the parting address of a warrior in the South Sea Islands, when he was taking leave of his friends, before going, as he expected, to battle.
>
> Nothing can surpass their efforts on some of these occasions, when their addresses abound with figure like the following:
>
> "Our ranks are rocks in the ocean, unmoved by the dashing waves; each warrior moves a sea porcupine, whom none dare handle."
>
> "Let the king's troops advance, and they shall rise before his enemies as the lofty breadfruit rises before the slender grass."
>
> "In the combat the warrior shall stand like the deep-rooted palm, and nod over the heads of their enemies, as the tall cocoa-nut nods over the bending reed."
>
> On urging the attach by night,
>
> "Our torches' glare shall surprise them like the lightning's flash; and our shouts, in the instantaneous onset, terrify like bursting thunder."
>
> The effect was greatly heightened by the conciseness of their language, and the euphony with which it abounds; and probably on one side of the place where they were assembled, the rocks arose, and the waves dashed; while on the other, groves of stately bread-fruit trees appeared, or towering cocoa-nuts, seventy, or eighty feet high, waved over their heads. (Ellis, 1825, pp. 98–99).

Thus, although neither the Hawaiians nor the Samoans had developed a writing system for their languages before the arrival of the missionaries, they both had developed highly literary styles of spoken discourse (Tannen, 1982) upon which great value was placed.

VERNACULAR LITERACY AND RELIGIOUS LEARNING

Within this context, the missionaries introduced native language literacy "to make [the Polynesians] acquainted with letters; to give them the Bible with the skill to read it..." (Kuykendall, 1938, p. 101). In both Hawaii and Samoa, this was accomplished within a generation.

The first missionaries arrived in Hawaii in 1820; by 1926, there were 400 native teachers in schools there (Kuykendall, 1926, p. 131). By 1830, one third of the population, predominantly adults, was enrolled in schools (ibid.) and 85,000 individuals, mostly adults, were able to read the Hawaiian language (Wist, 1940, pp. 22–23). By 1850, "the entire [adult?] population was able to read and write in their mother tongue" (Kloss, 1977, p. 204).

The first Western-style schools in Samoa were established by missionaries from the London Missionary Society in 1830. By 1839 there were 10,000 literate Samoans. By 1850, 15,000 copies of the New Testament had been published in Samoan; 5 years later, another 10,000 copies of a revised edition were in print (Turner, 1861, pp. 170–171). Although the accuracy of the population data for that time is difficult to assess, Oliver (1951, p. 211) estimates the population of Samoa in 1851 to have been 56,000. If these figures even approximate the actual population, they suggest almost universal access to written text.

Spolsky et al. (1983) report similar success rates for the introduction of vernacular literacy in other Polynesian societies. They list five necessary conditions for the introduction of vernacular literacy: (a) willingness by those introducing literacy to have literacy in the vernacular; (b) perceived utility of literacy by traditionally influential members of the community; (c) the establishment of native functions for literacy; (d) the continued widespread use of the vernacular as spoken language; and (e) the support of the maintenance of vernacular literacy by a powerful educational system under local control.

Spolsky et al. do not distinguish between the acquisition and the maintenance of literacy. Clearly, the first two of their conditions are features of the social context at the time of introduction of literacy which facilitate its success. The latter three appear to be conditions involved in the successful maintenance of native language reading and writing subsequent to its introduction.

Perceived Utility
The initial success of native language literacy in both Hawaii and Samoa can at least in part be attributable to the perceived utility of societal literacy by members of influential members of society. Because literacy and schooling were so closely tied to Christianity, it is impossible to understand support for the teaching of reading and writing apart from a consideration of the reciprocal relations between literacy and the role of Christianity in the islands.

In Samoa, support for the mission schools came from the *matais,* the decision makers in the existing institution, the village. The fact that literacy was made a prerequisite for church membership cannot be overlooked as a motivation for learning the written word.

Church membership was highly desirable. Churches were organized around villages (Gilson, 1970, p. 98) and since the matai often served as deacons and elders in the church, Christianity provided additional institutional support for the existing political structure. The practice of monthly intervillage services provided an opportunity for those deacons/matais to demonstrate their position beyond the village. Second, Christianity provided an additional literature to draw upon for oratory in the fono and elsewhere. Moreover, members of the congregation were often called upon to give sermons, thereby providing a new forum to display oratorical skill (Holmes, 1974, pp. 60–62). Thus, aside from the intrinsic appeal of its philosophy, the benefits of Christianity to the existing social structure were considerable.

At the same time, the schools taught only that knowledge and those skills which were not available through existing modes of education. They did not attempt to teach those skills and to pass on that knowledge which were being taught and passed on already through existing channels. The craftsman still had his place. The matai system remained intact. Thus, within the village, the arrival of a new Samoan pastor caused minimal changes in the village hierarchy. All these factors can be seen as contributing to the appeal of Christianity and the success of literacy can be seen in part as a result of that appeal.

In Hawaii, the perceived utility of Christianity and the concomitant literacy skills must be viewed in the context of socio-historical factors at play during the 35 years prior to the arrival of the missionaries. When the first fur traders stopped in Hawaii in 1785 to pick up provisions on their trips between the west coast of North America and China, Hawaii was parcelled into districts ruled over by a stratified hierarchy of chiefs often in combat with one another over domains of power. This social structure was reinforced thorough a system of *kapu,* or sacred laws said to be derived from the Hawaiian gods which restricted the ways in which members of various classes could interact and whose violation was punishable by death:

> Hawaiians lived in constant awareness of the presence of gods, and the gods gave high-ranking chiefs their mana, their power and their prestige. Royal incest kept the most valuable bloodlines pure, and the highest chiefs, with the authority of the gods behind them, could demand the kapu moe, prostration, from everyone. Elaborate prohibitions and regulations were enforced to make sure that superior and inferior elements in life were kept at a proper distance from each other, because only defilement and danger could result if they came in contact. (Daws, 1968, pp. 53–54).

Dealings with the early traders brought weapons which expedited the unification of Hawaii and the establishment of an absolute monarchy by Kamehameha during the last decade of the eighteenth century. But contact with westerners also brought about a weakening of the power of the kapu. Ships anchoring in Hawaii often violated kapus such as those forbidding women to eat with men or forbidding women to eat pork.

With the death of Kamehameha, the absolute power of the monarchy was dissipated, his 22-year-old son Liholiho assuming the throne, his nephew inheriting the power of the war god, and his favorite wife, Kaahumanu, assuming the position of executive officer. She convinced the new king to abolish the kapu, since she, as a woman, was prevented from exercising her complete powers as long as the kapu were in effect. This move also benefited Liholiho, since it neutralized the power of his cousin, who was a potential rival. The abolition of the kapu was viewed with favor among much of the general populus, and

> It is not surprising that the abolition of the tabu, effecting for them an emancipation so complete and an amelioration so important, should be a subject of constant gratulation, and that every circumstance tending in the slightest degree to revive the former tabu should be viewed with the most distressing apprehension. (Ellis, 1825, p. 281).

The lifting of the kapu also diminished the powers of the traditional priests and avoided the expenditure of both labor and property in support of that system.

Into this void came the missionaries preaching Christianity. Support for this new faith came first from Kaahumanu herself. The introduction of Christianity represented an alternative ensuring against the reintroduction of kapu. At the same time, with its admonishments against warfare, it represented a vehicle for preventing serious challenges to the legitimacy of the monarchy. For these reasons, those in power supported the introduction of Christianity, and their subjects followed suit.

In summary, the rapid acquisition of vernacular literacy in both Hawaii and Samoa can be viewed as resulting in part from the utility, as perceived by influential members of the community, of the institutions of literacy at least as much as from the perceived utility of literacy per se. Moreover, the institutions of literacy may be perceived as useful for a variety of reasons. In Samoa, Christianity was perceived as reinforcing the traditional social order, while in Hawaii it was perceived as reinforcing somewhat revolutionary alternatives to it.

Functions of Literacy

Although in Hawaii vernacular literacy probably enjoyed a wider range of functions than in Samoa, in both places institutional functions for reading and writing outside of the church appear to have been limited. In Hawaii, the first two Hawaiian language newspapers were published in 1834, but these were owned and controlled by the missionaries. Other publications from the same missionary presses included laws, proclamations, and port regulations for the government, small jobs for businessmen, and a small "textbook" of eight pages (the *Pi-a-pa*) containing "the alphabet, Arabic and Roman numerals, punctuation marks, lists of words, verses of scripture and other reading matter, including a short poem giving the thoughts of "Kings Iolani and Kaumalii in reference to Christianity" (Kuykendall, 1938, p. 107).

In Samoa, functions for native language literacy were even more limited. There is evidence that the new skill was used for love notes during courtship

(Pritchard, 1866, p. 139) but oral speeches, even those at religious functions, appear to have been committed to memory or performed extemporaneously, rather than composed in writing and then read. While the harbors of Apia and Pago Pago were developing into minor commercial centers, the businesses there were controlled by foreigners and consequently most literacy events associated with them were in European languages. Although the British drew up and presented to the chiefs for adoption a set of port regulations (Gilson, 1970, p. 149), there was no government bureaucracy dependent on forms and reports. Vernacular print seems to have been reserved primarily for scriptures, prayer books and primers.

Thus, the functions for vernacular literacy in both Hawaii and Samoa were somewhat circumscribed. Since the primary functions of literacy in both situations were associated with the newly introduced church, they cannot be considered "native" functions. Nevertheless, the new literacy events (Heath, 1983) appear to have been remarkably compatible with speech events existing in preliterate Polynesia. For example, although learning in preliterate Polynesian society in large part involved the acquisition of procedural knowledge through observation, a high priority was also placed on the refinement of oral language for specialized functions. This included the use of metaphor and simile, mythological and historical allusions, meter, and rhyme. It also involved the development of memorization skills.

A typical religious service in Samoa, for example, consisted of readings from the Bible, hymns from hymnals, a sermon, and an offering. Members of the congregation (and the community) were involved in these activities. During the offering, the deacons would read the church roll and as each family presented its offering, would announce it to the congregation and record it. The literacy skills involved in the church consisted not just of reading of religious texts but also at least a modicum of bookkeeping (Holmes, 1974, p. 71). Family Bible reading became a regular evening activity. There is no reason to assume that in Protestant Hawaii, services followed a significantly different format.

Many of these functions of literacy appear to have been compatible with existing preliteracy speech events. The bookkeeping activity was similar to existing oral activities involving the exchange of gifts conducted at ceremonial events in preliterate Polynesia. Moreover, the literary style of the scriptures and sermons, characterized as they were by the use of proverbs, similes and highly stylized language, shared many feataures with traditional public oratory. In both Hawaii and Samoa, the ability to memorize long passages of Scripture and the Polynesian appetite for religious oratory have been subjects of frequent comment in journals and histories. Evidence can be found in the accounts of missionaries and others of the use of traditionally valued oral skills in the acquisition of literacy. Writing of Hawaiians, Ellis states,

Rude as their poetry is, they are passionately fond of it. When they first began to learn to read and spell, it was impossible for them to repeat a column of spelling, or recite a lesson, without chanting or singing it.

They had one tune for the monosyllables, another for the disyllables, etc. and we have heard three or four members of a family sitting for an hour together in an evening, and reciting their school lessons in perfect concord. (Ellis, 1825, p. 337).

One can speculate that the acquisition of vernacular literacy was facilitated by the compatibility of the skills involved in the functions of reading and writing introduced with skills already highly developed for functions of oral language in preliterate society.

LITERACY IN A LANGUAGE OF WIDER COMMUNICATION

Although the situations in Hawaii and Samoa with respect to the introduction of vernacular literacy into a preliterate context share many common characteristics, more dramatic contrasts are seen when examining the shift from religious to secular schooling and the introduction of literacy in a language of wider communication. Both Hawaii and American Samoa became territories of the U.S. around the turn of the century. In Hawaii, however, secular education was introduced during the latter half of the 19th century and signs of diminishing vernacular literacy skills were evident prior to colonization. In American Samoa, on the other hand, high vernacular literacy rates have been reported well into the 20th century, subsequent to colonization and the institution of secular schooling. In both cases, however, high rates of native language literacy persisted when strong, locally controlled school systems supported it. But the strength of school systems supporting native language literacy was subject to changing currents of noneducational forces.

Hawaii

In Hawaii, although native language literacy was initially supported by a strong school system, that school system was never under local control. By 1840, the year in which the Hawaiian legislature passed a compulsory school law, 15,000 students were enrolled in three kinds of schools: (a) church-affiliated boarding schools for adolescents of promise; (b) mission stations which both taught students and prepared Hawaiians to teach; and (c) common schools, staffed by native Hawaiians (Kuykendall, 1926, p. 133).

Nominally, the government had taken over the management of this last type of school in that year. However, the curriculum and staff remained unchanged from that of the mission schools. The continuing influence of the missionaries on the education system can be seen in the fact that in 1846,

Richard Armstrong, an American Protestant missionary, was appointed Minister of Education and later President of the Board of Education.

At the same time, local support for vernacular schooling was undermined by the fact that from 1839, Hawaiian royalty was being educated in an English-medium school, administered by appointees of the mission. There was also strong sentiment among the growing foreign-born population (mostly Americans) and among some Hawaiians for education in English (Kuykendall, 1938, p. 361).

In 1849, the school was opened to children of American and European residents of Honolulu. By 1853, Caucasians constituted 79% of the enrollment of that school. In the same year, the Hawaii legislature appropriated funds for the establishment of English-medium schools for Hawaiians. By 1856, 758 native Hawaiian students were enrolled in such schools.

Not all Hawaiians, however, welcomed this change. By 1860, Armstrong had died and King Kamehameha IV appointed his own father, Matai Kekuanoa, President of the Board of Education. In 1864, Kekuanoa warned the legislature that

> The theory of substituting the English language for the Hawaiian, in order to educate our people, is as dangerous to Hawaiian nationality, as it is useless in promoting the general education of the people . . . . If we wish to preserve the Kingdom of Hawaii for Hawaiians, and to educate our people, we must insist that the Hawaiian language shall be the language of all our National Schools, and the English shall be taught whenever practicable, but only, as an important *branch* of Hawaiian education. (*Biennial Report of the President of the Board of Education to the Legislature of 1864,* cited in Kuykendall, 1953, p. 112).

Though his sentiments were shared by many, there was no organized attempt to prevent the introduction of English-medium schools, and in fact, demand for them continued.

By the middle of the nineteenth century, a number of social and economic changes had occurred in Hawaii. By that time, foreigners had become landholders. In 1841, for example, American sugar producers obtained a franchise from the King that "gave them the priviledge of leasing unoccupied land for 100 years at a low rental" (Dole, 1895, p. 577). English speakers were gaining influence not only in religious and educational aspects of Hawaiian life, but perhaps more important, in the economy of the islands. The growing importance of the English language in economic spheres was also reflected in Article 44 of the 1864 Constitution, which specified that the Ministry of Finances present the budget in Hawaiian and English (Kloss, 1977, p. 207). Those economic ties to English-speaking, specifically American, interests were consummated with the Reciprocal Trade Treaty of 1876, which had the effect of dramatically increasing the amount of sugar exported to the United States.

The influence of English was also being widely felt in government. In 1834, the Reverend William Richards became advisor to the king, "to instruct them in matters of government' (Kuykendall, 1926, p. 137). The American Board of Commissioners for Foreign Missions, an interdenominational body from New England which oversaw the administration of the mission schools, devised a plan in 1848 to stop the "homeward current" (Kuykendall, 1926, p. 340) of the missionaries in the islands, many of whom now had families. The plan included the granting of lands and houses held by the board to missionaries and their families. The missionaries were also encouraged to become Hawaiian citizens. The effect of these changes was that "the American missionaries and their families became an integral part of the Hawaiian body politic" (Kuykenall, 1926, p. 341).

These changes in political, economic, and social factors, combined with the dramatic decline in both the number and the percentage of Hawaiians in Hawaii due both to the lack of immunity against unfamiliar diseases and the lure of the whaling industry for many of the eligible males resulted in not only the decline in native language literacy skills, but also the loss of Hawaiian as a first language. It has been estimated that in 1778, the population of the Hawaii was around 300,000. By 1840, the total population of Hawaiians had fallen to 82,000 (Kloss, 1977, p. 202). In 1872, over 10% of the population of Hawaii was foreign. By 1900, the population of Hawaiians and part-Hawaiians in Hawaii had dropped to 37,656 (only 26% of the total population of the new territory).

Educational change followed on the heels of these social and economic changes. In 1854, there had been 412 common schools with a total population of 11,782 pupils, who received instruction in Hawaiian by Hawaiian teachers (Kloss, 1977, p. 109). By 1874, the number of common schools had declined to 196, with only 5522 students enrolled (71% of the student population). By 1878, 61% of the students were still enrolled in Hawaiian-medium schools. By 1882, that figure had dropped to 33% (Kloss, 1977, p. 204). By 1888, less than 16% were found in such schools, with the number of common schools falling to 63 (Wist, 1940, p. 72). Only 7 years later, in the year of the overthrow of the Lili'uokalani government by Americans in the community, the enrollment in Hawaiian-medium schools had dropped to less than 3% of all students in public schools in Hawaii.

In 1896, English became the language of instruction for all public elementary schools, and Hawaiian was not reintroduced into the curriculum until 1919, and then only as an elective subject in normal and high schools. That banishment was preceded by 80 years of changing economic, political, and social conditions which influenced that language policy. Long before English became the official language of instruction, it had already replaced Hawaiian as the language of economics, politics, and consequently education. The majority of the Hawaiians educated during the last quarter of the

19th century were taught neither content nor literacy skills in their own language but rather in a second language, English.

American Samoa

From 1830 until the beginning of colonial administration in Samoa in 1900, there was little need for anything but the vernacular as a spoken language outside the port towns of Apia and Pago Pago. The population of American Samoa in 1900 has been estimated at 5,579 (U.S. Department of Commerce, 1984). Outside of the ports, the internal administration of villages and districts was little affected by international jockeying for port privileges which eventually resulted in the division of Samoa into Western and American territories.

Perhaps because of the relative lack of outside influence, Samoans were better able to maintain control of their school system than the Hawaiians. Another key to the issue of control of educational institutions in Samoa was that, unlike other areas where Christianity was introduced to preliterate societies, Samoans were unwilling to relocate around mission settlements. Instead, the missions, if they were to prosper, had to go out to the villages. This was one more way in which the newly introduced religious learning was compatible with existing cultural patterns in preliterate Samoan society. The locus of the learning was on site. This, in turn, contributed to the degree of control which the matais could maintain over the institution, since its representatives became totally dependent upon the generosity of the village matais for their lodging and food. Congregational rule gave the village congregations an even greater independence, which contributed to the nativization of the institution (Oliver, 1951, p. 213; Gilson, 1970, pp. 127–37).

The strength of the new school system can be seen from the fact that by 1850, over 150 Samoan teachers were in place in village schools throughout Samoa (Gibson, 1970, p. 102). For more than 50 years after that, church-affiliated schools provided the only western-style instruction in Samoa. Even after the establishment of secular schools during the U.S. naval administration of American Samoa, the pastors' schools remained the most influential institution of formal schooling there. Support for the religious schools among the general population can also be seen in terms of resistance to secular schooling. In 1922, students enrolled in government schools represented only 15% of the total student population, the rest being enrolled in religious schools. In 1927, concerned about the quality of English education and the qualifications of the teachers (Gray, 1960, p. 233), the territorial fono, which functioned only in an advisory capacity to the government, entertained a resolution to recommend the curtailment of public education. With the introduction of universal free public education in the 1920s, the pastors' schools continued to provide the only source of formal instruction in native language literacy (Wallace, 1964, p. 167), with children attending them each day before and after their regular public schooling.

Increased domains for English created by the establishment of colonial government, the disruptions of World War II and its aftermath, and the introduction of educational television all served to weaken the influence of the religious schools and to contribute to shifts in language patterns, including the decline of native language literacy skills.

The annexation of American Samoa and the establishment of a naval station brought both wage-paying jobs and a western-style government bureaucracy. The government employed a Samoan guard (*Fita Fita*), whose duties included acting as prison guards, radio operators, yeomen, hospitalmen, cooks, fire fighters, chauffeurs, butchers, truck drivers, stewards, orderlies, enginemen, and boat crews. In addition, village chiefs (elected by village matai and subject to approval by the governor), county chiefs, district governors and district judges (all appointed by the governor), received either salaries or a portion of the fines and fees collected as a part of their duty. This marked the beginning of the government as the major source of employment in American Samoa. By the outbreak of World War II, approximately 10% of all adult Samoan men in American Samoa were employed at the naval station.

By 1917, the regulations and orders which had evolved over the previous 16 years were codified in English and 4 years later were translated into Samoan. They entailed a set of literacy events which, unlike those introduced by the church, were alien to existing ways of speaking in traditional Samoan society. They included written records of all village fono proceedings and laws enacted and of all cases tried before the village magistrate; written warrants for arrests; birth, death, marriage, and adoption records and certificates; registration of matai titles; monthly audits of government offices; building permits; licenses for firearms, livestock, dogs, and the importation of goods; and bank checking and savings accounts. Not all of these literacy events were conducted in English. Certainly at least some of the written reports of the proceedings of the village fono meetings, for example, must have been written in Samoan and translated into English. But with the establishment of the centralized top layer of bureaucracy by a colonial power, the "unmarked" (Fishman, 1980; Spolsky, 1982) language of government shifted from Samoan to English. The Codification of Regulations and Orders, for example, stipulates that in the case of a dispute over the interpretation of the Samoan and English versions of the texts, "the English shall govern the decision of all cases" (Noble, 1921, p. 1). Furthermore, while both an American and a Samoan judge presided over the district courts, in the case of a difference of opinion between them, "the opinion of the American district judge shall prevail..." (Noble, 1921, p. 14).

These changes together with the rise of a small commercial center at the port of Pago Pago (by 1922 it had grown to a town of 568 people and eight retail businesses, five of which grossed more than $2000 per month in sales) created a situation in which at a certain point it becomes no longer convenient, economical, or profitable to use the vernacular. Around the urban centers, Apia and Pago Pago, where whites and mixed bloods are concentrated, Samoan leaders and young people find that they can make their way better in matters not purely Samoan if they can understand and use English. (Keesing, 1932, p. 313).

The outbreak of World War II not only interrupted the schooling of many children, but also created a need for labor which drew many teachers away from the profession. During the war "almost every able-bodied male Samoan was either a member of the armed forces or in the employ thereof" (Navy, 1947, p. 13). With the discharge of Samoans from the military after the war, the number of Samoans living in American Samoa and employed for wages dropped to less than 10% of the estimated 17,000 total population. Of these, nearly two thirds worked as civilian employees of either the Navy Department or the Government of American Samoa.

In 1951, the administrative responsibility for American Samoa was transferred from the Navy Department to the Department of the Interior. The subsequent reduction in government payroll resulted in a drop in local employment in private enterprise. By 1952, it was reported that less than 200 Samoans were employed outside of the government. These economic conditions motivated large scale emigration from American Samoa to Hawaii and the U.S. mainland. Emigration figures for 1952 alone were estimated as high as 1500 (Holmes, 1974, p. 105), over a 500% increase from the year before.

But perhaps the event which inititated the most rapid chain of effects on the everyday lives of Samoans since the advent of Christianity more than a century before was the massive implementation of educational television in the 1960s to facilitate the learning of English. (The development and demise of this program have been well documented; see, for example, Wallace, 1964; Kaiser, 1965; Platt, 1969; Nelson, 1970; Anderson, 1977; Baldauf, 1981, and Schramm, Nelson, & Betham, 1981). The introduction of educational television into the public schools required the installation of electricity in virtually all villages, which in turn necessitated the construction of new roads. All of this provided new jobs, both in government and in the private sector (Holmes, 1974, p. 101).

This technological innovation also has had a dual impact on patterns of language use in American Samoa. First, it has increased opportunities for exposure to English. In 1979, it was reported that there was one television for every six persons (and nearly one radio for every person) there (U.N., 1983). Only 12% of the evening programming is in Samoan (Baldauf, 1982). Second, it has, together with the introduction of new protestant sects, also contributed to the decline in attendance at pastors' schools, which students previously attended after regular school hours (Thomas, 1981, p. 42). Since these schools have traditionally assumed the major responsibility for vernacular literacy instruction, the decline in enrollment has been identified as one cause for declining native language literacy skills (Baldauf, 1982, p. 3), as evidenced by both community concern and student performance on criterion referenced tests (Thomas, 1981, pp. 45–46). This situation vis-a-vis native language literacy is not ameliorated by the fact that approximately 10% of the current public school enrollment in American Samoa don't speak Samoan at all. Most of these are children of the emigrants of the 1950s through the 1970s (van Naerssen, 1979).

DISCUSSION

These two case studies provide both lessons for those involved in the formation of language education policy and proposals to consider in the development of a sociolinguistics of literacy. In Hawaii, the cross-generational maintenance of Hawaiian may no longer be a viable issue. The percentage of native Hawaiians for whom it is a first language is small indeed and there are very few functions for reading and writing it. But work by the Kamehameha Early Education Project (KEEP) has demonstrated how the language patterns and skills traditionally developed in oral language can successfully be incorporated into the teaching of literacy in the language of wider communication, even after several generations during which literacy in the ancestral language has not been taught (Au, 1980). This suggests that linguistic traditions can be transmitted from ancestral languages into a language of wider communication as that language becomes a first language. It also suggests that those linguistic traditions can continue to influence literacy development in the face of nearly complete societal language shift.

In American Samoa, which has been experiencing partial language shift accompanied by the attrition of native language skills, literacy in both Samoan and English might be enhanced through the approach taken by the Kamehameha Early Education Project, incorporating participant structures and skills employed in existing oral uses of language into the teaching of reading and writing. Some of the ethnographic groundwork for such an approach has already begun (Ochs, 1982). This assumes, however, that community members perceive vernacular literacy as a skill to be retained. Without some perceived use for it, it is unlikely to be retained. It would also involve the identification and perhaps even institutionalization of functions of written Samoan to be retained. Given the distribution of students across various kinds of schools, that would involve the public schools in a role traditionally reserved for religious schools, namely the teaching of vernacular reading and writing.

The two case studies also suggest several points to be considered in the development of a theory of the sociolinguistics of literacy. First, it is not always just literacy per se, but the institutions associated with it which are perceived as useful. Furthermore, the introduction of literacy may be useful in preserving existing social structures, as was the case in Samoa, or in

strengthening new ones, as in Hawaii. Third, any examination of the introduction of literacy, either in the vernacular or in a language of wider communication, must view that process in terms of both the skills involved in
the functions for which literacy is to be used, and the skills already employed in language functions in the society. Fourth, traces of these skills
may be evident even across instances of language shift. Finally, the retention of literacy entails attention to changing social, political, and economic
conditions and to the changing roles for educational institutions which these
conditions necessitate.

REFERENCES

Anderson, J.A. (1977). Samoan TV: 13 years of change. *Pacific Islands Communication Newsletter, 7*, 1+.
Au, K.H. (1980). Participant structures in a reading lesson with Hawaiian children. *Anthropology and Education Quarterly, 11*, 91–115.
Baldauf, R.B. (1981). Educational television, enculturation, and acculturation: A study of change in American Samoa. *International Review of Education, 27*, 227–245.
Baldauf, R.B. (1982). The language situation in American Samoa: Planners, plans, and planning. *Language Planning Newsletter, 8*, 1–6.
Daws, G. (1968). *Shoal of time: A history of the Hawaiian Islands.* New York: Macmillan.
Department of Education. (1941). *Annual Report.* Pago Pago: Government of American Samoa.
Dole, S.B. (1895). Evolution of Hawaiian land tenure. *Overland Monthly,* pp. 565–579.
Dorian, N.C. (1982). Language loss and maintenance in language contact situations. In R. Lambert & B. Freed (Eds.), *The loss of language skills.* Rowley, MA: Newbury.
Duranti, A. (1981). *The Samoan Fono: A sociolinguistic study.* Canberra: Australian National University.
Ellis, W. (1825/1979). *Journal of William Ellis: Narrative of a tour of Hawaii, or Owhyhee: With remarks on the history, traditions, manners, customs, and language of the inhabitants of the Sandwich Islands.* Rutland, VT: Tuttle.
Fishman, J.A. (1977). The spread of English as a new perspective for the study of "Language maintenance and language shift." In J.A. Fishman, R.L.cooper, & A.W. Conrad (Eds.), *The spread of English: The sociology of English as an additional language.* Rowley, MA: Newbury.
Fishman, J.A. (1980). Bilingualism and biculturalism as individual and as societal phenomena. *Journal of Multilingual and Multicultural Education, 1*, 3–15.
Fishman, J.A., Cooper, R.L., & Rosenbaum, Y. (1977). English around the world. In J.A. Fishman, R.L. Cooper, & A.W. Conrad (Eds.), *The spread of English: The sociology of English as an additional language.* Rowley, MA: Newbury.
Gardner, H. (1983). *Frames of mind: The theory of multiple intelligences.* New York: Basic Books.
Gilson, R.P. (1970). *Samoa 1830 to 1900: The politics of a multicultural community.* London: Oxford.
Gray, R.P. (1960). *America Samoa: A history of American Samoa and its United States Naval Administration.* Annapolis, MD: United States Naval Institute.
Heath, S.B. (1983). *Ways with words: Language, life, and work in communities and classrooms.* Cambridge: Cambridge University Press.
Hinojosa, M. (1980). The collapse of the Zapotec vowel system. *Penn Review of Linguistics, 4*, 28–39.

Holmes, L.D. (1974). *Samoan village*. New York: Holt, Rinehart and Winston.

Kaiser, T. (1965). Classroom TV comes to Samoa. *Saturday Review, 25*, 58.

Keesing, F.M. (1932). Language change in relation to native education in Samoa. *The Mid-Pacific, 44*, 302–313.

Kloss, H. (1977). *The American bilingual tradition*. Rowley, MA: Newbury.

Kuykendall, R.S. (1926). *A history of Hawaii*. New York: Macmillan.

Kuykendall, R.S. (1938). *The Hawaii kingdom, 1778–1854: Foundation and transformation*. Honolulu: University Press of Hawaii.

Kuykendall, R.S. (1953). *The Hawaiian kingdon, 1854–1874: Twenty critical years*. Honolulu: University Press of Hawaii.

Lewis, E.G. (1979). A comparative study of language contact: The influence of demographic factors in Wales and the Soviet Union. In W.C. McCormack & S.H. Wurm (Eds.), *Language and society: Anthropological issues*. The Hague: Mouton.

Mead, M. (1928). *Coming of age in Samoa*. New York: William Morrow.

Navy Department. (1947). *American Samoa: Information on American Samoa transmitted by the United States to the Secretary-General of the United Nations pursuant to Article 73 (e) of the Charter*. Washington, DC: Author.

Nelson, L. (1970). *Report of the Educational Television Task Force*. Honolulu: University of Hawaii—American Samoa Contract.

Noble, A.M. (1921). *Codification of the regulations and orders for the Government of American Samoa*. San Francisco: Phillips and Van Orden.

Ochs, E. (1982). Talking to children in Western Samoa. *Language in Society, 11*(1), 77–104.

Office of the Governor. (1952). *Information on the Territory of American Samoa for the fiscal year ending June 30, 1952, transmitted by the United States to the Secretary General of the United Nations Pursuant to Article 73(e) of the Charter*. Pago Pago: Author.

Oliver, D. (1951). *The Pacific Islands*. Cambridge: Harvard University Press.

Oxford, R. (1982). Technical issues in designing and conducting research on language skill attrition. In R. Lambert & B. Freed (Eds.), *The loss of language skills*. Rowley, MA: Newbury.

Platt, W.J. (1969). *Educational television in three developing areas: A report of a UNESCO mission to Niger, American Samoa, and El Salvador undertaken to assist the government of the Ivory Coast*. Menlo Park, CA: Stanford Research Institute.

Pritchard, W.T. (1866/1968). *Polynesian reminiscences or, life in the South Pacific Islands*. London: Dawsons.

Sanchez, P. (1956). *Education in American Samoa*. Unpublished Ed.D. dissertation, Stanford University, School of Education.

Schramm, W., Nelson, L.M., & Betham, M.T. (1981). *Bold experiment: The story of educational television in American Samoa*. Standord, CA: Stanford University Press.

Scollon, R. & Scollon, S.B.K. (1982). *Narrative, literacy and face in interethnic communication*. Norwood, NJ: Ablex.

Scribner, S. & Cole, M. (1981). *The psychology of literacy*. Cambridge, MA: Harvard University Press.

Spolsky, B. (1981). Bilingualism and biliteracy. *Canadian Modern Language Review, 37*, 475–469.

Spolsky, B. (1982). Sociolinguistics of literacy, bilingual education, and tesol. *TESOL Quarterly, 16*, 141–151.

Spolsky, B., Englebrecht, G., Guillermino & Ortz, L. (1983). Religious political and educational factors in the development of biliteracy in the Kindom of Tonga. *Journal of Multilingual and Multicultural Development, 4*, 459–469.

Tannen, D. (1982). Oral and literate strategies in spoken and written narratives. *Language, 58*, 1–21.

Thomas, R.M. (1981). Evaluation consequences of unreasonable goals—The plight of education in American Samoa. *Educational Evaluation and Policy Analysis, 3*, 41–49.

Turner, G. (1861). *Nineteen years in Polynesia: Missionary life, travels, and researches in the Islands of the Pacific.* London: John Snow.

U.N. Department of International Economic and Social Affairs. (1983). *1981 statistical yearbook.* New York: United Nations.

U.S. Department of Commerce. (1984). *Statistical abstract of the United States.* Washington, DC: U.S. Government Printing Office.

van Naerssen, M.M. (1979). *A pan-Pacific Samoan population/language dominance survey.* Unpublished manuscript.

Wallace, B. (1964). English language teaching in Samoa. *Language Learning, 14,* 167.

Williams, J. (1846). *A narrative of missionary enterprises in the South Sea Islands.* London: John Snow.

Wist, B.O. (1940). *A century of public education in Hawaii, 1840–1940.* Honolulu: Hawaii Educational Review.

PART V
TECHNOLOGY IN EDUCATION

Chapter Ten
New Technologies, Basic Skills,
and the Underside of Education:
What's to be Done?[1]

PEG GRIFFIN
MICHAEL COLE
University of California, San Diego

There is a rather disconcerting type of internationalism operating nowadays. Parallel to the trade deficit, there is a sense of information deficit signaled by perceived imbalances between countries and leading to a loss of power by the countries that are in arrears. Many believe that something should be done, but there is no unanimity about what is to be done. Responses to the perceived information deficit fall into these categories: (1) make sure the "other" fails to get further ahead; and (2) increase your own standing. Worries about technology transfer and brain drain are examples of the first; worries about the adequacy and efficacy of education are examples of the second. Those, like us, who are interested in improving education could take advantage of the second type of response and argue that, in order to be competitive internationally, more financial and human resources need to be expended on education in the United States.[2] We do not believe that this is

[1] We would like to acknowledge the constructive involvement of the faculty, staff, and students of the University of California at San Diego in the conduct of the field experiments relied on in this paper. Thanks are also due to the children, parents, and school and church officials who have participated in the fieldwork. We appreciate the assistance of Judith Langer in the preparation of this chapter for publication. The work reported draws on more general efforts that have been supported by the Carnegie Corporation of New York, the Grant Foundation, and the Third College at UCSD.

[2] Roger Shuy (personal communication) reports on this strategy being used in a local arena where literacy was placed in competition with mathematics. A relatively rich and successful school district used discrepancies between standardized test scores in a creative way: One year the average math scores would be higher than the average reading scores and a reading crisis would be declared, funding would be supplied to the county educators and research and development on literacy education could proceed: since each year scores in one or the other domains would be lower, the "crisis" funding allowed the county to spend a great deal on educational research. Unfortunately, the most clear way to improve the test scores—to develop ways to teach to the tests—is not necessarily the way to improve literacy or mathematics education. The adoption of this competition strategy as a way to finance educational research can become so deeply involved in the research program that the real end is replaced by what started as a means to it.

the way to go. We believe that international cooperation rather than competition is a more productive approach. "A Nation at Risk" could be written about any of a number of countries, and an understanding of the risk in any one can profit from an understanding of the risk in all. In effect, our stand is that to accomplish the second response (increase our own standing), we must reframe the issue so that the first type of response does not arise as a possibility.[3]

Much of our thinking on the issues indexed by the title of this paper occurred during our interactions with colleagues from other nations. Often this work has been via new technologies for communication, so the contact with scholars from different traditions has been more casual, more sporadic and in some ways more communicatively complete than when we were limited to meetings at international conferences, reading published articles, exchanging visits, letters and phone calls. We have tried this sort of joint work with colleagues in Japan, the U.K., Spain, Canada, and the U.S.S.R. We find common cause with respect to education on two bases:

1. Part of our societies are not equitably educated. The people that different countries fail to educate are not too dissimilar: girls, members of the ethnic or language minorities, children of poor or less powerful families, communities, and regions.
2. Our education systems stop short of delivering on full education. We have worries about whether we know how to provide education that will result in creativity, flexibility, adaptability to a rapidly changing world.

In general, in spite of a great deal of effort expended on education in the different countries, we all have what we will call in this paper a *parts problem,* such that we suspect we are missing *part* of the population and *part* of the goal of a full education.

What we fear is that failing to accept the international nature of the problem will promote analyses of the problem based on epiphenomena and have us invest in pseudo-solutions that will not only fail but lose us credibility, reducing future chances for productive work on educational issues. Just as studies of the "old" technology of literacy have gained by examining a wide variety of cases (e.g., Scribner & Cole, 1981), so, too, should studies of the broader problems of education and the new technologies gain by the

---

[3] There are two parallels to our strategy, one in psychology and one in current events. There is a too seldom recognized experiment, "Robbers Cave" (Sherif & Sherif, 1956, pp. 301–328), which is reflected in our stand; in that case, youngsters with some history of inter-group conflict were effectively organized when they faced an adverse situation in common. The recent Reagan and Gorbachev conversations evidently included a similar recognition of the advances that could be made in the face of a common problem; we believe, however, that the common problem is here, making it unnecessary to wait for an invasion from another planet.

study of many diverse cases. We have come to believe that, by making common cause through comparing and contrasting our problems, we can contribute to each of the national educational efforts. We do not believe that progress will come in the form of a single solution that can be imported everywhere effectively, but via the differences that will appear in the futures of solutions that we jointly devise; i.e., solutions with common histories (in problems and in theoretical interpretation) as they are embedded in educational action within the different national and cultural systems.

Consciously preparing for co-cultural comparative research and practice provides the impetus for a broader framing of the issues than psychologists and educators might otherwise provide. We need to attend explicitly to the analysis of the larger societal setting (i.e., to include both a longer time span as well as influences from institutions adjacent to education) in order to provide a context in which international collaborators can make sense of related efforts and contribute to each others' work. We believe that influences from the larger setting are always present in the conduct of educational research and practice; the call to attend to them explicitly and consciously in order to promote international cooperation has the side benefit of making more accessible to us the background considerations that subtly affect our work.

In this chapter, we first review descriptions of the changing situation in the United States relating new technology to education. We then consider the current use of computers in education and the role of "basics" in the situation. We conclude with some descriptions of computer use that we think fit well with our strategy of co-cultural work and that can be motivated within a framework that directly addresses the two goals implicated in the common cause we have with other nations: education for more members of the society and education for more functions in modern society. We hope that this approach can engineer profitable discourse with researchers from other traditions, who may be able to comment on our problems and proposed solutions with different viewpoints.

THE LARGER SETTING

The Conservation of Human Resources Project at Columbia University recently released a series of analyses of changes that have occurred in the United States. Noyelle's 1985 study deals with the "parts" problem—the parts of society we do not educate well and the parts of activity (social or cognitive) that we too often fail to educate. Noyelle (1985: pp. 38–39) summarizes the issue thus:

> Notwithstanding the fact that the economy will continue to produce large numbers of jobs demanding low-level skills, the general tendency to shift from manual to cognitive processes both in the workplace and in the sphere of daily

life and consumption makes better basic schooling more necessary than ever before. Not only has the high school diploma become the proof of basic socialization required by employers as a precondition of employment, but the move toward increasing use of teletex and televideo systems—whether for home banking, home shopping, or perhaps even electronic work at home—will place the less than fully literate person increasingly at a disadvantage.

As skill acquisition becomes increasingly externalized out of firms and out of the labor market, the role which vocational and higher educational systems play in employment opportunity and mobility becomes all the more critical... Increasingly, workers' positions in the labor market are determined prior to their entry into the labor market, in the course of their access to the vocational and higher educational systems. This stands in sharp contrast with the way employment opportunities used to be determined in the "old economy."

It is [Noyelle's] impression that the vocational and higher educational systmes will need to undergo fundamental changes if they are to respond to these new pressures; in other words, if they are to provide both a more efficient and a fairer vehicle for upward mobility. Most likely, what is called for is an evolution toward a truly continuing educational system—one that is more equitable, more flexible, better adapted to shorter term passages, more ubiquitous, and perhaps less specialized in orientation than it has traditionally been.

The important implication for those concerned with education is the move toward "off-the-job training." It may have been true in the past that education outside of the workplace was largely simple credentialing (of the ability to stay in school or in particular courses rather than mastery of any content or skill domain), and thus it may have made sense for school achievement to be considered (by students [cf. Ogbu, this volume] as well as by social analysts and activists) largely irrelevant to making progress in the world of work. The new economy, however, appears to require that schooling provide education, not just credentials.

Just as new technologies raise new challenges for education, new technology is seen as a way to meet these challenges. A good example is the rush to increase computer use in schools, as a variety of reports show:

1. The Center for Social Organization of Schools (CSOS, 1983–1984) at the Johns Hopkins University: School districts are quickly adding computer literacy to educational programs.
2. Quality Education Data (1984) (Naval Materials Council): The number of school districts with microcomputers *doubled* from 1981 to 1984; the percentage of districts having computers rose from 38% to 75% in the same period; the number of schools with computers *tripled*—numbering 55,000.
3. The Center for Children and Technology at Bank Street College of Education: There are now "close to a half million microcomputers in schools"; parents are more involved with computers (even raising funds to get them) than with other educational innovations. (Sheingold, Martin, & Endreweit, 1985)

COMPUTER USE

Given the eager jump into computer technology, we ask whether the technology is actually helping with the "parts" problem; that is, is education more equally accessible to all and is it getting to the more open-ended, more challenging tasks? The evidence on computers is not encouraging. Maybe the introduction of computers is not making matters worse, but computers are certainly not a magic remedy. The CSOS reviews many studies that confirm this judgement (CSOS, 1983–1984, p. 56). Over and over, they find the following constellation of facts:

1. More computers are being placed in the hands of middle and upper class children than poor children.
2. Female students have less involvement with computers when they are found in schools, irrespective of class or ethnicity.
3. When computers are placed in the schools of poor children they are used for rote drill and practice instead of the "cognitive enrichment" that they provide for middle and upper class students.

The first two problems are not surprising. We can expect a relation between the socioeconomic status of the children and the availability of funds for computers in their neighborhood schools. The gender difference problem with respect to computer access can be related to prior problems: It has often been pointed out that girls are less likely than boys to have access to mathematics, science and machinery courses in schools; when computers are introduced, it is often in these settings which have been less welcoming to girls than to boys.

How to redress either or both of these imbalances is a complex issue: To argue for more equitable distribution, we need a more clear idea of what "good" distribution is. That is, we do not want to rob Peter to pay Pablo and Pauline; but rather to provide what is needed for all three. Yet, there is not sufficient information available for us to describe clearly what the goal is, nor to argue for cost-benefit advantages of making changes in current allocations. In particular, how many computers should we have available for those currently underserved, if we are to make educational use effective? The national average is one or two computers in classes that have any microcomputers at all (CSOS, 1983–1984). In most of the CSOS classrooms, only one child actively worked on a computer at a time, with some assistance from other children. The number of students at a computer at one time varied among the schools, however; the CSOS reports:

> Our data show that in schools where use is concentrated among above-average students, the primary computer-using teacher reports a more 'individual use' pattern than in schools where "average" students get a proportionate share of student computer time. Use by "average" students is instead associated with students using computers in pairs (CSOS, 1983–1984).

There is little information available about what is a "good" number for education or even about how much time each child should spend with the computer.

At one extreme, Papert (1984) recommends one computer per child for classroom use and one to take home. Considering the costs of such an undertaking, it is a good thing that existing research suggests that one computer per child is probably *not* an optimum number, as least at the elementary school level where the issue has been most extensively studied. There is growing evidence that *two* students working on a machine reduce low-level errors and create support for more sophisticated activities when compared with students working individually (Levin & Souviney, 1983; Laboratory of Comparative Human Cognition, 1982; Trowbridge & Durnan, 1984). Students are likely to have different skills. By working together and dividing the labor of the task, they can bring their separate strengths together to get the task accomplished. Trowbridge and Durnan's research points out that when group size is increased, the organization of work breaks down and students are observed to engage in less effective learning at the computer. These findings are *very* limited, considering the importance of the issue.

At present no systematic research exists on the interaction of student characteristics, number of machines per classroom, and curricular content. We may argue that there is a de facto "parts" problem: It must be the case that computer technology is not equitably serving poor children and girls, since they are less likely to use computers; however, we have little to say about how much of a change we should make so that it would matter.

The third problem area addresses both "parts" problems—are all parts of the population getting all parts of education? Shavelson, Winkler, Stasz, Fiebel, Robyn and Shaha (1984) point out that even "exemplary" programs suffer the "parts" problem. By means of interviews and observations, Shavelson's group studied the patterns of computer use of 60 elementary and secondary teachers who had been nominated as exemplary users in mathematics and science instruction. They found one pattern, which they labeled "orchestration," to be the most effective, in terms of the kinds of education that was promoted: "Orchestrators" fit the computer into the ongoing streams—the child's development, the curriculum sequence, the ordinary classroom day. Other patterns of use, which proved considerably less valuable than orchestration, were called enrichment, adjunct instruction, and drill and practice. In looking at the distribution of the four types of use, Shavelson et al. found that classrooms with students above average in ability and with a low percentage of minorities tended to be taught by orchestrators, while in the classrooms with a high percentage of minority students or with students rated low in ability, computers were used in the less effective ways.

In a detailed study of carefully guided introduction of computers into four classrooms, Mehan, Moll and Riel (1983, 1985) found some positive changes in the status quo in classrooms varying in ethnic composition and ability: Although microcomputers were assimilated to pre-existing classroom arrangements, they were associated with some beneficial changes in teacher–student relationships and curricula. Cooperative peer interaction emerged and teachers were able to achieve educational goals that could not have been achieved as readily had a microcomputer not been available for their use. However, the researchers' remarks at the end of the first year of work offer sobering thoughts for computer enthusiasts:

> The computer easily becomes an intruder whose potential benefits are outweighed by the inconveniences they create. . .: The strategy of choice then becomes, not by design but by necessity, to accommodate the machine to the prevailing constraints. This decision, although pragmatic in the short-run, is absolutely fatal, especially for language minority students, because it assumes, uncritically, that the status quo is the appropriate context for computer use. Inevitably, existing curricular practices become the "model" for computer use. Why should we expect that the same practices that have produced widespread academic failure will create propitious environments for computer use? (Mehan et al., 1983, p. 226)

The Mehan et al. project was able to provide the resources in the classrooms so that the status quo could change somewhat; Cazden, Michaels, and Watson-Gegeo (1984) provide a detailed study of two classrooms as computers are first introduced and complement the mixed notes sounded by the Mehan et al. study. Michaels (1985) describes how the classrooms differed in the way student interactions around the computers were organized and how text-editing procedures were introduced. She provides a provocative analysis of the consequence of the variations on the students' knowledge about computer text editing. On post-tests, more children evidenced more sophisticated knowledge in one of the classrooms than in the other classroom, where the children appeared to learn less and where the distribution of the knowledge favored boys over girls. In our terms, one classroom experienced the "parts" problems and the other did not.

Michaels makes it clear that the classrooms were similar in many respects: the entering ability of the children, the use of the computer in the "publishing" part of a process-oriented approach to writing instruction, the lack of direct formal lessons on the use of the text-editor, the age-expected homogeneous sex groupings whenever the children had power to select group or pair membership. The differences between the classrooms involved the media for the indirect teaching of the use of the computer and the personnel involved in teaching and use: In the classroom without the "parts" problem, the teacher became expert at using the computer, providing varying gradations of help to the children while they were using the computer and supplying them with successively more complete wall charts that summarized the text-editing procedures which could be used. In the other classroom, one of the boys became the expert and instead of wall charts, only copies of a standard manual were available for reference. Furthermore, in the "parts" problem classroom, children worked on the computer in same-sex groups of their own choosing, while in the classroom with the more extensive knowledge spread, children worked in pairs as assigned by the teacher, and the pairs were often mixed in terms of the sex of the children and the abilities they displayed with the computer and elsewhere in the classrooms.

Michael's study confirms both the pessimism and optimism of the Mehan group's study. Where they could, the structures supportive of sex-differentiation expanded into the use of the new technology and made the "part of the population" problem worse, at least to the extent that they found a new arena to operate in. On the other hand, when an expert teacher becomes an expert user of the new technology, old technology (e.g., a wall chart, and sequenced or "titrated" information supply) made more extensive knowledge available to the students, making inroads on the problem about restricting education to "part" of the domain of activity. Although limited to a few cases, these detailed studies give us reason to worry that a laissez faire attitude toward social organization or a "teacherless" instructional strategy during computer introduction may contribute to the recapitulation of the status quo, including less effective education for part of the population and limited education for all.

THE BASICS

Detailed studies of computer use in schools are few and far between, but those that use broader strokes to study patterns of diffusion of microcomputers into the schools indicate that pessimism should have the upper hand in our evaluation of current computer use. Impediments to equal and full education that already exist in schools are magnified. The distinctive impediment we will focus on here arises from widespread acceptance in educational practice of a "two-level" approach to curriculum sequencing which is often justified in terms of a "two-level" theory of mental abilities.

The two-level approach assumes that some groups have more "upper level" abilities, which can best be stimulated by "upper level" experiences, while the remaining groups can best be stimulated by "lower level" experiences. Likely candidates for the "lower level" experiences are children from families that are ethnically and economically in a different group than the theorists and educators, i.e., groups we call minorities. The computer adapts all too well to this approach, reflected by the fact that, even when minority group schools obtain computers, the quality of usage is judged low (CSOS, 1983–1984; Shavelson et al., 1984). "Low quality usage" is variably defined: In the Shavelson et al. report, it refers to "non-orchestration" methods of organizing computer activities, which happens most often with minority group schools. In the CSOS report "low quality" refers to drill and practice programs in place of "enrichment activities."

The "drill and practice" emphasis in minority group schools implicitly adopts the recommendations of Arthur Jensen (1973), who has developed a two-level theory of mind and instruction that characterizes "level 1" as "rote learning" (which easily translates into "rote drill and practice") and "level 2" as "transformations on the input" (which easily translates into "more flexible and intelligent mental work"). Drill and practice computer use fits with level 1 curricular strategies that require, for example, mastery of speed and accuracy criteria at letter and word recognition before the student is allowed to engage in comprehension lessons, or that require automaticity of basic math facts as an entry requirement to other mathematics activities (e.g., word problems or the use of mathematic reasoning and concepts in science and other domains).

The widespread use of this educational strategy has, where proper management techniques are used, brought children up to grade level on "the basics" but failed to "boost" them into the higher order activity. Widely discussed as the 3rd–4th grade watershed, the heavy focus on level 1 skills seems to help children do only what they were trained to do in a rote way; There is no "transfer" of the achievement up into the "higher level" of learning. A number of minority group children get stuck at level 1: They are not exposed to practice with activities at "higher" levels of the curriculum when they do not demonstrate mastery of "the basics." This failing is then attributed to the children's own lack of ability for the "higher" skills, which they were neither tested on nor taught.

The circularity and incoherence of such pedagogical moves are apparent. There are empirical objections as well. Mandler (1977), for example, shows that there are excellent reasons to believe that the "level 1–level 2" theory is wrong, even for the experimental data that justified the distinction in the first place. Mandler's work displays that the complex integration and elaboration that characterize what might have been called "rote learning" make it impossible to dichotomize this activity from other "transformations on the input."

THE ALTERNATIVE

Essentially, the alternative position, and the one we prefer, is that *many roads can lead to excellence*. We can entertain a unified non-relativistic goal: flexible, creative use of mental and cultural tools. But, we can expect that precise definition of excellence and new inventions of mental and cultural tools will be varied and enriched if we are able to overcome the gatekeeping established by level 1 type practices in education. In effect, we propose to admit many different "first" level activities into computer use in schools and to test whether our educational system can capitalize on them to serve our goal. This position provides a clear impetus for engaging seriously in work with members of other cultural groups that have different practices and different traditions. We are impelled to work with as much cultural and individual variation as we can find.

Many different, even contradictory, sets of activities are rote or routine at different times in different societies. In the socio-historical context of education and psychology, a certain set of activities (e.g., letter–sound decoding) came to be routinized along with a certain variant of approaching them (e.g., with speed and accuracy). A cursory view of the history of reading (Wolf, 1976), writing (Schmandt-Bessarat, 1978), and literacy pedagogy (Resnick & Resnick, 1977) shows it could have been otherwise—was in fact otherwise at different times, in different places. But, events ranging over time from the adaptation of an alphabetic system, the inventions allowing print to be a mass media, the use of written standardized tests for military selection, the appropriation of educational systems for selection devices in general—such events made appropriate particular activities performed in particular ways. Concurrently existing mechanistic theories and metaphors of mental activity provided a placement of these as reducible components of other activities which were not currently seen as routine. These same theories and metaphors also provided a rationale for sequencing these reducible components as prior in skill development to other skills, as well as a rationale, based on a zero sum notion, for the "automaticity" of these routines being linked to successful performance on the whole task including those parts not seen as routine. Hence, we, currently, have arrived at level 1 and level 2. Seeing some variation in the population with respect to the appropriate routine activities, social policy promotes a prosthetic device to make routine the activities which appear to be lacking in some members of the population. Hence, we have arrived at drill and practice.

We do not believe that we need or should arrive at these places. As Rohwer (1980) points out, or psychology and social policy provides treatment for children in difficulty based on what we assume the successful children have passed through. But those successful children, unburdened by our treatment, continue to achieve, while those we treat "get poorer." We can only assume that with rapid change in our technology and economy, we will get worse and worse at guessing which activities should be at a rote or routine level for future success and worse yet at guessing which variant of those activities will prove most valuable and most amenable to effective educational treatment.

In our understanding of the processes of change, we need not follow this course. We can, instead, support many courses of development of expertise around larger activities. In the course of these activities, we can appropriate whichever approach the child uses for subordinated parts of the activity, providing not only for practice at the kinds of routines that work for the child in the activity, but also providing for their integration into the larger activity system which makes it sensible to routinize them in the first place. Although we want to end with uniformity of access and contribution to the developing repertoire of cultural tools and activities, we must begin with the variety that is currently available.

Thus, our definition of an educational activity: a medium, constituted of and coordinating cultural tools, which provides for the invention and growth of routine and nonroutine flexible activities on the part of the child. Educational activity takes advantage of the variation within and among children to promote activity suitable to current and changing conditions. The bonus here is that even if our guesses at the larger activities valuable for the future are not very good, we will have preserved the variation needed to meet them when we have a better idea.

AN EXAMPLE OF THE ALTERNATIVE

We provide only one example of research/pedagogy that is motivated by our view. We do so in order to provide the extended narrative detail that is needed to present work which is outside the currently standard paradigm. The example involves writing, computers, and children whose school experience usually consists of writing and computer use experiences that are very restrictive, easily characterized as strict rote drill and practice.

Some years ago, we started doing our research with children who had been identified as being in the bottom 20% of their elementary school population, according to standardized tests and teacher report. We built "American style jukus" (see DeVos, 1978 for the Japanese origins of jukus) so that we could engage the children in activities and social structures not usually found in elementary schools, at least for those in the "low" group.[4] Jukus are after-school schools that meet somewhere in the community for a few hours a few times a week. The communities and the children in our projects are diverse in their cultural and language backgrounds but are mostly work-

---

[4] The "we" involved in jukus include other members of the Laboratory of Comparative Human Cognition, especially, in addition to the authors, Catherine King, and members of the Community Educational Resource and Research Center, especially Alonzo B. Anderson, Esteban Diaz, and Luis Moll. By joining our research efforts with CERRC we were able to profit from the diverse expertise they bring to the enterprise by virtue of their history and affiliation with Hispanic and black communities.

ing class. While school-related tasks are involved in the jukus, neither the curriculum sequence nor the social relations common to schools need be involved. One visitor to one of our jukus, Marge Martus, an educational researcher, captured the flavor of the setting best when she commented that there was a great deal of movement and talk and a great variety of participants milling around, but, in the midst of the hubbub, it didn't seem that any child was "off task." Our response was that it would be like running through a rain storm trying to avoid the raindrops—there are so many tasks in the jukus that any child is bound to be "on" one of them. And so it is with writing in the jukus: the children can hardly fail to engage in some tasks that implicate writing of some sort.

The particular sort of writing in this example is quite unusual. If two parties are logged onto the same large computer via two different remote terminals, they can "write" or "chat" to each other in real time. The mode is like a phone conversation, but it uses the technologies of the written alphabet and the computer as well as telephones. The deaf community has a routinized practice involving this mode, using TTY's (teletypewriters). Our juku sites use microcomputers with telecommunications hardware (acoustic couplers or modems) and software, and ordinary telephones. The participants make a local phone call to connect with a large multi-user time-sharing computer on which we have established an account for use in the jukus. The account can be used for electronic mail and a variety of other activities as well as for the "write" function. A record of the written conversation can be stored in a computer file for later analysis, editing, or revision.

Our interest in "write" is quite simple: It can be a part of a variety of activities in which writing is used; some of those activities may be of interest to children who might otherwise resist engaging in literacy. It has potential as a *means* for development of literacy and for microgenetic, ontogenetic and sociogenetic research on literacy development. Thus we are working to create activity systems that can serve the purposes of research and of teaching/learning.

In principle, we want a strong contrast to a level 1–level 2 system. We want to severely underspecify what counts as the initial writing acts by the children (in contrast to the heavily specified acts of a level 1 theory). Furthermore, we want to promote the accomplishment of an end state which is open-ended, creative, and flexible, and which allows access to the culturally elaborated processes and products of literacy in order to elicit inventions of new products and processes to be incorporated into the cultural store (in contrast to the current level 2 theory). To evaluate our success in these activities we judge whether the activity has elicited writing of various types from various children and whether we are able to elaborate on the children's initial activities so that a variety of sophisticated uses and functions of literacy are available to them, no matter how they started.

The chronological account which follows details the ups and downs in our progress: the plans, the accidents, the reflection and analysis, and the recalibration of our goals and plans. We end with new beginnings.

1. International Exchange

The very first appearance of real-time written communication in our work with children was in an unusual international event. It gave us ideas about trying to use the mode in a more systematic way. Children in Pistoia, Italy,[5] had exchanged electronic mail, ordinary postal service mail, newspapers and videotapes with children from our San Diego jukus. We arranged for a written conversation via computer between the two groups of children. The researchers primarily in charge (Diaz in the U.S. and Duranti in Italy) had quite modest goals for the half-hour event: They wanted to see how this mode of communication would further substantiate the exchange between the children. Four observations were made about the children from the U.S. jukus during the event:

1. *Audience.* At first the children's participation in the event was limited. They responded to adult questions and carried out adult initiatives. Although the children were interested and pleased to be involved, much of the control and direction of the activity resided in the adults. Then we brought in a newspaper article that had been sent from Italy. The headline mentioned San Diego; a large photograph of a child seated at a computer had an Italian child's name under it. In many respects, the children already "knew" that the communication was with peers in Italy, but the introduction of the newspaper article produced such changes in the children's behavior that it seemed as if the knowledge was new. Suddenly, the children came up with many topics to put on the floor (screen?): names, ages, sexes, favorite computer activities, favorite singing groups, school and home daily events, and, eventually, the issue of time differences.

   This more active involvement of the children following the introduction of the newspaper from Italy demonstrates the interrelatedness of different modes of communication as well as the effectiveness of the larger activity (in which the real-time written conversation was embedded) to motivate children's communication. It also points to the need to understand the concept "audience" and the mechanisms by which a potential audience becomes an effective audience for youngsters.

---

[5] Our colleague, Alessandro Duranti, had participated in our jukus in San Diego and found Italian researchers and educators who had an interest in developing some related activities. He, Mary McGinnis, Sasha Cole, David Keenan and Elinor Ochs worked with Italian colleagues, including Laura Benigni, Patrizio Zini, and Sonia Iozzelli to set up a computer component of an educational effort in the town of Pistoia.

2. *Time*. The children "knew" in many ways that the time of day in Italy was different than the time of day in San Diego. Besides having school exposure to this, the children had their schedules disrupted, arising very early and coming to the computer room in order to communicate before the Pistoia children had gone home for the evening. Still, time differences were treated as an interesting and novel topic of the written conversation. That the Italian children already knew what happened in the afternoon, while it was still morning in San Diego, was a topic of conversation in the face-to-face setting among the American children and adults as well. The real-time nature of the written conversations gave substance to the rather abstract notion of time zones.

In a sense, the telecommunication event functioned as a laboratory experiment for a study of time differences. While there is a movement to foster "writing across the curriculum," including writing in science classes, this experience suggests a somewhat different relationship, where science moves in on written communication activities.

3. *Language*. As bilinguals whose home language is considered a minority language, many of the San Diego children had experiences with interlingual successes and difficulties. They "knew" that the children in Pistoia spoke and wrote Italian and studied English as a foreign language. All three languages appeared on the computer screen during the written conversation. Bilinguals, available both in Pistoia and San Diego, played a very important role. In addition to the functional value of bilingualism, another observation about language was made by several of the children. Afterwards, while reflecting on the event, they puzzled over their ability to understand some of the written Italian without the assistance of the Italian bilingual or the bilingual dictionary. This expertise contrasted with their experiences with written English and Spanish. Quite often, they could ignore some of the Italian spelling and look at the middles (roots) of the words in order to get the gist of the meaning in the context. The ability was lacking on the part of the English monolinguals or monoliterates present, even the adults. The children concluded on a note of comparative linguistics: To say that Italian and Spanish are different languages is not the same as to say that Spanish and English are different languages.

The telecommunication provided an opportunity for the recontextualization of the children's bilingualism, including an opportunity to engage in sophisticated analytic activity about this everyday fact of the children's lives.

4. *Initiative*. Each "breakthrough," about time, audience, and language was associated with (and noticeable because of) disruptions in the orderliness of the face-to-face interactions. As the children became

more active subjects, they jostled to get nearer to the keyboard or screen, spoke in overlapping turns and code-switched between English and Spanish, complained about the slowness of the current typist or translator, and worried that the latency preceding an answer from Italy was due to some infelicity in what the last turn-taker had written. As the children found motives for composing, typing, reading and rereading, there were reverberations in the social ordering of the event. Some of the children became upset about their own perceived lack of ability. Some became upset about the inability of adults to help. Each "wave" of disruption settled down in the flow of the demands of real-time communication with the Italian interlocutors, but each settled period had more children physically positioned in the forefront of the activity and more "authoritatively" in control of the direction of topics and distribution of turns.

These observations compel us to reconsider two notions related to studying literacy: a) the role of social discord in processes of change in contrast to assumptions underlying current practices that focus on classroom management techniques designed to minimize discord; b) the active development of "authorship" or ownership in contrast to assumptions underlying current practices which arrange for ownership of literacy products merely by guarding against the possibility of some other "owner" being introduced into the writing event.

Overall, the "computer chat" with children in Italy showed us the value of real-time written conversations for fulfilling our goals: Children who were stuck with simple rote writing in their ordinary school experience could become very active participants in literacy events that involved interesting topics in some depth. We brought this lesson home and started engaging the children in our jukus with "writing" in real time on a regular basis.

2. Children's Written Phone Calls

The children first used "write" among themselves: children from one neighborhood juku contacted children from a distant neighborhood. The content was about names, ages, grades and "favorites" in sports, music, colors. The typical pen-pal routines were broken only by two sorts of discussions, both peculiar to the jukus. First, there was some discussion about computers and particular programs. For example, a math game (Levin, 1979) with an authoring system was used by the children to make up games that were fiendishly clever, and the "write" system was used to issue challenges, negotiate rules and make other arrangements. Second, there was some discussion of the individual child's ability with respect to using the computer; for example, a dispute arose about the trade-offs involved in the mechanics of writing: the trade-off between speed and accuracy in real-time communication was one part, and the trade-off between a child typing independently or having a speedy adult helper was another.)

This use of "write" appealed to some children. We collected information about the interest and capability of the children to use alphabetic literacy that seemed beyond them when they engaged in standard academic tasks. But, there were four drawbacks: First, some children were not interested in this as a literacy activity or did not maintain an interest in it. For instance, when Adriana and Martha finally came to grips with the fact that the computer was using an ordinary telephone line, they wanted to stop doing the computer "write" and call by voice phone to their electronic pals. Second, some children seemed interested and content to maintain a great deal of adult control of the activity by the "helpers" with whom they were face-to-face in their juku setting. Third, changes in the time schedules for the jukus made child–child sessions difficult. Finally, when the communication was child-to-child, there were few chances to develop topics that would stretch the children's writing skills. The usual content was quite stereotyped and a far cry from creative writing or problem solving writing that would be useful in a variety of other ways in the children's lives.

In summary, the "parts" problem was not addressed to our satisfaction. We were still missing some of the children and we were still missing some highly valued uses of literacy.

3. Low Performance in the New Mode

Trying to overcome these problems, we switched to discourse between adults and children, still using the "write" mode. The participants were children at the jukus and adults at the University. The discourse consisted of questions and short answers, with little disjunction between social role and discourse role. The only thing the children asked about was the adult's name. This was quite a setback. We had session after session of monosyllabic responses from the children, the sort of language use that is common in stressful testing situations and the very sort that Labov (1972) criticized as a poor representation of children's true language ability. We did get them in writing; but monosyllables they were nonetheless. According to field notes taken at the juku sites, the children's "yes," "no," one-word, and "I-don't-know" responses were enthusiastic and optimistic in contrast to the stress exhibited in test situations. However, we were not able to reduce the effect of the asymmetry between researcher and children enough to get written language that was any better than the sorts of language use the children experienced in their "level 1" ordinary classroom practice. We had a visitor well versed in interviewing children, Charles Crook from the University of Durham, try his hand at it; it seemed that the adult–child asymmetry combined with the literacy mode was too difficult to overcome.

Two indicators of what might help were apparent in the record of these exchanges: Playing with the keyboard and screen elicited long exchanges from the children; that is, when the adult made designs by using nonalphabetic symbols (* : | % $ #), the children entered the activity with great fluency and verve and invented some non-modeled strings. They also initiated this kind of play without invitation or instruction or request from the adults. The second indicator involved an adult deficiency: when the children used a Spanish word, the adult asked for information about it and the children proceeded to "run" a series of exchanges, carefully including some Spanish that would have to be asked about in each bit of information that was given. This, too, had a playful character, but, more importantly, it broke into the asymmetry by reversing the social power relations and discourse roles. Nothing of substance was developed as a topic in either of these kinds of exchanges however, and so we sought for other solutions that could build on these.

4. The Birth of the Electronic Written Rap

A clear potential in computer communication was our first ally. It is difficult to tell much about who the interlocutor is when communicating on the computer. We could ward off the monosyllables by not assuming personas that supported the asymmetry between adult and child. Our second ally was the liberating effect of play, but using full verbal means (not asterisks and percent signs, not the adult's deficient language skills). When we engineered the written conversations to take advantage of these potentials, we found that the discourse roles were reorganized, that the children's fluency in writing was unleashed, and that a genre that is effective for many of the children, the "rap," made an appearance in written form.

Here and in the next sections we will provide some transcripts of the "write" sessions. To read the data, some aspects of the situation must be kept in mind:

1. The "speakers" are separated by many miles but are communicating in real time. In a public room in a working class neighborhood, there is a dyad or group that constitutes one "side" of the discourse; the participants there include one or more elementary age children who are low performers and a university undergrad (often one who shares the ethnic and class background of the children). In an office at the university, the other "side" of the discourse is carried on by an adult researcher or a group of them.
2. The "speakers" are actually typing and reading on a computer hooked to a telephone line.
3. The ubiquitous "ga" in the data records means "go ahead". It is necessary to signal turn completion in this mode. "ga" is similarly used over Citizen Band radio and with teletypewriters in the deaf community.

4. We have added the name identifiers to indicate who is the "writer" for
    each turn. These names do not show up during the written conversa-
    tion. Field notes and interviews with the undergraduate participant ob-
    server were used to identify the speakers. For this presentation of the
    data, we have omitted some of the elements that are introduced by in-
    terference from the telephone lines or the computer systems. Any other
    discontinuities in the discourse are remarked upon in the transcripts.
    The line length as transmitted during the event is preserved in this pres-
    entation of the record. Since the listener/reader does not receive any-
    thing until the return key is hit, short lines help to signal that the
    speaker/writer is still there.
5. Everything after the colon (:) shows up on each party's computer
    screen, line by line, as the sending party hits the return key. New lines
    are added to the screen at the bottom; eventually earlier parts of the
    message scroll past the top of the screen. The discourse is simulta-
    neously saved in a computer file and interpreted with reference to par-
    ticipant observation field notes.

Example 1 illustrates the change in the discourse that preceded the emergence of the "written rap." Teresa has an opportunity to question and challenge in this discourse; the adult still has information ("-csh" and "control-d")
that indicates asymmetry, but the child introduces and pursues the topics.

Example 1   (Teresa and Aida are on a terminal connected to a phone down-
                   town at the Mt. Erie juku; Teresa is a fifth grader and Aida is a
                   college undergraduate; the adult is a researcher on a terminal on
                   the UCSD campus.)
Teresa: hi who is this ga
Adult: who wants to know ga
Teresa: teresa
                   what does -csh stand for? ga
Adult: csh? csh? maybe csh stands for
                   cash
                   ga
Teresa: well, it is what you were doing before we wrote to you. ga
Adult: how did you find that out ga
Teresa & Aida: because we used "w" to find out who was on
                   and that's what you were doing. -csh ga
Adult: so, are you guys spys or something?
                   How do you know so much about this machine? ga
Teresa: I learned it from Aida ga
Adult: So, you are a spy for Aida! ah hah!!!!!! ga
Teresa: you never told me who you are
                   and i am not asa spy ga
Adult: well, I'll tell you the other thing you asked about---
                   if you remember what it is you asked AND
                   if you promise not to tell Aida. ga
Teresa: I'm going to make Aida close her eyes,

(The connection between the parties is temporarily lost. The Adult screen shows "EOF" [for end of file]; the child's screen shows a "%" that indicates the "write" function was terminated and that something new can be done. Teresa and Aida "write" to the adult again; so that a "Message from..." shows on the adult screen and then Teresa resumes:)

Teresa:	what happened? ga
Adult:	I don't know -- seems like the
	computer thinks that you or the telephone
	line is sending a <control-d> because that sign off
	is what happens when there is a <control-d>
	Now do you remember the thing you asked
	me about that wasn''t the bi secret of my name?
	ga
Teresa:	yes, what is -csh
	?ga
Adult:	-csh means this:
	sh is for shell a c is the name of the language that
	this computer system understands so -csh means hat I
	was sitting there at the shell level and
	about ready to do some fancy work. Now don't tell Aida. ga

This seems to us to be the trick: have the child be an active subject as indicated by discourse roles while not pretending that the adult fails to have information and experience advantages that are useful for the child's pursuit of learning. There is a certain involuted nature to the topics in this discourse: They are about the computer being used, but the discourse holds promise.

Later on the same day, Teresa went about other activities at the juku and Renee and Veronica (sixth graders) joined Aida to have a written conversation with the adult at UCSD. Again, in response to the children's request for identification, the adult responded by asking who they were. The identified themselves as a group, using the name of their juku, the Computer Breakers. Example 2 picks up the discourse at the adult turn. The ease with which the children are controlling the situation here is apparent. Veronica's complaint ("we going to tell you just wait") is fully justified: there had been no "ga" and the adult was jumping the gun, not being responsive to the turn change at the remote site when Vernoica took over from Renee.

This disruption in Veronica's turn nicely displays the hybrid nature of this written conversation: The complaint part sounds like an oral exchange, but the clauses that follow appear "written." According to the field notes, no notice was taken of the copula absence in the complaint (we going to) as is appropriate for the dialect of oral language spoken in the neighborhood; but the other clauses were monitored in ways appropriate for written language. There was monitoring for meaning ("iwe" was an imperfectly executed attempt to change from I to we), for written language mechanics (the

Example 2

Adult:	why do you call yourselves the computer breakers? ga
Renee:	But Veronica has been here longer than I have
	so she will tellyou why we call
	ourselves the computer breakers.
	(There was a lengthy pause.)
Adult:	hello hello ga
Veronica:	WE call ourselfs computer brwe going to tell you just
	wait
	iwe are called computer breakers because
	we know how to break and we are like a
	club and use computers. we are a o.g.
	team so we wanted a o.g. club

ga

change from the reflexive "WE call ourselfs" to the passive construction "we are called" solved a spelling problem that Veronica commented on as a problem) and for written language syntax (the appearance of the "are" form of the copula and the use of periods was discussed by Veronica).

Example 3 illustrates the preconditions for the emergence of the rap. First, the adult was taking full advantage of the vague identity afforded by this mode so that some activities would not be ruled out based on her actual identity as an white adult university researcher. At one point there is a "bluff" about "O.G." lest the children dismiss her as a lame for not knowing what it stood for ("only girls" as Veronica later subtly reveals); at another point there is "gossip" (I heard...) and a comment on the usual gender patterns for raps which suggest that the interlocutor is in a social network with the children.

Very important for the future developments of our enterprise, this exchange named a language genre, the *rap* and provided some material for use in a rap, namely, the girls' prowess at double dutch jump-rope. The rap had recently developed as a nationally recognized form of verbal art: it is a form of discourse with complex rhythm and rhyme characteristics that had gained prominence as an accompaniment to the popular "break dancing" performances/contests that had entered popular culture. It is an oral discourse form. In addition to being recently highlighted in records and movies throughout the country, raps have a special significance and history in the black community of which these children are members. Rap discourse not only promulgates information but is an entertainment and a means of establishing social ranking in the community. It is most often and most artfully used by adolescent males. Very important for our purposes, the rap is a genre that affords monitoring of performance, evaluation of performance, and the notion of improvement of performance over time. It is a cultural tool with great promise as an element in educational activity.

Example 3

Adult:	O G you are an O G team? I don't believe that! Do you mean to tell me that you think that I will believe that you are an OG team Humph!!! If I believed that I would believe just about anything!! prove it. ga
Veronica & Renee:	come over to m.t. and we'll tell something to prove it! we'll even tell you a rap we made by our selfs! <div style="text-align:center">ga</div>
Adult:	girls made a rap? now I know you don't expect me to believe that! ga
Veronica:	aha thats why we made a video but we let the boys do the breaking because we had on dredresses. i hope you saw it so you can see what the boys did and the girls said ga
Adult:	I heard about a video but I heard that the girls moved more thantheir mouths I heard that they did some things with a jump rope that would make everybody sit up and pay attention. Are you those girls? ga
Veronica & Renee:	yes we played a little double doutch and jump rope. we have another club but it is only girls and no boys no grown ups eather

While raps had been mentioned and we can see the potential of using them, there was still the problem of their mode: they were oral language tools, not written language, not computer communication. The attempt to make a transition to another mode turned out to be very simple, a fact no doubt related to the oral/written hybrid nature of the "write" mode. Immediately following Veronica's turn concerning double dutch and her reinstitution of the O.G. topic, the adult attempted to construct a rap (Example 4). Our response to this example, even now nearly a year later as we engage with it as an object of study, is amazement. There was a virtual explosion of language. It was fast—word-finding and key-finding were so subordinated in the written raps that it seemed as if the raps jumped from the mind of one interlocutor to the other's computer screen!

The interruption in the third line of the adult's turn (of Message from...) indexes this significant moment: When the children saw the first couplet (a little double dutch/that ain't such much—last line courtesy of Dave Van Ronk, a musician who bridges traditions of black and white

Example 4

Adult:	a little double dutch
	that ain't such much
	but a lot ofMessage from......
	oops you interrupted me want to see the rest of my rap?
Veronica & Renee:	yes
Adult:	a little double dutch
	that ain't such much
	but a lot of double dutch jump rope?
	then all the rest better give up hope.
	ga
Renee:	you think you are cute
	and you think you are
	live you need to cut
	it out cause its all
	in your mind.
	ga
Adult:	you know I am cute
	and that's double to boot
	and you gotta mind because you
	got not mind !!!
	ga
Renee:	you wis you were cute
	you wish you were cute
	but you are a mute
	ga
Adult:	I don't mind
	cuz I can sign
	ga
Veronica:	you got no sence in your head
	cause your rap is dead ga

American music), they jumped toward their computer screen, accidentally
closing off part of the communication channel as they leaned on the keyboard; with no assistance or prompting from the undergraduate, Aida, they
executed the "write" function again, causing the system to print "Message
from..." on the adult's terminal. It is very important to know that their accident did not cut them off as listeners/readers; it just cut off their opportunity to respond. To be the recipient of a rap is to be ready to respond; the
children demonstrated their status as active subjects of the rap event, as well
as knowledgeable users of both the computer and the rap as cultural tools.

Renee, who earlier (Example 2) had contributed only an explanation of
non-contribution, found her voice/fingers in this genre. Her first rap is not
just a mimic, having a different rhyme scheme than the adult's prior turn (a
quatrain, not two couplets). The hybrid oral–written nature of the "write"
mode and, consequently, of the written rap is clear in Renee's turns:

Although the "live" and "mind" rhyme depend on Renee's oral language dialect, the spelling is standard for written English; In her second turn, she noticed the missing "h" on wish only after she had hit the return key and transmitted it; The only way to act on this monitoring and evaluation, at this point in the "write" mode, was to retype the line. Notice also Veronica's "cause" following the adult nonwritten standard spelling of "cuz." Again, it is not a mimic and it demonstrates the writing in "write."

At the time of the rap, and now, Veronica's Vygotsky-esque message is especially appreciated by our research group: The relation between thinking (sense in your head) and speech (rap) is brought to the forefront (cf. Vygotsky, 1962). Unfortunately, the adult, in ignorance of the rules for ending a rap, complimented Veronica's turn, unwittingly signaling the end of the rap in Example 5. Renee properly interprets the ending the adult didn't intend (but that the rap genre determines) suggesting that to the winners should go the spoils of the adult's "big secret"—the name. The adult lamely tries to carry on, ignoring the closure that had been invoked, but both children reject this anarchy. They provide appropriate closings by the "winners:" ones that demonstrate their superior control of the rap genre. Veronica responds, now adding social relations (forget you then) and affect (you are mean) to her Vygotskian comment about raps, moving to a quatrain rhyme scheme. Meanwhile, Renee enlisted Aida's help to fashion a closing of some com-

Example 5

Adult:	I like your style
	you beat my by a mile
	ga
Renee:	now that we finished
	our game
	what is your name?
	ga
Adult:	my name is mine but I'll give you a sign
	for every letter in my name
	there''s a number in this game
	ga
Veronica:	forget you then you are mean
	thats why your rap is a bean
Renee and Aida:	take it slow cause
	i've got to go
	carla going to run this show
	ga
Adult:	16 5 and 7
	that's my name and it's heaven.
	ga,Carla, ga
Veronica:	your name is peg and your rap is dead
	ga

plexity: a couplet with an internal rhyme in the first line and with a complex rhythm pattern: /uuu/u(u)/. At the same time, Renee and Aida perform another part of the rap ritual, turning the floor over to the next rapper who is waiting in the "wings." The adult, incoherently for the rap genre, tries to reinstitute the name and number game topic but does accept the change in speakers. Veronica beats the adult at her own game and delivers the final end to the rap among these interlocutors.

Word of what was going on in the telecommunications center of the juku spread. First, in the middle of Example 4, the word spread among the children attending the juku that day. Many people arrived along with Carla; they jostled for turns to do written raps, made alliances to share turns, discussed issues if equity and excellence as a means to decide who should have turns and eventually had to be cajoled to go home and stop writing. Second, in the university, the researchers looked for aids to work with this genre: A member of the University community, Billy Vaughn, who is also a member of the black community was enlisted to help out; A writer, Sheila Cole, provided a rhyming dictionary to help out the non-native users of the rap. Third, in the seven following days, the word spread through the neighborhood of the juku and older children not previously involved in computer communication started to come by and "check it out."

5. Untoward Consequences of Written Raps

In the next meeting of the juku, two days later, the written raps continued. The artistry and fluency of the children, their speed and flexibility with the "write" mode in the rap genre, was truly impressive. All of the children were intrigued, involved and active; some were recognizable and lauded as more expert practicioners. Then, a weekend intervened and seven days after the birth of the written rap, a truly dismal experience occurred.

Important background knowledge to interpret Example 6 is the role of the rap in the schooling in the neighborhood. It was outlawed. Raps were not done on computers, they were not written, they were not supposed to be engaged in on school grounds, not even in the playground. Raps were classified, along with other verbal genres native to the community, as not permissible in polite educated company. There has been enough said and written about the problems engendered when the school requires that children give up their cultural and language heritage in order to succeed at literate activity. It is clear that the fluency with language displayed by the children in raps was not available for educators to appropriate in the language tasks that were allowed in school. It is also clear that their implicit familiarity with the mechanics of poetics as demonstrated in the written raps would be good entry points for advanced literature courses that most of the children would never be allowed to take, since they would fail to meet the existing entry requirements for them.

We could know all this in a theoretic sense and argue against such stulti-
fying policies. But the brute force experience of the consequences in this
concrete case is more enlightening, and more depressing. The children had
time and opportunity to discuss the sudden appearance of the rap in writing
and on the computer in the juku setting which involved school-like tasks.
Example 6 shows that they did not remove raps from the category "inappropriate" because of their experience the week before. Rather, the analysis
appears to be "anything goes: if raps are allowed, talk about bums and
fools and wiping butts and shutups are also allowed."

Example 6 (Many children are present, including some that do not usually attend
the juku. They are older and have heard the news of the written raps
around the neighborhood.)

Children: weare computer breaker and
we are live
we are rapping on the
mike from 9 to 5
ga

Adult: rapping on the mike
What's that like?
This is a comcomputer
and I'm a straight shooter!
ga

Children: you dont know you must
be dum cause you can't
afford no gum you bum
ga

Adult: Sure
Sure I inow know
My mind is HARD
I dop do my business
With the main WizARD!
ga

Children: your group is mad
your brothers sad
cause we are going
yo wipe your little
butt
ga

Adult: come on folks
no more jokes
we have a fine time
when we all rhyme
but you lost your stroke
and your broke
so what will you do?
Go to thje zoo?

(The rhyme and rhythm are not re-instituted; only the challenging nature of the discourse remains as an indicator of the rap. The turns continue but there is disarray in the discourse; only the conventions of the mode ("ga" and "o" for over or out) are available for coordinating the discourse partners. The children name an alternate genre "basing" that appears to be emerging in the place of the rap but the adult does not/ will not engage in this genre. The following excerpts are samples:)

Children:	we dont answer you nowe dont answer you kno
Adult:	ga??ga??
Children:	says og funky fresh
	ga
Children:	areyouareyou basing
	ga
Adult:	heavy duty dont get snooty
Children:	aretyouareyou are YOU BASING?
	ga
Adult:	well, you yes
	ga

(The adult, unable to regain coordination with the children, finally terminates the session:)

Adult:	have a fine holiday
	see yhou soon
	time we headed
	rouhd the moon
	when we get back
	we'll check the slack
	see you on line
	have a fine time
	doln't feel bad, you guy are fine!
	ga
Children:	xd}i}iyou think your cool
	but your a fool
	ga
Children:	shetup
	ga
Adult:	get down
Children:	oao
	ga
Adult:	o&o
System:	%EOF (% consequence of Adult < control-d > and EOF consequence of children's < control-d >)

The rhyme, the rhythm, the intricacy, the fluency—it all disappears. The historical relation of raps to broadcasted oral language (rapping on the mike) is in the opening turn. The adult attempt to indicate the computer mediation of the current rap is not taken up, nor is his attempt to change topics to involve the computer wizard with whom the juku members are familiar. The confused typing of single line turns in Example 6 are only excerpts from a long chain that betrayed no rhythm, rhyme, evaluation, monitoring, or coordination among interlocutors, but did contain various bits of "bathroom talk." To borrow from Veronica's earlier comment, there was no sense when the rap was dead.

The social organization around the telecommunication center at the juku was chaotic. Aida, the undergraduate, could barely function as an assistant to the children or as an observer. The overall impression is that the children had not maintained their respect for the artistry of the rap genre; instead they had accepted the implicit message of the school that it was just another part of "street stuff" or "bathroom talk." The merciful closing of the channel, indicated by the System turn, was the only successful element. There was no need to cajole the children to go home—nothing was happening.

6. Content Transformation in Written Raps

We were intent on reclaiming the rap genre and the "write" mode from the categorization that seemed to be operating in Example 6. We wanted to take advantage of the children's evident ability to write while rapping (Examples 4 and 5) so the children could take advantage of a fuller range of literacy activities. We wanted to introduce a range of topics that were worthy of extended thought and discussion and that could profit from literate activity. From work with children on electronic mail, computer-produced newsletters, and reading groups, we know they could have a lot to say and reason about on topics of current events and social justice. We reasoned that some "content" focus during the rap could prevent the kind of disintegration found in Example 6. The combined activity of "written raps" and discussions of importance would interact to support each other and leave no room for testing the appropriateness of other aspects of oral language in this setting. Substantive topics could be, in Luria's term (1932), "functional barriers" that would help to regulate the responses.

This indirect approach to the problem worked to reclaim the written raps that we and the children admired. Example 7 features a child from a different juku; he is not that much of an active participant in oral rapping, but the genre still does some work for him.

The adult uses a slogan promulgated throughout California over television and on posters, and suggests that child abusers like gun users should suffer dire consequences, using the word "bail." Pablo initiates the minilesson on the lexicon. In this juku setting, it is commonly the case that the children grapple with the problem, rather than attempting to "pass," when confronted with a word or language structure that is unfamiliar to them. Pablo's involvement in the rap and the topic of child abusers is indicated by his interest in the word "bail." It is clearly a side-sequence, firmly related to

Example 7   (Pablo is a sixth grader whose home and neighborhood language is
Spanish. Pablo is being assisted by undergraduates; they report that he
was not interested in participating initially, but changed to be actively
in charge by the time the following excerpt occurred. The lead in to this
topic was a claim (in rhyme) by Pablo that he wanted to communicate
with Spain because he wanted to know if they thought about the same
things that we did, this topic being an example.)

Adult: Hey thast''s not nonsense,
             that's no bluff
             let's get on a rap
             about serious stuff
             There's a war going on
             and there's no truce
             it's the war against child abuse
             ga

Pablo: that/s very sad
             and very bad
             it makes me very mad
             and I hope that we could have
             some peace ga

Adult: yeah -- use a gun and go to jail?
             huh! hurt a kid and there''s no bail
             ga

Pablo: i don/t understand the word bail
             could you lead me on the trail? ga

Adult: no bail?
             without money, without greens,
             you ain't never gonna get o}iut of jail!
             that''s what it means
             and that's how it seems
             ga

Pablo: so even if you are rich
             you don/t have to stay stiff
             and can stay out if it if you wish
             but if you are poor that/s it? ga

Adult: if they let you have bail that's true
             so for a child abuser what should we do?
             ga

Pablo: stick themj stick theml rich or poor
             leave them in there and close the door ga

Adult: that's a rap and you got style
             you'll beat those bad guys by a mile
             ga

Pablo: now we played your game
             will you tell us your name
             it/s been fun have this rap
             and I hope we have another chat ga

the topic, as demonstrated by his ability to integrate the sequence into the topic with his suggestion about what to do with child abusers, rich or poor.

Even in this short example, it is clear that a literacy device is being effectively used. Pablo has a chance to delve into his second language (English) and into topics of social concern. We had similar "content written raps" about apartheid, Ethiopian famine, and children born drug addicted. In general, the raps were faster, longer and more sophisticated with the children from the juku in the black neighborhood than with the children in the Hispanic neighborhood. It became common that the rap on a given day would be "about something," and that the first order of business was to negotiate the topic for the content filled written rap.

WHAT'S TO BE DONE?

The answer to this query has two parts. One aspect is the continuation of the narrative about our work with the children in the jukus; the other is the more general development of research that can grapple more productively with new technologies, basic skills, and the "parts problems" in education.

In our own work, we are focusing on two different developments from the use of the "write" mode on the computers with the children. One keeps the "content rap," but not the telecommunication; the other keeps the telecommunication and the content, but not the "rap." In one juku, the "content written rap" has become a genre to be included in the group's newsletter. Two young boys published the one shown in Example 8 in a recent issue of their newsletter. The joint activity of the "write" mode remains; but the

Example 8   Why I Don't Use Drugs

Drugs are dangerous to your health
You do them anyway and see your death
Drugs ain't good they make you die,
then your whole family will start to cry.
Baseball and drugs are very silly,
If you use them anyway you'll do a willy!
Chuck Muncie is good, but he used drugs,
if he keeps on doing it he will pull the plug!
People who use drugs and go to school,
keep on doin' it, they are a fool!
We were walking down the street and saw this drug addict,
He asked us for some drugs and we started to panic!
We said, "NO WAY be on your way
or else we'll kick you into the next day!"
So that's what we think about using drugs,
We don't do it because we don't want to pull our plug!

Darell S & Atim S

composition was done outside of any telecommination activity. The "write" mode in this juku sometimes functions like the initial phases of a process approach to teaching writing: a topic is discussed in a "write" and then, after this brainstorming, the children compose pieces on the topic or a related one, which can later be revised and published.

In another juku, the "content written raps" turned into what we call "composations." As the word suggests, the activity is an amalgam of a conversation and a composition. The conversation from the "write" mode is stored in a computer file and later edited and revised into a composition with a word processor. The "first draft" of the composition is a joint activity. The adult interlocutors can, in a natural way, provide the audience constraints that a child would have to imagine in more ordinary writing activities. Furthermore, the adult interlocutor can conversationally request the "more concrete detail" or "more explicit organization" that the child's writing might need. As the child edits the "written conversation" with the goal of producing an essay, a newspaper article or a letter, there are some unusual opportunities for thinking about writing and computers. The differences between dialogic real-time language use and language used in more usual kinds of writing are there to be reflected on, if only because the child needs to edit out the infelicities. The adult's preoccupation with details or organizational issues can be noticed and used by the children before they have independent ability to manipulate their writing based on such concerns. Since the written conversations produce quite a large computer file, the children get a chance to use the parts of a computerized word processor that their usual slender compositions would not encourage them to use. Instead of concentrating on "inserting" and "deleting," the children can work with the features that truly distinguish between a computer and a typewriter: global substitutions, cutting and pasting, spelling checkers, etc.

We do not believe that computers themselves, telecommunication itself, the "write" function itself, "written raps" themselves or "composations" will work automatically to make children better writers. We believe that each can, however, play an important role in organizing a system of activities that allow us to elicit more variable beginning points among the diverse children in our classrooms, beginning points that can be appropriated for the development of writing. By not insisting on uniform starting points or uniform roads to progress, and by capitalizing on the unity of joint activity, we think we can make progress toward more equitable and successful education. In the opening part of this section, we emphasized the importance of underspecifying the beginning point of a writing curriculum and working toward an open-ended, creative and flexible end state. We wanted to evaluate our work relative to the variation we could elicit and the use we could make of that. So far, our work on computer communication in writing development suggests that we have found an opening for productive work on the "underside of education."

The potential suggested by our first experience with the children in Italy has held up over time. We have a reasonable vehicle for research and teaching, one that brings out writing on issues of substance, effectively engages "audience" constraints in the teaching/learning of writing, promotes the inclusion of abstract concerns about language *qua* language, and allows for child initiatives where discord may be harnessed for growth. We see, too, that computers can be used in systems which have the properties that genres like "raps" in the black community provide for developing expertise— notions of monitoring, evaluation and improvement of performance over time.

A theoretical stance underlies the narrative that we have provided in this chapter. It influenced our observations and judgements about what to modify and what to take advantage of as we explored the educational potential of real-time computer-mediated written conversations. Set in a framework developed in the 1920's by Vygotsky (1962, 1978), Luria (1932a, 1932b), and Leont'ev (1981), this viewpoint on psychological research requires that attention be paid to the role of cultural tools in learning and development. By cultural tools are meant material artifacts (e.g., computers and telephones), materialized systems (e.g., alphabetic literacy), social interactions among people (especially those between novices and those more expert in a domain), and the historically elaborated techniques, genres and strategies (e.g., raps or essays) that sometimes differentiate among, but sometimes unify, cultural groups.

Clearly, then, our general orientation places particular value on our continuing to learn from investigations that involve cultural variability. This applies to domestic co-cultural work with researchers whose involvement with children from nonmajority cultural backgrounds allows us to see the ways around inadequate theories and practices that rely on a level 1–level 2 theory of cognitive change. It also applies to concern with the temporal variations in our domestic culture, with the changes that are beginning in what Noyelle (1985) calls the "new economy" and the consequent changing articulations with educational institutions. And, very clearly, it motivates us to find out what happens with new modes like "written computer mediated conversations" and unusual genres like "written raps" and "composations" as they interact with the theories and practices developed in cultures different from ours around the world.

REFERENCES

Cazden, C.B., Michaels, S., & Watson-Gegeo, K. (1984) *Microcomputers and literacy project* (GRANT #NIE G-83-0051). Washington, DC: National Institute of Education.

Center for Social Organization of Schools (CSOS). (1983–84). *School uses of microcomputers: Reports from a national survey* (Issues 1–6). Baltimore, MD: The John Hopkins University.

DeVos, G. (1978). The Japanese adapt to change. In G.D. Spindler (Ed.), *The making of psychological anthropology* (pp. 219–257). Berkeley: University of California Press.

Jensen, A.V. (1973). *Genetics and education*. New York: Harper & Row.

Labov, W. (1972). The logic of nonstandard English. In P.P. Giglioli (Ed.), *Language and social context*. Harmondsworth, England: Penguin Books.

Laboratory of Comparative Human Cognition. (1982). A model system for the study of learning difficulties. *Quarterly Newsletter of the Laboratory of Comparative Human Cognition, 4*(3), 39–66.

Leont'ev, A.N. (1981). *Problems of the development of mind*. Moscow: Progress Publishers.

Levin, J.A. (1979). *The shark family: Estimation arithmetic games. Computer programs*. San Diego: LCHC.

Levin, J.A., & Souviney, R. (Eds.), (1983). Computers and literacy: A time for tools [Special Issue]. *Quarterly Newsletter of the Laboratory of Comparative Human Cognition, 5* (3).

Luria, A.R. (1932a). *The nature of human conflicts: Or emotion, conflict and will*. New York: Liveright.

Luria, A.R. (1932b). The development of writing in the child. In M. Cole (Ed.), *The selected writings of A.R. Luria*. New York: Sharpe.

Mandler, G. (1977). Organization and repetition: Organizational principles with special reference to rote learning. In L.G. Nilsson (Ed.), *Perspectives on memory research*. Hillsdale, NJ: Erlbaum.

Mehan, H., Moll, L.C., & Riel, M.M. (1983). A quasi experiment in guided change (NIE Project Rep. No. G-83-0027). Washington, DC: National Institute of Education.

Mehan, H., Moll, L.C., & Riel, M.M. (1985). *Computers in classrooms: A quasi-experiment in guided change* (Final Rep. No. NIE-G-0027). Washington, DC: National Institute of Education.

Michaels, S. (1985). Classroom processes and the learning of text editing commands. *Quarterly Newsletter of the Laboratory of Comparative Human Cognition, 7* (3), 69–79.

Noyelle, T.J. (1985, August). *The new technology and the new economy: Some implications for equal employment opportunity*. Paper presented to the Panel on Technology and Women's Employment of the National Research Council.

Papert, S. (1984, December). *Steps toward a national policy on education in a technological society*. Paper presented at the National Conference on Industrial Innovation, Los Angeles.

Quality Education Data. (1984). *Microcomputer data*. Unpublished raw data available from Naval Materials Council, Dallas, TX.

Resnick, D.P., & Resnick, L.B. (1977). The nature of literacy: An historical exploration. *Harvard Educational Review, 47* (3), 370–385.

Rohwer. W. (1980). How the smart get smarter. *Quarterly Newsletter of the Laboratory of Comparative Human Cognition, 2* (2), 33–39.

Schmandt-Besserat, D. (1978). The earliest precursor of writing. *Scientific American, 238* (6), 50–59.

Scribner, S., & Cole, M. (1981). *The psychology of literacy*. Cambridge: Harvard University Press.

Shavelson, R.J., Winkler, J.D., Stasz, C., Feibel, W., Robyn, A.E., & Shaha, S. (1984, March). *"Successful" teachers' patterns of microcomputer-based mathematics and science instruction* (Report to the National Institute of Education). Santa Monica, CA: Rand Corporation.

Sheingold, K., Martin, L.M.W., & Endreweit, M. (1985). *Preparing urban teachers for the technological future* (Tech. Rpt. No. 36). New York: Bank Street College of Education, Center for Children and Technology.

Sherif, M., & Sherif, C. (1956). *An outline of social psychology*. New York: Harper and Row.

Trowbridge, D., & Durnan, D. (1984). *Individual vs. group usage of computer based learning materials*. Unpublished manuscript, Educational Technology Group.

Vygotsky, L.S. (1962). *Thought and language*. Cambridge: MIT Press.

Vygotsky, L.S. (1978). *Mind in society: The development of higher psychological processes* (M. Cole, V. John-Steiner, S. Scribner, & E. Souberman, Eds.). Cambridge: Harvard University Press.

Wolf, T. (1976). *A new theory of skilled reading*. Unpublished Ed. D. dissertation, Harvard University, Cambridge, MA.

Author Index

A

Alexander, P., 37, *48*
Allen, H., 135, *145*
Anderson, J.A., 192, *194*
Anderson, R., 13, *20*
Anthony, P., 23, *48*
Applebee, A.N., 6, 7, 9, 12, 15, *18, 93, 106*
Ash, S., 142, *145*
Astington, J., 112, 116, *126*
Au, K.H., 6, 13, 14, *18*, 193, *194*

B

Bach, K., 122, *126*
Bachman, L., 51, *61*
Bakhtin, M.M., 3, *18*
Baldauf, R.B., 192, 193, *194*
Bateson, G., 70, *87*
Bateson, M.C., 83–85, *87*
Becker, A.L., 67, 71, *87*
Benveniste, E., 123, *126*
Ben Zeev, S., 58, *61*
Bernstein, M., 30, 32, 34, *48*
Besnier, N., 100, *106*
Betham, M.T., 192, *195*
Bialystock, E., 58, 59, *61*
Bleich, D., 67, *87*
Bloodgood, F.D., 72, *87*
Bloomfield, L., 113, *126*
Bond, H.M., 157, 169, *174*
Boyd, S., 130, *145*
Boykin, A.W., 150, 156, *174*
Branscombe, A., 94, *106*
Brinton, D.M., 61, *63*
Britton, J., 72, *87*
Bruner, J.S., 6, *18, 19*
Bryce-LaPorte, R.E., 153, *174*
Budwig, N.A., *20*
Bullock, H.A., 157, *174*

C

Canale, M., 51, 52, *62*
Castenada, A., 150, *176*
Castile, G.P., 163, 165, *174*
Castle, S., 153, *174*
Cazden, C.B., 14, *18*, 205, *229*

C (continued)

Chafe, W., 3, 6, *18*, 69, *87*, 113, *126*
Christian, D., 137, *146*
Clanchy, M.T., 7, *18*
Clifford, G.J., 1, *18*
Cochran-Smith, M., 5, 14, *20*
Cohen, P., 132, 138, *146*
Cole, M., 5, 6, 8, *20*, 41, 42, 44, *48*, 56, *62*, 150, 155, *175, 176*, 179, *195*, 200, *230*
Collins, A., 61, *62*
Collins, J., 14, *19*
Conway, B.E., 30, 32, 34, *48*
Cook-Gumperz, J., 13, *18*, 155, *175*
Cooper, R.L., 180, *194*
Cressey, D., 5, 7, 13, *18*, 150, *175*
Cummins, J., 58, *62*

D

D'Angelo, F.J., 68, 69, *87*
Dasher, R., *127*
Davidson, J.E., 42, *48*
Daws, G., 184, *194*
DeAvilla, E., 58, *62*
DeVet, C.V., 23, *48*
DeVos, G.A., 163, 165, *175*, 209, *230*
DeWare, H., 157, *175*
Diaz, R., 58, *62*
Dole, S.B., 188, *194*
Dorian, N.C., 180, *194*
Dornic, 58
Duncan, S.H., 58, *62*
Duran, R.P., 7, 52, 55, 56, *62, 63*
Duranti, A., 100, *106*, 181, *194*
Durnan, D., 204, *231*
Dweck, C.S., 37, *48*

E

Eckert, P., 139, *145*
Eisikovits, E., 139, *145*
Ellen, R.F., 94, *106*
Elliott, E.S., 37, *48*
Ellis, W., 182, 185, *194*
Endreweit, M., 202, *230*
Englebrecht, G., 180, 183, *195*
Enright, M., *63*
Erickson, F., 14, *18*, 150, 167, *175*

F

Farran, D.C., 149, *175*
Feagans, L., 149, *175*
Feibel, W., 204, 207, *230*
Feldman, C., 58, *62*
Fillmore, C.J., 60, *62*
Fisher, J.C., 119, *126*
Fisher, J.H., 119, *126*
Fishman, J.A., 180, 191, *194*
Flavell, C.J., 49, 57, 59, *62*
Flores, F., 56, *63*
Florio, S., 14, *20*
Fordham, S., 163-165, 168, 169, *175*
Frake, C., 113, *126*
Fraser, B., 116, 118, *126*
Freed, R.S., 151, *175*
Freed, S.A., 151, *175*
Freedle, R., 56, *62*
Freedman, S.W., 91, *106*
Friedrich, P., 69, *87*
Fry, P.S., 32, *48*
Furet, F., 7, *18*

G

Gardner, H., 178-180, *194*
Gay, J., 41, 42, *48*, 150, *175*
Geis, M.L., 125, *126*
Gibson, M.A., 150, 152, 155, *175*
Gilson, R.P., 183, 186, 190, *194*
Glick, J., 41, 42, *48*
Goldman, S., 58, *62*
Goody, J., 3, 6, 7, *18,* 67, *87,* 100, *106*
Graff, H.J., 2, *18*
Graves, D., 9, *18*
Gray, R.P., 190, *194*
Green, E., 122, *126*
Green, J., 14, *18*
Green, V., 163-165, *175*
Greenbaum, S., 53, *63*
Greenfield, P.M., 6, *18*
Griffin, 8
Guerra, E., 56, *62*
Guillermino, 180, 183, *195*
Gumperz, J.J., 13, *18,* 53, 54, *62,* 155, 156, *175*
Guy, G., 130, *145*

H

Hakuta, K., 58, *62,*
Haley, A., 164, *175*
Halliday, M., 97, *106*

Harnish, R.M., 122, *126*
Harris, L., 86, *87*
Harris, W., 140, *146*
Havelock, E., 67, 71, *87*
Heath, S.B., 1, 6, 13, 14, *18, 19,* 38-46, *48,* 68, 91, 94, 99, *106,* 113, *126,* 179, 186, *194*
Herzog, M., 114, *127*
Heyneman, S.P., 151, *175*
Hinojosa, M., 180, *194*
Holmes, L.D., 181, 186, 192, *195*
Holt, G.S., 165, *175*
Hundert, E.J., 112, *126*
Hymes, D., 53, 55, 56, *62*

I

Ito, H., 150, *175*

J

Jensen, A.V., 207, *230*
Joag-dev, C., 13, *20*

K

Kaestle, C.F., 1, 2, *19*
Kaiser, T., 192, *195*
Kane, P.T., 35, 37, *48*
Kay, P., 60, *63*
Keesing, F.M., 192, *195*
Ketron, J.L., 30, 32, 34, *48*
Kirshenblatt-Gimblett, B., 77, *87*
Kloss, H., 182, 188, 189, *195*
Kluger, R., 169, *175*
Kochman, R., 156, *175*
Kosack, G., 153, *174*
Kushner, G., 163, 165, *174*
Kuykendall, R.S., 181, 182, 185, 187-189, *195*

L

Labov, W., 69, 77, 79, *87,* 114, *126, 127,* 132, 135, 138-140, *145, 146,* 214, *230*
Lakoff, R.T., 4, *19,* 70, *87*
Lambert, W.E., *63*
Lancey, D.F., 150, *175*
Langer, J.A., 1, 6, 7, 9, 10, 12, 13, 15, *18, 19,* 60, *63*
Laughren, M., 114, *126*
Leech, G., 53, *63*
Lehmann, W.P., 136, *146*
Leont'ev, A.N., 229, *230*
Lessard, R., 130, *146*
Levin, J.A., 204, 213, *230*

LeVine, R.A., 154, *175*
Lewis, E.G., *195*
Lewis, J., 132, 138, *146*
Liskin-Gasparro, E., 53, *62*
Luria, A.R., 11, *19, 43, 48,* 225, 229, *230*
Lyons, J., *126*

M
MacLean, K., 23, *48*
Mailloux, X., 98, *106*
Maitland, F.W., 116, *127*
Mandler, G., 207, *230*
Martin, L.M.W., 202, *230*
Matute-Bianchi, M.E., 163, *176*
McDermott, R., 13, 14, *19,* 42, *48*
McLare, J.B., *20*
McLaughlin, B., 59, *63*
McLeod, B., 59, *63*
McNamee, G.W., *20*
Mead, M., 181, *195*
Mehan, H., 56, *63,* 206, *230*
Mellinkoff, D., 116, *126*
Michaels, S., 14, *19,* 205, *229, 230*
Mohatt, J., 150, 167, *175*
Moll, L.C., 205, *230*
Mullis, I.V.S., 9, *18*
Myers, M., 104, *106*
Myhill, J., 140, 142, *145, 146*

N
Nelson, L.M., 192, *195*
Ninio, A., *19*
Noble, A.M., 191, *195*
Noyelle, T.J., 201, 229, *230*

O
Ochs, E., 69, *87,* 100, 101, *106, 107,* 193, *195*
Ogbu, J.U., 13, 68, 138, 150–152, 154, 155, 157, 159, 160, 162, 163, 169, *176,* 202
Oliver, D., 183, 190, *195*
Oller, J., 51, *63*
Olson, D.R., 3, 6, *19,* 67, *87,* 101, *106,* 112, 113, 116, 118, *126*
Olver, R.R., 6, *18*
Ong, W.J.S.J., 3, 4, 6, 8, *19,* 67, *87,* 100, *106,* 115, *126*
Ortz, L., 180, 183, *195*
Ott, M.M.B., 77, *87*
Oxford, R., 180, *195*
Ozouf, J., 7, *18*

P
Palmer, A., 51, *61*
Papert, S., 204, *230*
Paris, S.G., 57, *63*
Pattison, R., 113, *126*
Payne, A., 135, *146*
Penfield, J., *62*
Petroni, F.A., 168, *176*
Phillips, S.U., 14, *19,* 150, 156, 167, *176*
Platt, W.J., 192, *195*
Pollock, F., 116, *127*
Pritchard, W.T., 186, *195*
Proust, M., 94, *106*

Q
Quirk, R., 53, *63*

R
Ramirez, M., 150, *176*
Resnick, D.P., 1, 2, *19, 20,* 208, *230*
Resnick, L.R., 1, 2, *20,* 208, *230*
Reyes, M., 58, *62*
Richardson, M., 119, *126*
Ricks, C., 68, *87*
Riel, M.M., 205, *230*
Rist, R., 153, *176*
Robins, C., 132, 138, 139, *146*
Robyn, A.E., 204, 207, *230*
Rohwer, W., 208, *230*
Rosaldo, M.Z., 122, *127*
Rosen, H., 70, *87*
Rosenbaum, Y., 180, *194*
Rosenblatt, L., 98, *106*
Rossman, T., 59, *63*
Ryan, E., 58, 59, *61*

S
Sanchez, P., 181, *195*
Sankoff, D., 130, *146*
Saville-Troike, M., 94, *106*
Scherer, J., 169, *176*
Schieffelin, B.B., 5, 14, *20,* 101, *107*
Schiffrin, D., 69, *88*
Schlieben-Lange, B., 119, 123, *127*
Schmandt-Besserat, D., 208, *230*
Schmidt, C.R., 50, 57, *63*
Schramm, W., 192, *195*
Schultz, J., 14, *20*
Scollon, R., 6, 13, 14, *20,* 179, *195*
Scollon, S.B.K., 6, 13, 14, *20,* 179, *195*
Scribner, S., 5, 6, *20,* 42, 44, *48,* 155, *176,* 179, *195,* 200, *230*

Searle, J.R., 122, *127*
Shade, B.J., 150, *176*
Shaha, S., 204, 207, *230*
Sharp, D.W., 41, 42, *48*
Shavelson, R.J., 204, 207, *230*
Sheingold, K., 202, *230*
Shen, M., 58, *62*
Sherif, C., 200, *230*
Sherif, M., 200, *230*
Siebert, E., 122, *127*
Silber, J., 73, *88*
Simons, H., 150, *176*
Slawski, E.J., 169, *176*
Smith, A., 4, *20*
Smith, E., 61, *62*
Snow, A.M., 61, *63*
Souviney, R., 204, *230*
Spicer, E.H., 163, 165, *177*
Spolsky, B., 51, *63,* 180, 183, 191, *195*
Stansfield, C.H., 53, *62*
Stasz, C., 204, 207, *230*
Steffenson, P., 13, *20*
Sternberg, R.J., 6, 30, 32, 34, 38, 42, *48,*
    49, 50, *63*
Stock, B., 113, 116, *127*
Stubbs, M., 3, *20*
Styron, W., 164, *177*
Suarez-Orozco, M.M., 153, *177*
Suben, J.G., 38, *48*
Suchmann, R.G., 42, *48*
Sung, G.L., 154, *177*
Svartvik, J., 53, *63*
Swain, M., 51, *62*

T

Tannen, D., 3, 6, *20,* 67–70, 73, 77, *88,*
    113, *127,* 182, *195*
Thomas, R.M., 192, 193, *195*
Thomplins, J., 98, *107*
Toon, T.E., 115, *127*
Torrey, J., 140, *146*

Trabasso, T., 42, *48*
Traugott, E.C., 2, *127*
Trowbridge, D., 204, *231*
Turner, G., 181, 183, *196*

V

van Naerssen, M.M., 193, *196*
Varnhagen, C.K., 58, *62*
Vendler, Z., *127*
Viberg, A., 115, *127*
Vygotsky, L.S., 5, 6, 7, *20,* 221, 229, *231*

W

Wallace, B., 190, 192, *196*
Wallat, C., 14, *18*
Watson-Gegeo, K., 205, *229*
Watt, I., 67, *87*
Weinberg, M., 169, *177*
Weinreich, U., 114, *127*
Weis, L., 170, *177*
Wellman, H., 59, *62*
Wells, G., 14, *20*
Welty, E., 71, 72, *88*
Wertsch, J.J.V., *20*
Williams, F., 149, *177*
Williams, J., *196*
Williams, W.C., 90, 91, 101, 102, 103, 105,
    107
Winkler, J.D., 204, 207, *230*
Winograd, T., 56, *63*
Wist, B.O., 182, 189, *196*
Wolf, T., 208, *231*
Wolfram, W., 137, *146*
Wong-Fillmore, L., 57, *63*

Y

Yussen, S.R., 35, 37, *48*

Z

Zupitza, J., 115, *127*
Zwicky, A., 125, *126*

Subject Index

A

Ability and instruction, 206
Abstract reasoning, 113, 121
  see also higher level skills
Analytic abilities, 26

B

Biculturalism, 8
Bilingualism, 49, 55, 57, 212
Black Americans, 151, 156, 157, 159, 162,
  165–168, 170
Black English, 133, 140, 141, 142, 143

C

Castelike minorities, 156, 157, 172, 173
Co-culturalism, 8, 201
Cognition: emotion in, 83
Cognitive scripts, 56
Cognitive strategies, 12, 56
Collaboration, 12
Collective action, 161
Communication, 9, 11, 50, 68, 71, 73, 95, 187
  computer, 215, 218, 229
  content, 224
  contexts for, 4, 7, 11, 43, 54, 56, 94
  functions of, 54
  learning community (*see also* interaction),
    90, 91
  literary, 89
  modes of, 4
  non-linguistic cues, 54
  purpose for, 12, 43, 57, 98
  technologies for, 200
  written, 211, 212, 217
Communicative competence, 52, 53, 50
Communicative interactions, 14, 105
Communicative style, 156
Community effects, 128, 133, 135, 143
Community: minority, 161
Comprehension monitoring, 61
Computer chat, 213
Computer raps, 215–227
Computer use, 202, 205, 206
Computer use: bias, 202
Computers and writing, 230

Constructed dialogue, 69, 70, 73, 76, 78
Conversation, 69, 71, 73, 81, 86
  computer, 213, 216
  written, 82, 84, 85
  see also dialogue
Conversational inference, 53, 55
Conversational narrative, 69
Conversational style, 68
Cultural differences, 13, 155, 156
Cultural domination, 155
Cultural inversion, 166
Cultural opposition, 155
Culture: and learning, 7, 149, 208

D

Deculturation, 151
Diagnosis, 10
Dialogue, 71, 77, 81, 98
  see also conversation
Discourse analysis, 53

E

Education and jobs, 162, 202
Education
  bias, 159, 160, 169, 170, 172, 200
  exclusion from, 157
  segregated, 158
  Western concepts, 181
Educational activity, 209
Educational change, 209
Educational policy, 178, 193
Ethnography, 90, 91, 94–96, 160, 161, 164,
  193
Evaluation, 93

G

Goals: barriers to, 154

H

Hawaii, 179, 187, 188, 189
Higher level skills, 7, 60, 207
Human resources, 199

I

Ilongot, 122

Immigrants, 135, 151, 153, 155, 163
Instruction, 11, 17, 128, 189
  interaction, 12, 16, 204
  writing, 90, 91
Instrumental attitudes, 161
Intelligence, 23, 58
  and culture, 38
  children's views, 35, 37
  conceptions of, 23, 26, 28, 31, 33, 36, 47
  creative, 45
  implicit theories of, 28, 33
  lay and expert views, 30, 31
  objective sense, 28
  professors' views, 31
  school views, 25, 38
  societal views, 23
  subjective sense, 28
  synthetic, 45
Intelligent behaviors, 33, 50
Interaction, 13, 15, 56, 70, 92, 97, 98, 100,
    104, 125, 203, 205
  control of, 15
  see also dialogue, conversation
Intercultural learning, 164
Internationalization, 11
Internationalism, 199
Interpsychological processes, 6
Intrapsychological processes, 7

J
Job ceiling, 157, 172
Juku, 209, 214, 217, 227

K
Knowledge transmission, 10, 11

L
Language, 2, 3, 95
  analysis of, 96
  and cognition, 3, 41, 111, 121, 125, 150
  and culture, 39, 128
  contexts for, 95
  genres, 70
  history, 111, 114
  learning, 128, 129
  mental state verbs, 112
  oral, 6, 67, 68, 72, 77, 85, 86, 92, 93, 97,
    100, 115, 116, 150, 181, 224
  social bases, 43, 91, 92, 93, 111, 118, 122,
    125, 131, 133, 136–139, 141, 144, 145
  speech act verbs, 111, 112, 115–118, 123,
    125

Language (cont.)
  structure, 91, 97, 102
  uses of, 95, 96
  vernacular, 178
  written, 3, 4, 67, 68, 85, 86, 97, 100
  oral, 3, 4
  structure, 3
Language and cognition, 59
Language change (see also language
    history), 128
Language instruction, 137, 144
Language learning, 130, 140
Language proficiency, 51
Language shift, 180, 193
Language stereotypes, 132
Linguistic differences, 13, 69, 154
Linguistic function, 14, 118, 124
Linguistic patterns, 69, 78, 86
Linguistic system, 128, 129, 141, 144
Linguistic traditions, 193
Literacy, 1, 67, 116, 150, 156
  and cognition, 6, 103, 124, 179
  and economics, 179
  and status mobility, 153–154
  barriers to, 164
  cognitive aspects, 12
  context for, 6, 8, 42, 100, 161, 180, 179,
    222
  cultural bases, 2, 5, 6, 7, 8, 42
  definitions, 1, 2, 3
  economic bases, 189
  functional, 1, 149
  functions of, 4, 5, 58, 59, 151, 180, 185,
    193, 194, 210
  socio-history, 113, 121, 151, 157, 178,
    179, 185
  intellectual effects (see also literacy: and
    cognition), 6
  learning, 11
  opportunities for, 151
  political bases, 179, 184, 189, 191
  programs, 5
  purpose for, 13, 100
  social bases, 5, 8, 11, 14, 100, 101, 104,
    105, 113, 150, 157, 179, 189, 192,
    213
  uses of, 183, 214
Literacy activities, 227
  socially embedded, 7
Literacy and society (see literacy: cultural
    bases), 6
Literacy development, 178

Literacy learning, 2, 13, 91, 149, 151
Literacy problems: social origins, 152
Literary discourse, 68, 69, 73
Literary style, 186
Literate conventions, *see* writing, 4
Literate thinking, 1-4, 6, 10, 17, 46, 60, 101, 103, 113, 116, 125
Literature, 70
  deconstruction, 89
  essay, 89, 90, 102, 103
  narrative, 78
  prose, 116

M

Meaning and saying, 112
Media, 4
Memory, 182, 186
Mental state verbs, 124
Metacognition, 3, 12, 49, 51, 53, 57, 58, 112
Metalinguistic knowledge, 2, 3, 12, 101, 105, 112
Middle English, 118, 120, 122
Migrant workers, 152
Minorities
  autonomous, 152
  castelike, 153, 155
  immigrant, 152
Minority adaptation, 152
Minority distrust, 169, 170, 173
Minority education, 13, 160
Minority groups, 149, 151, 159, 163, 207
Minority students, 14, 68, 204
Modern consciousness, 122, 123
Modern English, 118
Mother tongue, 180

N

National Assessment of Educational Progress, 1, 9
Nonliterate languages, 114, 115

O

Old English, 118, 121, 122, 123
Oppositional identity, 173
Opposition process, 163, 166
Opposition process: collective, 165
Oppositional identity (*see also* social identity), 165
Oratory, 182, 184, 186

P

Paralinguistic cues, 75, 76, 85

Parent goals, 161
Participant role, 89
Pedagogical function, 14, 16
Polynesia, 181, 183
Prelerate learning, 178
Preliterate society, 180

R

Reading, 3, 50, 60, 61, 85, 101, 150, 187, 193
Reading achievement (*see also* student achievement), 9
Reading instruction, 136
Reading: attitudes towards, 42
Religious literacy, 178, 182, 184, 186, 190
  see also literacy: functions of
Rule learning, 12

S

Samoa, 179, 187, 190-192
School segregation, 169
School success, 163
School: attitude toward, 173
Schooling, 8, 156, 173, 187, 190
  alienation from, 13, 139, 158, 162, 164, 166, 167
  attitudes toward, 161
  curriculum, 9, 10, 187, 205, 228
  instrumental barriers, 159
  minority education, 159
  resistance (*see also* alienation), 167
  minority education, 158
  functions of, 153
Second language learning, 49, 55, 57, 104
Social abilities, 27
Social function, 14
Social identity, 156, 165, 167, 168
Socio-historical context, 179, 208
Sociocognitive activity, 13
Sociocognitive perspective, 1, 10, 11, 14, 17
Sociolinguistic markers, 131
Sociolinguistic variable, 138
Speech act verbs, 122
  see also language: speech act verbs
Speech community, 129
Story reading, 58
Storytelling, 45, 70-72, 85, 103
Student achievement, 9
Survival strategies, 160-162
Synthetic abilities, 26

T

Task structure, 14

Technology, 199
Telecommunication, 212
Tests, 9, 10, 17, 28, 93, 205
Third World countries, 178

V
Vernacular literacy, 179, 182, 183, 185–188,
    193
    see also language: vernacular

W
Walpiri, 123

Writing, 3, 187, 193
    approaches to, 99
    as tool, 6, 113, 210
    audience, 211
Writing achievement (*see also* student
    achievement), 9
Writing instruction, 9, 10, 79, 80, 92, 93,
    98, 104, 136, 211
Written conversation, 228, 230

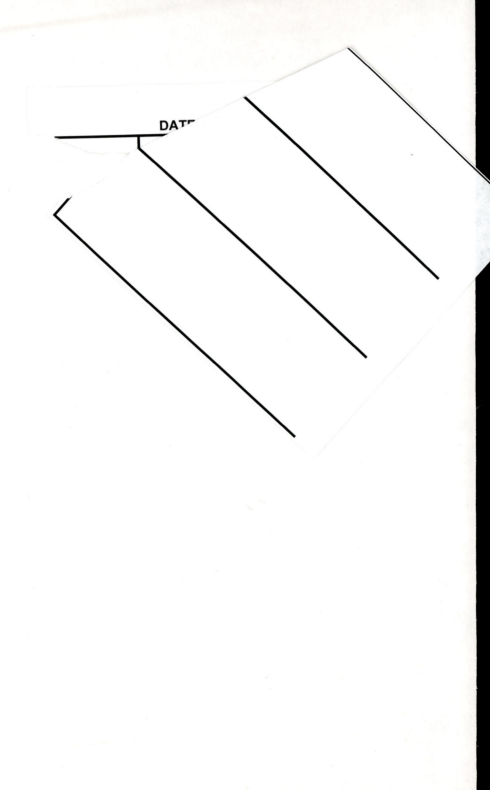

DATE